# THE MOUNTAIN NEVER CRIES

## A MOTHER'S DIARY

Ann Holaday

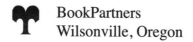

BookPartners
Wilsonville, Oregon

Due to the sensitive and highly personal content of this book, BookPartners has opted not to exercise its editing privilege.

David W. McClure, Ph.D., has kindly given permission gratis to use an edited version of the rescue report *The OES Climbing Tragedy on Mt. Hood,* ©1986.

***BookPartners, Inc.***
P. O. Box 922
Wilsonville, Oregon 97071

*Dedicated to my mother, Ann Beatrice Graddon,*
*and*
*Sergeant Richard Harder*


*In loving memory of:*
*Alison, Susan, Erin, Father Tom,*
*Tasha, Pat, Richard, Erik, Marion.*

*What we have once enjoyed*
*We can never lose.*
*All that we love deeply*
*Becomes a part of us.*

—Helen Keller

# CONTENTS

# ACKNOWLEDGMENTS

In this book I only speak for myself and do not second-guess what The Mount Hood Tragedy was like for anyone else—even Giles. The vivid memories flooded back from hidden compartments of my mind as I recalled my story and although time has dimmed many details, I will never forget the people who were around me. It was impossible to mention everyone; in order to make my story clear to those who were not there, I named but a few. However, I recognize and thank every person involved in the Tragedy during the rescue, the hospital stay, rehabilitation and beyond. I thank those who remembered us by writing, sending gifts and giving blood on behalf of the climbers. I thank: the staff and parents of Oregon Episcopal School who graciously supported Giles and the family in our greatest hour of need; all those who were there for Giles in school, college and when he skied; and my family and friends who stayed close to me both in body and in spirit.

I am forever indebted to you.

I thank all those who have in any way helped me with this book, particularly: Joan at BookPartners; the Oregon Clinic and doctor friends including my husband, for helping me accurately describe medical details; Dave McClure for permission to use the rescue report; Michael Henderson for his contribution; the Very Reverend Roy Coulter for his tireless support; my friends Ann Bennett and Hilary Lipman, who encouraged me to keep going; my family, especially my husband, Bill Holaday, who fended for himself during the long hours of writing and Giles Thompson, my son, who allowed me to write his story.

Some of the names in this book have been changed to protect the privacy of those closely connected to the 1986 Mount Hood Tragedy.

Giles Thompson

# INTRODUCTION

## The Oregon Episcopal School Climbing Tragedy on Mount Hood

—from a report written for the Mountain Rescue Association
by David W. McClure, Portland Mountain Rescue

At approximately three o'clock in the morning on Monday, May 12, 1986, four adults and fifteen students from Oregon Episcopal School (OES) in Portland left Timberline Lodge (6,000 feet) to attempt a south-side climb of Mount Hood (11,235 feet). The anticipated time of their return was six o'clock that evening. Thus began what was intended to be a routine sophomore "Basecamp Program" graduation climb, but instead, the event became a climbing tragedy of monumental proportions.

A few hours into the climb, five students and one adult decided to return to Timberline Lodge, leaving three adults in charge of the remaining ten children. Oregon Episcopal School priest Father Tom, who was the climb's leader, had the overall responsibility and decision-making authority for the climb. He was assisted by Ralph, a hired guide, and Marion, a teacher at OES, who was making her first ascent.

The weather prior to Monday had been very unsettled, with new snow, and another storm front was forecast to move in sometime Monday. However, conditions were quite stable through the late morning hours; in fact the climbing party could see Timberline Lodge and the summit from approximately 9,600 feet as late as eleven o'clock.

Progress through the calf-deep snow was very slow, and it took the party more than five hours to ascend to the top of the Palmer Ski Lift (8,600 feet). The weather was windy and cold, and snow conditions required that team members take turns breaking trail. By 11:00 A.M. the party reached the area near "triangle moraine," at approximately 9,600 feet. As indicated above, the weather was relatively stable up until that time, but then began to change perceptibly.

It should be noted that normally a successful south-side climb of Mount Hood takes approximately seven hours from the lodge. Most parties make a concerted effort to be off the summit by noon in order to avoid the dangerous snow and rockfall conditions attendant with the afternoon sun. Yet the OES party still had more than an hour of climbing ahead of them when they left the Hogsback (10,500 feet) at approximately two o'clock in the afternoon, almost twelve hours after the climb began.

Due to rapidly deteriorating weather (visibility was now down to fifty feet or less), and the poor condition of the party, the decision was finally made to turn back a short distance above the Hogsback. At this point, approximately an hour was spent attempting to warm one of the children who had become demonstrably hypothermic. Meanwhile the storm front had arrived, bringing with it increasing winds and diminishing visibility.

By four o'clock in the afternoon the party began their descent, through knee-deep snow, along a line that was basically south. Weather conditions were severe with wind gusts in excess of forty miles per hour and visibility of ten feet or less. This southerly heading was followed until eventually one of the party's wands was found at approximately 9,400 feet. For reasons that are unclear, the descent line was shifted to 160 degrees, i.e. towards the southeast. In addition, the party was ordered by the climb leader, Father Tom, to "bear left" several times, thus exaggerating this southeast trajectory.

It is important to comment here that the descent on the south side is straightforward in good weather, but can be very tricky in limited visibility because the lodge is known to be directly south, i.e. 180 degrees from Crater Rock. The tendency in bad weather is to let gravity do the work by descending the natural fall line back to the lodge. However, this logic is dangerously erroneous, as this southwest route leads to the cliffs of Mississippi Head, approximately a mile west of the lodge. Since this problem is now widely known, many climbers, not using compasses, deliberately compensate to the east on their descent. Unfortunately, overcompensation leads one to the crevasses of White River Glacier, and that is exactly where, although unknown to them at the time, the OES party found themselves at approximately seven o'clock on Monday evening. The weather and the condition of some of the members of the party had by then deteriorated to the point where the leaders found it necessary to build a snow cave for survival. Ralph dug a cave approximately the size of a four-man tent while the rest of the party took shelter under a tarp. However, the cave was so cramped with thirteen people in it that it was necessary for individuals to take turns outside in the storm every few minutes.

For the most part, the group was reasonably well dressed, i.e. wool clothing, etc. However, the cave was too small to accommodate packs as well as people, so additional resources (including the stove) were not available. In any case, the packs were soon buried in the snow. This meant that people were, except for a space blanket, in direct contact with the snow because neither the packs nor their contents could be used for insulation. In fact, it was later noted by one of the survivors that people were sitting in a pool of ice water, generated of course, at the expense of body heat.

By ten o'clock in the evening the party was four hours past due. Worried parents and OES officials contacted the Clackamas County Sheriff's office who, after a short investigation, activated Portland Mountain Rescue (PMR) at 12:25 on Tuesday morning. The weather at Timberline Lodge was reported to be light rain and a temperature of about thirty-six degrees. However by 5:00 A.M., when the unit was fully field ready, there were forty-mile-per-hour winds at Base Operations (in the lodge) with heavy snow, visibility of approximately five hundred feet and a temperature of twenty-eight degrees. In short, conditions were rapidly deteriorating and the extreme seriousness of the situation was apparent.

At this point, we had no knowledge of the probable position of the OES party, except that the descent route had to be down the south side. This meant that a roughly two-square-mile triangular area from the summit, southwest to Mississippi Head and southeast to White River Canyon (which includes White River Glacier) had to be searched. Furthermore, because of the heavy snowfall and the concomitant avalanche hazard, probing seemed likely. From the climbers' registration form, we knew that the party had a stove and a sleeping bag, but that they didn't have a shovel (it was later confirmed by Ralph that he did have a shovel which he used to dig the snow cave) or an altimeter. This latter omission proved particularly tragic in light of subsequent events.

Five teams were committed at first light to cover as much of the terrain as possible, but weather conditions made a search virtually impossible. With more than four feet of snow accumulating in less than twelve hours, this spring storm was extraordinary in its ferocity. Winds at the top of the Palmer Ski Lift (8,600 feet) were well in excess of sixty miles per hour (and later estimated by a meteorologist to have reached eighty miles per hour). In fact, a window in a sno-cat, used to transport search teams, blew in allowing over a foot of snow to accumulate in the cab within a few minutes. Several teams had to build snow caves for protection, and there were reports of rescuers falling over cornices and teams who were stranded. With visibility as low as two feet for most of the day, the issue became one of survival for the searchers themselves.

Meanwhile, with advancing hypothermia and dehydration, the situation in the snow cave was desperate. At approximately eight o'clock on Tuesday morning, Ralph and Molly (a seventeen-year-old student) decided to leave the cave, hoping to find help. As Ralph commented, "We had lost the ability to take care of ourselves...we would keep walking until we found help or died." In reality, they were the only ones who were physically able to make the attempt. The description of Father Tom, for example, who had spent a considerable amount of time outside the cave during the night, suggests a probable core temperature of approximately ninety degrees or less.

Heading southeast, with zero visibility and no actual knowledge of their position, across the crevasse field of White River Glacier and up the steep east moraine, they eventually made their way to the Meadows Ski area; and then by 10:30 A.M. to Base Operations.

During debriefing, Ralph revealed that he believed the snow cave to be in White River Canyon, probably on the east side of the moraine, situated above a fifty-degree slope, below a twenty-degree rise and within 150 feet of a crevasse that was 25 feet long, 30 feet deep and 5 feet wide. Lacking an altimeter, he estimated that the cave was at an elevation of 8,000 to 9,000 feet. He also indicated that the physical condition of the occupants of the cave had appreciably deteriorated during the night.

By 5:00 P.M. the weather had cleared to approximately 7,600 feet although the wind was still high. A helicopter flyover with Ralph aboard proved fruitless apart from the fact that Ralph now felt the cave was probably situated on the west side of the moraine; but even that was uncertain since the recent four feet of new snow had totally changed the character of the terrain.

During the night, a rescue team searching by head-lamp thought they heard cries for help coming from White River Canyon at approximately 8,500 feet, but were unable to pinpoint a location. Winds were still gusting at more than forty miles per hour, but the weather was clearing rapidly. On Tuesday night a sno-cat fell into a crevasse, fortunately without consequence to the operator.

Dawn broke on Wednesday morning with clear weather and a firm belief that the cave would be found as soon as the helicopters were airborne. The strategy for the day included the use of Nordic Patrol skiers to search the extensively wooded areas below Timberline, in case the OES party had tried to walk out after Ralph and Molly left the cave, and a saturation search by climbing teams of the west side of White River Canyon between 8,000 and 9,000 feet. We also made arrangements with Seattle to obtain the use of search dogs; and with a helicopter service for a flyover using an infra-red detector.

Six PMR teams were in the field by first light, followed throughout the day by an additional five teams from other Oregon rescue units, including the Crag Rats, Alpinees and Corvallis Mountain Rescue Unit.

At 5:58 on Wednesday morning, a 304th. Air Force Reserve unit helicopter, in the course of investigating a sleeping bag in White River Canyon, found the bodies of two of the OES children at the foot of a steep slope and a third body near the top of the west moraine at approximately 8,200 feet. These areas were coarse-probed without success. It was later thought that these children, in the course of taking their turn outside of the cave on Tuesday after Ralph and Molly left, were unable to regain access due to drifting snow filling the entrance to the cave. It should be stressed here that, because the areas in which the bodies were found bore no resemblance whatsoever to Ralph's description and what transpired next, the ridge and the location below it were considered to be very unlikely to contain the snow cave. Ironically, the cave was eventually found just a few feet from the child on top of the ridge.

Coincident with these events was the finding of three sets of footprints leading from approximately 9,000 feet to the near vicinity of the body on the ridge. The footprints were well defined, very recent, and clearly belonged to children or small adults. The prints did not have crampon marks—an important point since none of the children had crampons for the climb. This finding strongly corroborated the thesis that the cave was located at close to 9,000 feet on the west moraine because Tuesday's weather precluded other climbers on the ridge.

Wednesday morning and afternoon were spent coarse-probing parts of the west moraine and White River Glacier from 8,500 to 9,000 feet and the timbered regions below 6,000 feet. What was becoming very clear to everyone was that, in all likelihood, the snow cave was no longer distinguishable from the air and would require discovery by fine-probing of a considerable area by a large number of searchers. Fine-probing takes time—a lot of time for an area as extensive as this—and time was a luxury we no longer had. A sense of frustration and despair was clearly evident—in the searchers, parents and press alike.

This necessity for probing, and the fact that we were beginning to lose climbers to burnout and personal commitments, forced us to look out of state for additional manpower. Fortunately, Seattle Mountain Rescue Council (MRC) was quick to respond with fifteen fresh climbers, and another ten on standby, who arrived at approximately two o'clock on Thursday morning.

The German Shepherd Search Dogs (GSSD) unit from Washington and a helicopter fly-over with an infra-red camera on board were deployed early Wednesday evening...to no avail, although a false-positive finding was made at approximately 8,800 feet.

The warm weather on Wednesday made searching very dangerous. It was also postulated that, since our finding the three children, perhaps the rest of the group may also have left the cave on Tuesday to wander through the crevasse field of White River Glacier. This nightmarish possibility necessitated that climbers rappel into each crevasse to investigate. The high temperature during the day made this action very dangerous because anchors were totally unreliable in the soft snow. Snow bridges were also extremely unstable and we had at least one incident in which a group of three climbers took a long fall. The hazardous snow conditions and the obvious exhaustion of the searchers made a night search irresponsible, so Wednesday's operation was shut down around midnight.

The search plan for Thursday was based on the conviction that the cave was in the vicinity of 9,000 feet and was most probably located on or near the top of the west moraine ridge, since it seemed unlikely that a hypothermic and exhausted person would climb from a cave located in the canyon, up a fifty-degree slope, only to succumb on the ridge top. Besides, that would have required climbing into a sixty-mile-per-hour wind. Our best guess was that the three children had left the cave some time on Tuesday (hence the footprints) and headed south and down along the ridge top. Two fell over the steep slope in the prevailing whiteout and came to rest in the canyon below, while the other collapsed on the ridge.

During Thursday, we had eight teams deployed, five from Seattle MRC, two from Corvallis MRU and three from PMR as well as the GSSD unit. In addition, there were teams from the 304th. participating in the ground search. The intent was to do a detailed and systematic search probe from the highest probable elevation (approximately 9,600 feet) down along the ridge to an elevation of approximately 7,500 feet, thereby insuring that there would be no chance of missing the cave if we were right about its location on the ridge. The weather was even hotter than on Wednesday and the glacier was an oven.

At approximately 3:00 P.M. a group of operation leaders at base, including members from Seattle, Portland and the sheriff's office, held a conference. The general conclusion was overwhelmingly pessimistic; in fact, most of us felt that we were no longer looking for survivors and that in all probability the location of the cave would not be found until the snow melted. Between exhaustion (some of us had only slept for six out of the last sixty-five hours), frustration and the oppressive air of sadness everywhere, the mood in Base Operations was one of great depression.

At just about that time, events on the mountain were taking an interesting turn. Pete, a Seattle Field Operations leader, poignantly captured the spirit of the moment in his report following the rescue and I can do no better than quote, in part, from his observations.

*3:00 P.M.: By this time exhaustion and frustration had taken its toll. Some of the earlier searchers on the mountain were exhausted and ready for a break. It was decided that some of the personnel would come down, some would stay, and that any fresh searchers at base would come up and join the search until dark.*

*As we were organizing this (probe) team, Ralph…stated that he had a very "hot" feeling about the exact site we were standing on. At this time we decided we would search the immediate area, starting three hundred to four hundred feet higher, and work east toward the spot where the Wednesday victims were found (marked with wands). The PJs (304th. Air Force Reserve personnel) were very helpful in scouting the area in front of our two-hundred-foot, close-order probe line. Knowing that the PJs were looking for any crevasses large enough to endanger the advancing probe line gave us the peace of mind to allow us to concentrate on the probing.*

*Ralph…and the PJs seemed to be operating on a sixth sense, and all the time we were advancing on the wands the PJs had left at the Wednesday body site, they became more excited.*

*As we crossed the only open crevasse that Ralph seemed to remember, one of the PJs hit a solid object four feet under the snow, about six feet from the drop to the Steel Cliffs drainage. At this time we started digging and the equipment cache was found. Ralph immediately pointed to where the cave should be and members of the Seattle and Corvallis teams simultaneously hit the cave. Since the PJs were roped independently from the main probe line, they started digging. A void in the snow was hit approximately four feet below the surface and four to six feet from the edge of the drainage. It was discerned that this was either the top of a hidden crevasse or the air trap Ralph had dug out for the entrance to the cave.*

*One of the PJs stuck his head down, smelled the void, and said it had a bad smell. This immediately told us that we were on target and moments later we heard moaning coming from the main cave. Carefully we removed snow from the opening and assured the occupants that they were okay and would be out shortly.*

*[Brittany] was semi-conscious and seemed aware that we were helping her. Giles Thompson was unconscious but had vital signs.*

Sadly, the others in the cave were not so fortunate. In all, four children and the two adults, Father Tom and Marion, could not be revived after transport to local hospital facilities. Including the three children who died outside of the cave, the storm and the flawed response to it took nine lives; and all of this happened a little more than a mile from Timberline Lodge....

...[I] wish to acknowledge with the utmost respect and gratitude the self-sacrifice, dedication and professionalism of the individual volunteer rescue units who came when needed—no questions asked...[I] also acknowledge with thanks the help of the many volunteers such as the Red Cross who fed us and especially the sno-cat operators who risked their lives on that Tuesday and succeeding days. Last, but most surely not least, special thanks go to the SAR deputies of Clackamas County for their high level of professionalism and support. It was a real pleasure to work with people who cared as much as they did....To members of Portland Mountain Rescue, one can only say thank you. You know what you did and why. What we all shared during those three days in May will forever touch us all.

# PART I

Giles! Can you hear me! It's me, Giles...your mother! Where are you, my child? You seem to hear me, I think you recognize my voice, your eyes roll back when I call out to you and your head turns towards me, but you do not respond. There is a chasm between us and I cannot reach you; you are beyond our conscious world in a suspended state, which I do not comprehend.

I know it's you, Giles, but your bright youthful face is gray, drained of life-giving blood. Your eyes are partially open but unseeing and your face is puffy, distorting your handsome features. The ravages of the storm have left your skin with nasty cracks and red splotches; your soft rose lips are chapped and swollen. I thought you had long hair, but ah yes I remember, you had it cut for your part in the play, and yet I still recognize your ash-blond curls. It's you, Giles, there is no mistake. You are alive.

Beeping and pumping machines surround us; the liquid hiss of oxygen brings life to you through a thin, translucent line, which forks into your nostrils. I am horrified by the tube in your throat connected to the respirator. Your body writhes against the force of its mechanism as though it were sending an electric charge through you. I cannot bear to see you like this, but the doctors tell me they are pleased with your condition…I do not understand.

I have been waiting for three days at the mountain, Giles, while you were sleeping in the cave. Now I am here at your bedside and I want you to know how desperate with worry I have been, fighting thoughts of losing you. I hope it isn't too late to tell you how much you mean to me.

## *Monday, May 12th.*

I remember exactly where I was standing when I looked at the clock at 4:30 in the afternoon. I thought about you getting on the bus to go back to school after your expedition, glad to be in the warm safety of the vehicle and tired after more than twelve hours of climbing the mountain. You would be arriving at school about then, I mused, have a hot meal and go to bed. I didn't expect you to call.

Bill arrived home late in the evening, after a medical conference in Los Angeles. We went to bed early as we had a busy day ahead. The first inkling I had that something was wrong was when the phone rang. As I went to answer it, I had a feeling it was bad news. A woman from school was calling all the parents to let them know that the driver of the school bus had reported that the climbers should have returned to Timberline Lodge by 6:00 in the evening, but they weren't back. It was assumed that you had probably run into a storm, she said, and were staying at Silcox Hut, a little shelter approximately halfway up the mountain where climbers often find refuge from bad weather. Portland Mountain Rescue (PMR) had been called, and it was expected that they would bring the climbers down the next morning. She sounded optimistic, convinced me that there was no cause for concern and assured me I would be notified as soon as there was any news.

Disturbed by the call, I woke Bill up to tell him about it. He laughed and said that you were probably having a ball up there, people stay on the mountain all the time, and there was no reason to believe that you would not be safe. He told me not to worry.

Nevertheless, I lay awake most of the night waiting for the phone to ring. My mind wandered far and wide, imagining untold catastrophes and building scenarios of what could have happened.

## *Tuesday, May 13th.*

B y four in the morning I had worked myself into a frantic state, as parents do, who wait and wait for their children to come home. I needed to talk to someone and remembered Marion, the Dean of the "upper" school and the only other person on the Sophomore Climb whom I knew. We have become good friends of late. She married an Englishman and lived in England for a while, which gives us a lot in common. She has taken a special interest in both you and Ross, and often contacts me if she has any concerns about your well-being.

Unable to wait for daybreak for come, I called Marion's house and the woman who was looking after Marion's daughter, Amy, answered the phone. She didn't have any new information, but sounded confident that the climbers would be safe.

Worry and anxiety engulfed me as I struggled to remain calm by getting on with my daily routine. I managed to get to work, but felt I should drive to the school immediately. At approximately nine-thirty, Jeff called from the dorm office. I grabbed the phone only to hear him say that he was certain you were in good hands. He himself had checked your equipment and he was sure there couldn't be a problem. Father Tom was an experienced climber and Ralph a professional guide. We didn't have to worry.

However, there was still no sign of the climbers.

He promised to call me the minute he heard anything. A few minutes later he called again to say that Ralph and Molly had been picked up at Mount Hood Meadows and search and rescue teams were going back up the mountain to bring down the others. His voice was reassuring; I didn't think any more about it.

I didn't hear from the school again, and although I assumed everything was under control, I wanted to see for myself that you were safe. I remembered that I had promised to bring your tuxedo for the senior prom on Friday. I resolved to leave as soon as I finished work, which was before three o'clock. It was ironical really—we were having the first bereavement support group meeting at the clinic, and Pam, our social worker, didn't come. I ran the meeting for a while, but it ended earlier than it normally would have.

It was a beautiful day in Portland; the air was fresh and exhilarating after the recent storm, the sky clear and sunny. The trees were spectacular, laden with clouds of blossoms; the azaleas and rhododendrons were in full bloom. On my way to the school I dropped in to see Joanne at her apartment, where I found her with Ross and his girlfriend, Rachel. Ross didn't know anything about your staying on the mountain and was quite nonchalant about my worry saying you were probably asleep at school. I wasn't convinced. I picked up the phone to call Marion's number again; this time Amy answered.

"They haven't come back yet," she exclaimed when I asked her if she knew the whereabouts of her mother. "They will have to spend another night on the mountain." After a long pause, she added solemnly. "It's bad...it's really bad."

I was panic-stricken. Jeff hadn't indicated that there was any doubt the group would be found. The situation sounded simple; just a matter of helping you and the others off the mountain.

I couldn't wait a moment longer. I decided to drive to Mount Hood immediately, but I wasn't dressed for cold weather. Joanne found a warm coat and an old jumpsuit for me to wear.

On the spur of the moment, I changed my mind again and drove over to the school. It was about six-thirty in the evening and the campus was deserted except for a couple of boys wandering around. I asked them if they had heard anything about the climbers. It was their impression that the rescuers were with the group and you had blankets, but were waiting for the weather to improve. The boys directed me to the house of the Basecamp Program director on campus, who had set up a dispatch center at his home in order to maintain contact with the mountain and keep the school informed.

The little house was packed with people; students, teachers, the headmaster and his wife. There was a buzz of conversation and during a pause between persistent phone calls, the director acknowledged me, saying that they had information about what had happened. Apparently you had been trapped by a freak snowstorm and had dug a snow cave for shelter. I had never heard of such a thing and he explained that a snow cave is simply a large hole in the snow. He told me about a yellow raincoat which you had put over the entrance and he thought that was a good thing because the rescuers would see it easily.

He continued by saying that the group had plenty of equipment: a sleeping bag, warm clothing and a little stove to melt snow in order to have warm water to drink to prevent dehydration. "Snow caves are warm," he said, "in fact, heat can be a problem; they are often too warm." Search and Rescue were on the mountain and as soon as the climbers were located they would bring them into a sno-cat, a piece of equipment used to groom the slopes at night. These vehicles are heated and the director predicted everyone would be fine until the morning.

I tried to visualize thirteen people huddled together in "a hole" in the snow. I could not believe it would be warm despite what the director said, but then snow is a good insulator because of all the air in it although at night, it must be extremely cold.

Suddenly, I felt I had to be close to you. "I'm going up to Timberline," I said as I got up and put on my coat. "I would like to be there when they bring them down. I can't stay here guessing…I must see for myself."

"There are other parents waiting up there," the headmaster commented. "It's getting late; do you think you will get there before dark?"

At that moment the phone rang again; we stopped talking and listened, but there was nothing new…just another report.

I looked intently at the headmaster and said, "I suppose this is all character-building."

He smiled and nodded, but said nothing.

"Now please be careful," he added firmly, "it's one thing to have children missing, but we don't need to have parents lost as well. There could be ice on the road; please drive carefully."

The two-hour drive to Timberline seemed to take forever. My head was spinning; I didn't know what to think. I wanted to be optimistic; surely you would be alright, but why hadn't you appeared? Why hadn't they found you and the other climbers?

I arrived at the lodge shortly after nine at night. The mountain air was cold and calm and apart from deep snow on the ground, there was no sign of the recent storm. I climbed the steep stairs to the entrance of the lodge and there, huddled on a bench by the door, was a couple whom I recognized as parents. Their faces were pale and haggard. I asked them what was going on, but they were so distraught they could hardly talk. It was then I realized that the situation was very serious. I was bewildered. At the Basecamp Program director's house, we were led to believe that everything was under control, that the rescuers knew the location of the cave and it was just a matter of bringing everyone down when the storm subsided. Panic engulfed my soul...I had to find answers. Why didn't anyone know the truth? Frantically, I was looking for a familiar face, when I caught sight of Jeff. His pallid face was twisted with worry and he was far from being his usual cheerful self.

"What is going on?" I cried. He said nothing, but took my arm and led me to the dining room where a group of parents had gathered. I sat down apprehensively, anxious to find out more, but a part of me reluctant to hear what they would say. I discovered that many of the parents had been waiting at the lodge all day and I was irritated for a moment because no one had notified me of this critical situation. If I hadn't driven to Portland, I wouldn't have known anything, and as it was, I had been given a lot of misinformation. Maybe they didn't want to alarm me.

I learnt that the storm on the mountain had been extraordinary in its ferocity, with temperatures well below zero, a wind-chill factor of sixty below and wind gusts of more than sixty miles per hour. Four feet of snow had fallen with drifts of unimaginable dimensions and visibility was less than two feet. Apparently, other climbing parties had canceled because a cyclonic storm was forecast. Portland Mountain Rescue had attempted a search, but conditions had been impossible and extremely dangerous. It was believed that rescuers knew the location of the cave because they thought they heard cries for help, and what sounded like someone beating on a metal object. Search and Rescue (304th. Air Force Reserve) was standing by with huge military helicopters (Hueys), but they were unable to fly because of the weather.

"It's beautiful out there now," I exclaimed, "and there isn't any wind. I wonder why they can't go up, especially if they know the location of the snow cave."

"I don't know," someone said. "I don't think they can fly the helicopters in the dark. Portland Mountain Rescue have sno-cats up there, so if they do find the climbers they will stay in those overnight. They will go up at first light tomorrow, about four o'clock in the morning."

Ralph joined us at the table, conspicuous by his ruddy complexion and swollen lips, a result of his recent exposure to the elements. I questioned him about you, Giles; I needed to know how you were. You are strong, healthy and athletic, surely you would be alright after one night on the mountain. No...of course, I was forgetting. This was your second night.

Ralph said you are a fine young man and that you had been a big help to him on the Climb. You had carried his pack while he attended to a student who seemed to be suffering from hypothermia on the descent. He said the group stopped for an hour or so to rewarm the student by giving him warm water which you heated on a stove. Another student attempted to warm him with the heat of her body by getting into the sleeping bag with him. He was quite disoriented and wanted to go to sleep, and Ralph had to more or less drag him down the mountain.

Ralph told me about the snow cave which you built, but I must say I cannot imagine it. He said the conditions were dreadful, with the wind howling and the snow drifting at an alarming rate. He was the only one who could dig the cave because there was only one shovel. Finally, you all jumped into the hollowed out space, even though it wasn't anywhere near large enough for eleven people. He told me about Monday night. While I was in my warm bed worrying about you, Giles, you were having to take turns going outside in order to make room in the cave and to get fresh air. He said it was impossible for you to get your gear because your packs were buried, and when you attempted to dig them out, there must have been at least two feet of snow on top of them.

By morning the group had lost the ability to take care of itself, so Ralph and another student decided to get help. Initially Ralph asked you to go with him, but you were exhausted after working on the entrance to the cave. He said everyone's spirit was good when he left, and that you were well. He seemed quite nonchalant and confident about everything. "Nevertheless, he's not here with us, I thought.. I can't touch him and know that he is safe, nor can I listen to his voice or hear his laughter."

I wondered what you were doing. You must have slept a little, but I knew there was nothing to eat or drink.

I stayed a little longer and talked to the other parents. It was interesting to note how many of the children on the Climb had been in the play with you and Ross. We chatted about that for a while and it seemed to divert our preoccupation with the absence of our children.

It was almost midnight when I took a room at the lodge and I suddenly remembered that I hadn't called Bill. He sounded sleepy when he answered the phone, and surprised to hear I was at Timberline Lodge. "I will expect you back in Longview around noon tomorrow," he said.

"Probably. The climbers will be dehydrated and may have some frostbite. I'm sure they will be taken to hospital in Portland which means I might not be home until later. Ralph said Giles was fine this morning," I added.

"Oh, I'm sure they will be okay."

Settled in my room at the lodge, I lay in bed for a long time staring into space. I thought about the events of the day, particularly about my conversation with Ralph. The situation was obviously much worse than we had thought, even though Ralph was confident that rescuers would find the group now that the storm had subsided. I tried to visualize the cave. I had no concept of what it must have been like; eleven people in a hole in the snow trying to stay warm. Sixty below zero…I still can't imagine it. The fact that you had lost your packs unnerved me, because it meant that you couldn't use any of the "suitable" equipment you had taken.

I remembered my earlier feelings of foreboding about the climb. When Ross went on the day hike two years ago, I never felt like that—in fact, Ross hardly mentioned it afterwards saying there was nothing to it. Somehow, I felt that this was different.

Apparently, several parents had called the school and questioned whether the climb should take place at all because the weather forecast predicted a Pacific storm. They had been assured that the group would make just a token attempt to climb the mountain.

"What went wrong?" I wondered. "The peak is so close to Timberline Lodge. How could you be lost? How *was* the ferocious storm they tell me about?"

I suppose I dozed off for a short time because I thought I heard the drone of helicopters taking off, and the sound of boots on the floor above my room as rescuers prepared to leave…but it must have been a dream.

## *Wednesday, May 14th.*

By four o'clock in the morning, I was in the lobby of the lodge. There was already activity, as rescue crews bundled up and gathered equipment for their mission. Some were attaching crampons to their boots while others tied ropes and anchors to themselves. Groups of rescuers huddled together laying out their strategy to search the mountain. The atmosphere was electric with excitement and anticipation, and I felt sure that in just a matter of hours you would be brought down to safety.

Families and friends gathered by the ski patrol office, drinking coffee and chatting quietly. After introducing myself I wandered outside. It was extremely cold and I pulled up my collar against the biting air. The sky was clear as dawn broke on the mountain, the wind had dropped and conditions seemed perfect to fly the helicopters.

A Red Cross disaster van was set up in the carpark where volunteers were busy cooking and serving hot meals for the rescuers, to make sure they were well fed and hydrated before they left. I drifted aimlessly over to the van; the volunteers offered breakfast to me, but I couldn't think about food. I helped myself to coffee, the first of many cups which would sustain me through the upcoming vigil.

We watched the searchers climb into the sno-cats and like an army of soldiers they began their ascent. Soon the drone of helicopter engines filled the air. It was a comforting sound and we were confident that at last there was action. I thought the deafening roar would surely be heard by the climbers. The Huey lifted off and headed towards the mountain. The pilot flew in the direction of White River Canyon to the right side as we faced Mount Hood. As the morning clouds lifted we could see the Palmer chair to the left where the group had ascended just forty-eight hours earlier. The helicopter was a long way from there. It hovered for some time behind Plymouth Rock, about a mile away from where we were standing. The massive machine looked like a tiny mosquito against the huge expanse of snow on the south face of the mountain.

"They must be able to see them," someone exclaimed, "they are probably waving to get the pilot's attention."

At that moment, the helicopter dropped a flare which landed directly behind Plymouth Rock. Its red glow shone like a beacon, we could see it clearly even though we were a considerable distance away. That first flare landed exactly at the mouth of the snow cave, but it would be another thirty-six hours before rescuers would find the cave. The helicopter continued to hover for what seemed like an eternity; perhaps they were deciding what to do next.

"Maybe they can't land there," someone shouted.

Nothing happened. We waited…and we waited.

Eventually, an official asked us to go to the cafeteria in the day lodge to wait. He said it might be a while before there would be anything to report and it was warmer inside. He didn't say anything else—and we didn't ask. As we trudged up the stairs, I wondered why he had asked us to wait inside. Was there something he didn't want us to see?

The cafeteria was a cold, unwelcoming place, designed solely for the purpose of feeding hungry skiers. It was a large room with high ceilings and blue fluorescent lighting and even our anxious murmurs echoed in the hollow room. We continued to wait. There was a clock in the center of the wall and its hands inched slowly around marking the passage of time. There wasn't much conversation, just an occasional whisper. I could feel the tension mounting as time ticked by. By then it was almost eight o'clock.

"What's taking so long?" I thought to myself. "Why don't we have any news? They must have found the children by now."

I was sitting next to another parent; we chatted under our breath trying not to reveal our anguish. The atmosphere was so thick that one could have cut it with a knife. Suddenly, we heard sounds of activity outside and went out to see what was going on. At that moment a sno-cat emerged out of the fog carrying a dozen or so rescuers.

"Everybody alright?" my partner cried.

The searchers ignored us, glancing neither to the right nor the left—their faces were grim.

"Let's go inside," I urged. "We don't know anything yet; we are jumping to conclusions and tormenting ourselves by speculating like this."

We went back inside and we waited...and waited.

At approximately nine-thirty, an official came through a side door and marched determinedly to the center of the room, carrying a piece of paper. He turned to face us and introduced himself as the deputy sheriff of Clackamas County.

"We have found something!" he announced. He glanced at the paper, turned on his heels and marched out. A few minutes later he returned. His attitude had completely changed. Something was wrong...something was very wrong!

"We have found three bodies," his voice quivered and his hand shook as he spoke. "Two do not have vital signs and the other appears to be dead."

A deathly hush descended over the room as we attempted to absorb the meaning of the announcement. "What about the cave?" came a voice from the front of the room.

"We haven't found the cave. We have no survivors," he replied.

With that...he departed.

I couldn't believe my ears. No survivors! I hadn't even considered the fact that there might not be any survivors. Perhaps this was a dream and I would wake up momentarily and you, Giles, would walk through the door. How could this be happening? I wanted to escape, to run far, far away from that place.

Numbed by the tidings of sorrow, I gazed out over the snow. Oh no! Oh! No! A voice screamed within me. I wanted to cry, but no tears would come. I wanted to scream, but my throat was paralyzed. I turned, and there was Jeff at my side; his expression was contorted by grief. He gripped my hand, but said nothing. We were stunned.

Most of the other people in the cafeteria were standing, looking at one another and trying to make sense out of the news. After a few minutes, a man who introduced himself as a public relations representative from the sheriff's office called for our attention. "We are going to try something," he began, "we have decided to send the three bodies to Emanuel Hospital in Portland. They haven't been cold for too long and we feel there is a possibility that they could be revived."

It sounded quite hopeful—the three climbers probably hadn't been exposed for very long and probably weren't dead after all. It was difficult for me to believe that, after such a relatively short time, things could be so serious.

A few minutes later the deputy sheriff entered carrying a glove and a hat. He said they had been found near to the bodies and asked if anyone recognized them. A lady at the front thought the glove belonged to her daughter and another person recognized the hat. I didn't know what you had taken with you, Giles, so I couldn't comment.

The deputy marched out again, but soon returned and announced, "We think we have two boys and a girl...they are young."

Two boys and a girl! There were more girls among the missing than boys. Young! That ruled out Father Tom and Marion. I tried not to jump to conclusions and not to think the worst; after all, we didn't have any certain information; it was all speculation.

Over the next few hours, the deputy sheriff and the public relations representative marched in and out making announcements and giving information, none of which offered any indication as to where the cave might be located.

"We are continuing the search," the deputy's voice echoed off the stark bare walls. "As soon as we have any news at all, we will let you know. We ask that you stay close to this immediate area because we will announce new information to you here. There are a number of reporters in this lodge and at Timberline Lodge," he added. "You do not have to talk to them. This cafeteria has been sectioned off as a holding area for relatives and representatives from the school; the media is not allowed in here."

Some parents asked searching questions, querying whether the rescuers knew what they were doing. They sounded angry, frustrated and perplexed. I had those feelings too, but I didn't say anything. Surely the rescuers were doing their best, under very difficult circumstances.

I composed myself sufficiently to find a telephone to call Bill. "Three bodies have been found." The words sounded foreign as though said by a stranger. "They have been taken to Portland. They haven't been identified."

After a long pause, Bill replied in a guttural voice, "I will come up. I'll close the office right away."

When I returned, the atmosphere in the cafeteria was tenser than ever. There were probably about twenty people waiting: relatives and friends of the climbers, teachers and students from the school. Several had arrived from faraway places to wait. We passed the time talking about ourselves. It struck me how many parents were in transition; divorced or going through a divorce; step-mothers and stepfathers. My situation wasn't any different. Even though Bill isn't your real father either, Giles, I am glad I have someone in my life. It would be awful to be alone, going through something like this.

I spent many hours with Stan, whose daughter was on the Climb. We supported one another and tried to come to grips with what was happening to our children because of that awful storm. One parent kept going on and on about the school. Why hadn't they done this? Why hadn't they done that? Why hadn't they done the other?

Did we need to hear all that? Maybe she was right, but I didn't care whose fault it was. I just wanted to see you safe and sound.

The headmaster of the school arrived in the afternoon and gathered a group of us together. We stood in a circle and gripped each other's hands. We prayed and he gave us communion. As we prayed I tried to reconcile myself as to how this could be happening—the whole thing was so unreal. Why did I have to have a child on this particular climb? "Accidents like this happen to other people's children," I thought.

I met Father Roy, Dean of St. John the Baptist, the little church at the school. Roy is such a powerful figure; tall and distin-guished he seemed to take charge of our confusion. He laid his hand over mine and I felt his holiness penetrate my body and his commanding voice brought calm to my troubled mind. He said very little really, but his prayers gave me courage.

Time passed by and there were no more announcements; the atmosphere became too much for me and I had to get out. I walked up to Timberline Lodge, thinking perhaps it would be a "good news place." I have always loved that magnificent old structure, built during the depression to provide work for craftsmen and women in Portland. Subsequently, Government Camp developed, as a place where the workers lived. Everything in the handmade lodge is lovely, the light fixtures, the furniture, the curtains woven by hand. The circular lobby, the focal point of its architecture, has a warm and serene atmosphere with big fireplaces and comfortable chairs. The huge windows at the back looking out over the south face of Mount Hood present a spectacular, breathtaking view. I doubt whether such a lodge, with enormous timbers supporting the main structure, could be built today. Apparently there was a plan to pull the lodge down at one time, because it wasn't suitable for skiers. However, a conservation group in Portland raised money to build Wy'East, a day lodge, which stands adjacent to Timberline Lodge and allows it to be used exclusively as a hotel.

I paced around the lobby, around and around; praying to myself; willing you to be alright.

"O God! Please be with the climbers! Don't let anything happen to them."

Hour after hour I paced, hoping that perhaps good news would come, but it was to no avail. Nothing happened. I gazed out of the window at the south face and watched the ground rescue crews scattered like flies across the mountainside. Meanwhile, the helicopters went back and forth, back and forth. It was their job to guide the ground crews by dropping flares on the snow in areas which might indicate the location of the cave; a raised area perhaps; footsteps or grooves in the snow. Rescuers were able to follow a trail of footsteps made by Molly and Ralph, which ended where the bodies were found at approximately 8,300 feet. They obviously thought the cave must be in that area because they concentrated their search behind Plymouth Rock where the first flare had been dropped earlier.

It was a beautiful clear day without a cloud in the sky. The mountain seemed so close, as though I could just reach out and cradle you in my arms and bring you back to safety. I was puzzled as to why the searchers couldn't find eleven people. Surely that number of bodies would create quite a mound in the snow especially with all the gear you had taken. Surely there was something which would give the rescue parties a clue....Nothing happened.

I ran into a family member on one of my laps around the lobby. "They're just grasping at straws," I said. "It's obvious that they have no idea where those children are. I don't think they even know where to start looking. They are as confused up there as we are down here."

There was talk about how others had survived on the mountain and returned virtually unharmed. Apparently a group of teens had stayed on Mount Hood for five days and walked out unassisted. As much as I wanted to believe these stories, the fact that you didn't have your packs with you haunted me and robbed me of optimism. You didn't have any protection. I knew in my heart that there was something very wrong. Why couldn't you come out? Perhaps you were trapped or even buried. I didn't know how long a human being could last without protection from the bitter cold. How long would that be? I remembered the book *Scot of Antarctica*; from that I knew it couldn't be very long and how important it is not to fall asleep.

I called out to you in my mind and urged you to stay awake.

The day dragged on, hour after hour, with very little new information. We heard that the three children found earlier had been taken to Emanuel Hospital in Portland and the medical teams were trying to rewarm them. The news was hopeful and it sounded as though their lives would be saved. I began to hope that you were one of them. I didn't know whether you were in Portland or still in the snow cave, but I felt I needed to stay close to the rescue operation and I didn't feel quite so alone when Bill arrived later in the afternoon. Some parents went back to Portland to wait and the faces changed throughout the day. People came and went; many had jobs to go to and there were other children to take care of, but the vigil continued.

By five o'clock there were just a few of us left and a feeling of despondency pervaded. I was panic-stricken when it dawned on me that the rescuers were giving up the search for the night. The helicopters stood silent in the carpark, the searchers were taking off their boots and packing up their equipment. The bitter realization that you were going to have to spend another night on the mountain gripped at my soul…another freezing night.

"They're giving up for the night," said Bill. "There isn't anything that you can do here."

"I want to stay," I protested, "I need to be close to Giles. What if they find something?"

"I have given them the number at the cabin, they will let us know. Come on. Let's go."

Reluctantly I tore myself away and left with him.

O ur cabin is such a beautiful old place, with huge cedar trees which must be at least a hundred years old surrounding it, and Henry Creek winding its way through the garden at the back. Steiner built about thirty such distinctive cabins in the Mount Hood area around the time when Timberline Lodge was built, all of them hewn by hand, with hand-carved staircases and doors with unique door knobs. Who would have thought that our cabin, charming beyond words, and a place where we love to go, would be a refuge for us in a tragedy like this.

Joanne, Ross and Rachel were at the cabin when we arrived, their young faces grim and pale as the tragic events of a seemingly innocent climb unfolded before us. We were suddenly in the midst of an unimaginable nightmare, when just a week ago we didn't have a care in the world. We stared at the floor with nothing to say, until finally I suggested that the children return to Portland as it wasn't necessary for them to remain at the cabin. There was school the next day and I wanted them to leave before dark. I tried to be reassuring in my belief that the cave would be found; I would call as soon as we had any news. They departed, shoulders down and dragging their feet.

After they left us in the silence of the cabin, my worst forebodings assaulted me. I felt myself sinking, losing control. I began to cry and my body rocked with violent sobs.

"How can you worry about *stupid* things having to do with children?" I cried. "Whether they are out getting pregnant, or whether they are reading the right books or watching suitable television programs, it really doesn't matter, as long as they come home at night."

Bill stared into space and absentmindedly shook his head. "There is nothing to compare to the loss of a child."

The pain—the overwhelming pain. It felt as though my heart was being wrenched apart. I wailed uncontrollably as though my soul were possessed by another spirit.

Bill had to go out for a while and leave me alone. The deafening silence haunted me and I felt I had to talk to someone. I picked up the phone and called your grandfather.

"Just talk to me," I wailed. "Just talk to me. I can't bear the thought of losing Giles. He has always been so special to me."

I could hear Pop sobbing on the other end of the line.

"Oh please don't hang up," I cried, "Bill isn't here and I can't bear to be alone."

Finally, Bill came back and I said goodbye.

"Try to get some rest," my father added as he said goodnight.

"Rest? What does that mean?" I thought. "How can I rest knowing my son might be lying dead in a Portland hospital or trapped on Mount Hood?"

Bill poured me a glass of wine, filled up the bath and encouraged me to get in. The warm water and the wine soothed my aching mind. It was so painful, death would have been a relief.

"I don't think I will ever see Giles alive again."

"It will be a miracle if you do," Bill responded solemnly.

Bill's predictions on the prognosis of his patients are usually uncannily correct. Oh God! How I hoped he was wrong about this.

The phone rang at about nine-thirty; it was Joanne. I sobbed into the phone: "I'm afraid…I'm afraid I may never see Giles alive again."

"Mummy!… Listen to me! It was on the news tonight that the three climbers found this morning have died. I've been in touch with the city morgue and the lady to whom I spoke couldn't tell me who was dead, but she did say Giles isn't one of them. They are telling the families now—they can't release the names until they have been notified. Giles is still up there, Mummy!"

"But they don't have any protection," I cried. "It's so cold on the mountain. How can they survive another night?"

"Mummy, Giles is still alive: I know he is. They will find them tomorrow. You must not give up on him; he will need you when he comes back."

Joanne talked to me for probably an hour or more, keeping my mind occupied and trying to console me. By the time she hung up, Bill had gone to bed and it wasn't long before the somnolent sounds of his snoring came from the bedroom. "How could he sleep," I thought, "seemingly oblivious that my child is missing and I am in so much pain?"

I stared at the fireplace with no more tears left to shed. The cabin was as silent as a tomb, just the faint buzz of traffic in the distance and the sound of Bill snoring. The drone of helicopters still echoed in my mind and in my drowsy state, I imagined that the cave had been found and the climbers were being taken to Portland. But the phone didn't ring.

I must have dozed off because in a dream you called out to me saying, "I'm okay, Mom! I'm okay."

Perhaps you were okay! Somehow, I think I would have felt differently if you were dead. Your voice persisted in my mind. "I'm okay, Mom! I'm okay."

You often call me from school and say, "Hi, Mom!" I don't like to be called Mom, but I would have done anything at that moment to pick up the phone and hear you say, "Hi, Mom!"

The drone of helicopters burst in my ears: and all the time I could hear, "I'm okay, Mom!…I'm okay."

## *Thursday, May 15th.*

This morning I was unaware that sleep had engulfed my weary mind, but I seemed calmer and my head was clearer. Suddenly I thought of you. Where were you, Giles? I tried to picture you in my mind when an apparition of your blond curls and lean body appeared before me. Were you conscious? I prayed that you wouldn't be trapped under the ice unable to escape.

At three o'clock in the morning, I was driven by an uncontrollable urge to return to Timberline Lodge. I had to be there. I dressed, wrote a note to Bill, picked up the car keys and left. About an hour later, I pulled into the carpark with your tuxedo for the senior prom still hanging in the car.

Dawn was breaking and the first rays of daylight painted vermilion flames in the sky. Although it was cloudy and cold, it promised to be a good day for the rescue. There was already a buzz of activity as rescuers prepared for another day of searching, and the helicopter engines roared as they were fired up. I noticed a smaller helicopter which I hadn't seen the day before, standing by with the words "Life Flight" written on the side. Several nurses were on hand, presumably waiting to take the remaining climbers to Portland hospitals.

I walked up to Timberline Lodge and in the lobby, standing in a circle around the deputy sheriff, was a group of all too familiar faces. The parents were studying a map on the floor. I nudged my way in and listened intently. The deputy pointed to three crosses on the map which I assumed marked the places where the three bodies were discovered twenty-four hours earlier.

"We have been up all night devising a strategy," he explained. "Yesterday we concentrated our efforts in the area where the bodies were found and we think it might be the wrong place. We are going to search at a higher level today, along here—White River Ridge."

He pointed to a location on the map above Plymouth Rock and ran his finger along White River Canyon. "We think the children may have left the cave in an attempt to come down which would mean the cave is much higher."

What he said made sense, but the prospect of young, inexperienced people wandering in the storm made me sick with worry.

"A Bell Jetranger 206 helicopter was dispatched to the mountain last night. It has special infra-red probing equipment, capable of detecting variations in temperature as little as two degrees," he explained. "The ground crews will use dogs which are highly trained to detect any evidence of human presence, even under very deep snow."

He pointed to two beautiful golden retrievers lying close by waiting patiently, their ears perked for a command from their handlers, their eyes watching every move. The dogs had little packs on their backs presumably carrying first-aid equipment. I tried to pet one of them, but he was oblivious of me and only had eyes for his master.

"We think the cave may also be much deeper than we originally assumed," the deputy continued. "The snow must have drifted over the entrance after Ralph and Molly left, perhaps as much as six or eight feet. We will be using twelve-foot probes today and continue to search with metal detectors. We have planned a more systematic approach, to move in grid lines starting at approximately 9,300 feet. This way, we will comb the area more thoroughly.

"The rescue crews you see here have come from Seattle and Corvallis. The problem is, this work is very exhausting in the bitter cold; the maximum time that we can allow a crew to be working on the mountain is about two hours. In order to have rescuers up there at all times, we have to rotate the groups regularly. There are usually twenty to twenty-five crew members searching at any one time. Approximately one hundred and fifty have been here so far, and today's searchers are a different group than yesterday."

It all sounded very efficient and organized, as though everything was well coordinated and under control. The deputy was optimistic as he predicted, "We will find the cave in no time at all." He wasn't nearly as formal as the day before and gave us the impression there was no time to lose; no time for formalities; they had to get on with it and find the cave.

The rescuers climbed into sno-cats and started up the mountain and the first helicopter left the carpark. There was a definite feeling of renewed enthusiasm and hope; we were encouraged.

I went to the Red Cross van where volunteers had been cooking for several hours. I asked for coffee even though I must have had fifty cups the day before. I found it bitter, although warm and comforting. The volunteer recognized me and offered me some food; I hesitated, but then took something realizing I hadn't eaten since noon the day before.

"Perhaps it won't be very long today. Maybe we will be in Portland in a couple of hours." I opened a polite conversation with the volunteer. She nodded and smiled empathetically, but didn't respond.

I arrived at the cafeteria in the day lodge, which was still designated as a holding area for families and friends. There was some discussion about the three children who had been found the previous day and some parents were conspicuous by their absence. I prayed for them. A cold hand gripped my heart as I faced reality again. It must be extremely cold on the mountain at night, and those in the cave had spent an additional night. There wasn't any protection other than the cave. Would that be enough to protect them from such severe temperatures? Could they survive?

There were only a handful of us present preparing for the day's vigil. Marion's brother had spent the night at the lodge. He told me he had been reading about hypothermia and what had to be done to revive a victim. He said that both the abdomen and chest had to be opened up, and the organs massaged to rewarm the body. He doubted whether Marion could go through it. I was numb with pain and couldn't respond; it was more than my mind could absorb.

Throughout the day I asked questions, continuously searching for answers from whomever would listen. I wanted to know why the group had been on the mountain so late in the day because I had been led to believe there are strict rules associated with climbing this particular mountain. I thought that regardless of where a group is on a climb, they must turn back no later than mid-day because there is a predictable danger of severe storms blowing in the early afternoon. In order to get back to safety, climbers have to be off the summit well before noon to avoid being trapped.

"Why didn't the climbers take CB radios?" I asked, but the only explanation given was, because the signal is not a dedicated one, anyone can listen in. There were no plausible answers.

I had my first taste of the media frenzy associated with the Mount Hood Tragedy in the cafeteria this morning, when I caught sight of a newspaper article featuring a photograph of a searcher walking through the blizzard. I was intrigued that the rescue was even in the paper.

The ski patrol office in the day lodge was converted into a control center for the rescue where an official was explaining to a group of reporters about the strategy of the day's operation. The press kept interrupting him with questions, but he was guarded about giving out information. He requested that the media not intrude on the privacy of those involved, but nevertheless they would ambush an unsuspecting person if they recognized him or her as a parent. The deputy sheriff warned us that there were reporters in both Timberline Lodge and Wy'east Lodge, jostling for a picture or an interview. Journalists were difficult to recognize, only those with cameras were easy to avoid, but many were not identifiable. They hovered by the doorway of the holding area and took every opportunity to push their way in. The deputy shooed them out and finally posted a person to check people in and out of the room. It was quite a distraction for us and a problem for them.

I could not face talking to the press. My mind was confused, incapable of organizing thoughts sufficiently to make appropriate comments. What could I say? My emotions were on the surface and I couldn't have held back my tears long enough to give an interview. The presence of the media was quite intrusive, even though I understood it was necessary for there to be a record of the proceedings. I suspected that reporters didn't realize I was a parent at first. When I left our designated area, I walked with my head down pretending that I worked at the lodge. After a while they must have guessed who I was and even knew my name. On one of my excursions I met Mark Morris and Bob Crider from our local *Daily News*.

"Do you have any comments?" Mark asked me. "The people of Longview would like to hear from you."

"I don't want to talk to the press," I said. "I cannot find words to express how I feel. Just tell them we are hopeful."

Father Roy and I went to lunch at Timberline Lodge. Our brief encounter seemed to soothe the anguish which was tearing me apart. We talked about trivial things, about the school and the kids, avoiding the subject of the dead children, the missing snow cave and the search. As we parted, I confronted him with, "I'm certain that Giles is still alive, they are going to find them later today...I believe at 3:30."

"Would you settle for earlier?" Roy responded. "The searchers need to find the climbers soon."

J oanne and Ross joined me again this afternoon. Ross brought his guitar and settled down to practice. The music was ambrosia to our tormented minds and had a calming effect on those of us remaining. We stared motionless into the space in front of us; there was no more talk—no more conversation. Time was running out—hope was waning.

I was convinced that the group would be found at 3:30 in the afternoon. I don't know why, perhaps it was my way of maintaining sanity through the endless hours of waiting. Soon after three o'clock, I went outside to the parking lot, but I couldn't see any indication that things had changed. The sky which had been clear all day, blanketed us with dark, forbidding clouds gathering overhead.

Several reporters were lounging on the hoods of their cars, talking to rescuers and watching the activity on the mountain. Their cameras lay on the ground and they had long since stopped taking notes. They were part of the operation, caught up in the tension of the moment, caring about the children and even showing signs of giving up hope with the rest. I had casual conversations with them, but even at that critical time, all they wanted to hear was the emotional side and whom did I blame. They wanted me to point fingers—at whomever, at whatever. The school...the system... anything.

"What do you think?" I asked a young man standing close to me.

"I don't think anyone will be alive, even if we do find them now," he said.

"You mustn't think that!" I cried. "They could still be alive."

"It's very cold up there. They have been in the cave for two nights and we aren't any closer now to knowing where they are than we were when we started."

"But you must keep trying!" I pleaded, visceral panic welling up inside me.

He looked up at the sky. "Yes, and we only have a couple of hours left to search. There is another storm coming in."

I was firm in my conviction that you were alive, but time wouldn't stand still and wait for the rescuers. If only I could hold back the day just long enough for them to find you. I suggested that they take me in the helicopter. My instincts would know, I would be able to pinpoint the cave—I knew I would. I would feel your presence.

I even suggested that we bring our dogs from Longview; Rufus and Smoky would certainly find you, but at that late stage it was hardly a pragmatic solution. If only I had thought of it before. I grasped at straws as I drowned in the anguish of realization. Could you have passed beyond the chasm to eternity without saying goodbye? I'm sure I would know in my heart if you were gone. I just had to convince everyone else that you were alive.

"What are you, a witch or something?" a reporter asked.

Where were my supernatural powers? I must possess some trait which would find the cave. I was told that a psychic in Portland had been consulted, but she hadn't been any help. How could she possibly have the same instincts as those of a mother; my maternal powers would surely discover you in the labyrinth of snow and ice which defied the rescuers.

"We won't give up until we find them," Sergeant Harder from the 304th. Air Force Reserve affirmed. "Just when you least expect it, that's when you find people alive."

"I know my son is alive."

"Believe me...I hope you are right."

It was after four o'clock when I walked back to Timberline Lodge, where I found Molly and a parent watching the swarm of rescuers picking at the mountain. The crews were much closer together; they had worked their way down and were in the same area which they had searched earlier, behind Plymouth Rock. Molly was convinced that the cave was exactly where we saw the searchers. We knew that Ralph was with them, and that he too was sure the snow cave was there. The other parent mirrored my panic. He began to question Molly. Was there anything in particular that she could remember which might give the rescuers a clue? She gazed into space, connecting her spirit with the icy tomb. "I just know this is the place," she replied.

"Do you remember anything specific; anything at all which might be of help?" I explored her vacant stare, desperately hoping she would remember a significant clue.

It was 4:30 P.M. Infectious terror assaulted me. My body fidgeted as though out of control and I couldn't sit still; I had to pace the never ending circle of the lodge again. I screamed to you in my mind, "Giles! You must do something! Call out! Put your hand up! Do something! They are near to you, I'm sure they can hear."

I prayed—I called out to you; I racked my helpless brain. What else could I do? I felt defeated.

It was almost five o'clock when I wandered aimlessly by the registration office and saw the deputy sheriff.

"I'm Ann Holaday," I stammered. "My son is Giles Thompson; he is in the snow cave."

"I know who you are," he replied. We walked over to the old staircase where he sat down. His dispirited eyes sunken deep into the dark hollows of his drawn face, looked back at me in desperation. He ran his unkempt fingers through his hair and sank his weary brow into his hands.

"We have no clues...No clues at all. We are searching the original area again, but it's only a hunch. We don't know anything." He would not look at me as he spoke. "Those kids! It's so much harder when it's children." His eyes were filled with tears as we stared helplessly at one another.

"I think it's too late anyway," he muttered. "There is another storm coming and it's getting too dangerous up there for my crews. It will be dark soon and conditions are very treacherous. When this group comes down, it will be the end of the search for today."

"I believe that my son is still alive. In fact, I know he is. You must go back. You must go back one more time."

"You know," he looked at me with sad, despondent eyes, "I have been in this business for a long, long time, and if there is one thing which I can say is consistently dependable, that is the instincts of a mother."

"I know he is alive," I pleaded earnestly. "Please, please go back."

He pulled himself up from the stairs as though drained of energy, and left without a word. Would he listen to me? I couldn't tell. I prayed that he would.

I went back upstairs to sit with Molly. It took all of my strength to tell her that the rescue would soon be called off. "Maybe tomorrow—maybe they will find them tomorrow."

Molly disappeared for a moment; when she returned her eyes flashed with excitement. "They've found something! They have found the packs! One of the probes hit the tarp under the packs."

My heart missed a beat. This was the only news we had had in two days, but now I felt almost reluctant to succumb to hope. "Ralph recognized the trough in the snow where we slid down the slope as we left the cave. I knew it! It had to be there."

She ran off again and returned shortly after to tell us they had found the cave. I felt the blood rush through my veins with euphoric pressure. We raced out of Timberline Lodge, through the day lodge and down the stairs to the parking lot. "They have found them!" Our jubilant cries echoed through the building.

The drone of helicopters was deafening. The rescuers cleaved havoc, gathering up their equipment and scurrying to and fro. It was true! It was true! At last they had found the cave with only twenty minutes left before the search was to be called off.

A young woman ran past us, her ruddy face beaming with joy. "We have patients!" she cried. "We have patients!" Other rescuers were not so cheerful, their expressions were grim, but we did not want to acknowledge what it might mean. All we could hear were the words. "We have patients!"

Sergeant Harder took charge of the final stages of the rescue operation.

"The helicopters will bring the climbers down here," he shouted, as he marched purposefully across the macadam, "where they will be transferred to the Life Flight helicopter. We have to move the climbers very carefully; they mustn't be jolted at all, even the slightest movement can cause a heart attack. The Life Flight nurses are triaging the victims and giving them IVs on the mountain now. Stand back!" he shouted. "We have a lot of work to do. Stand back!"

My head turned towards the sky and my eyes came to rest on the peak of Mount Hood. The ominous clouds, heralding another storm, had parted; the late evening sunlight glistened on the snow, gleaming on the surface like jewels. It was a miracle. At last God had heard us. The rescuers could bring the climbers off the mountain safely without fear of encountering another blizzard.

The hectic activities transformed the solemn scene as some of the climbers were transferred from the Hueys to the Life Flight, and others flown directly to Portland from the mountain. By 8:00 P.M. the hum of the last helicopter faded into the distance. We stood and watched the uncanny scene, and soon the Red Cross personnel asked us to return to the cafeteria where they would inform us of the procedures.

There were just a handful of us—Nan and Pop, Joanne, Ross and Elizabeth were with me. A Red Cross nurse explained that the rescuers coordinated their efforts with medical teams in Portland and had triaged the climbers on the mountain, meaning they had assessed your condition. The victims had been flown to various Portland hospitals according to severity. Emanuel Hospital is the main trauma center, but it would be impossible for all eight victims to be treated there; as a result, the climbers were transported to hospitals throughout the city. The nurse could not tell us which victim was where and asked us to proceed to the Red Cross Center in Portland. She advised us not to drive because of "post-traumatic syndrome" and suggested we carpool if possible. She said the Red Cross staff was available to help with transportation.

We were served a delicious stew which we devoured voraciously and we even ordered a bottle of wine. We raised our glasses and toasted to the climbers. At last the cave had been found and our prayers were answered. In retrospect, I'm glad that we celebrated, because the future would not hold much cause for celebration.

Our family were the last to leave the lodge. A haunting silence seemed to swallow us up as we walked the familiar corridors for the last time with only the echo of our voices and the hollow thudding of our footsteps to be heard. Everyone else was gone, which seemed strange after all the activity of the last three days.

Outside, we gazed once more at the mountain. It rose before us, majestically fearsome in its beauty, entirely dominating the terrain. The spring melt revealed gray volcanic ash forming long fingers which reached down from the summit. The setting sun reflected an iridescent red glow on the western side and a halo of wispy clouds shrouded the top. Formidable crags of rock protruded from the vast monolith of ice and snow. A picture or photograph could never capture its indescribable beauty. The mountain looked so innocent, as though painted on the navy blue sky. There was no sign of the fury recently bestowed on our loved ones; no remorse for holding our children hostage in its icy tomb. It seemed to challenge us—defying us. Would I ever be able to look at this mountain again?

I drove to the Red Cross in Portland with another family. I lay down on the back seat and listened to their familial conversation. They were looking forward to the summer, their daughter was coming home and they were making extensive plans.

None of us knew what was in store.

My head ached mercilessly, my brain bursting inside my skull; finally released from the agony of uncertainty, my mind was otherwise numbed by exhaustion.

At the Red Cross headquarters we announced our names and were asked to wait once again. I saw the familiar face of a parent who mouthed the words to me that his son was dead. His son had suffered from hypothermia on the Climb, and so I believed he would be the only casualty. Ralph told me you had been working on the cave when he left you on Tuesday, which assured me that you would be alright. I scrambled to the phone and called Bill to tell him where I was. He already knew you had been brought to Providence Hospital. He had seen it on the news.

A Red Cross nurse took my arm and led me to her supervisor.

"I'm Giles Thompson's mother," I told her.

She looked at her roster. "He is at Providence Hospital," she mumbled. "We are guardedly optimistic."

My mind was blank. I didn't know what she meant. I think I preferred not to know, so I didn't ask her.

"I'll take her over there. I have my own car," offered my new-found Red Cross friend.

Her supervisor hesitated. "Okay," she said finally, "but do be careful."

We left together.


The nurse introduced herself as Jo. When we pulled into the emergency room parking lot, there were bright lights everywhere and a large group of people gathered outside. They were waiting for me, Giles. Can you believe that? It was the press waiting for a chance to take photographs and talk to me. Fortunately, Jo understood their motives and we sneaked into the building through a side door. I was surprised at so much media attention, apparently they are now focusing on you and Brittany; your names are all over the news.

Ross and Jack were in the ER waiting area when I arrived. I know how much you think of Jack. Much more to you than an art teacher, he is a good friend and I understand your admiration for him. He was at the mountain much of the time, bewildered as we all were facing up to the stark reality that the group was missing.

Jack was holding a boot. You had borrowed his boots for the Climb, but you were only wearing one of them when you were brought here. Where is the other boot, I wonder? Is it still in the snow cave on the mountain?

A nurse asked Jack what they should do with your clothes. The doctors cut them off your body and your clothes were in shreds in a plastic bag. Jack said he put his head in the bag and the odor was awful which isn't surprising, after all you have been wearing them for almost a week. He told the nurse to dispose of them.

It was Jack who told me that Marion and Father Tom and four students have died and only you and Brittany survived. She was taken to Emanuel Hospital. It's difficult for me to believe that there are only two survivors. How could this routine climb of Mount Hood have ended so tragically? What really happened?

The marketing director of the hospital, Dan Lagrande, asked if I would appear on *Good Morning America*. I had never heard of the program, much to everyone's dismay, because I don't watch the television in the morning. The network even offered to fly from New York to interview me at 3:00 A.M. After what we had been through, I couldn't think about being on the television. I would probably cry through the interview anyway and besides, I don't believe it would have been the right thing to do; we have to consider the other parents. I am still in the jumpsuit that Joanne lent to me on Tuesday. I haven't worn makeup in days and my hair looks like a haystack—I wonder why an invitation to be on TV has to happen when I look such a wreck.

Ross has already appeared on television, I think they interviewed him here at the hospital. He was wearing my pink sweater, but I don't think anyone even noticed that. The reporters asked him if he had ever experienced any other tragedies in his life and he said he was failing in math. I don't think he thought about the fact that Father Tom was his math teacher. He concluded the interview with the statement, "The mountain never cries. There are no answers from the hill."

Ross is here now; he needs to be close to you. He hasn't been far away during the nerve-racking days on the mountain and his confidence in you has never wavered. He has been a pillar of strength for the whole family. He was here long before I arrived this evening and he was asked to identify you. He was shown a picture of the top of your head and recognized your blond curls.

If only the rescuers had found you sooner, perhaps the others would be alive too, but I thank God you are off the mountain, at least you are safe here in the hospital. I could not have endured another night like last night.

The doctors who operated on you tonight told me that you arrived here at 7:30 P.M. by helicopter and you were taken straight to the operating room. Your arms and legs were completely frozen, and the medical team had to cut off your clothes to get at your body, in order to run the IVs. Your jaws were frozen tight, and you bit off the thermometer when they tried to take your temperature. While you were moved to the operating table you had a cardiac arrest. Your heart stopped, Giles! Death laid its hand on you.

Dr. Marx opened your chest and massaged your heart until it began to beat again. You were placed on a heart/lung machine to circulate blood through your frozen vessels and bring your temperature back to normal. You were so cold, so very cold; your core temperature was twenty-two degrees Centigrade, mean blood pressure 34 and pulse 40 to 42 per minute. A defibrillator cannot be used on hypothermic patients, so they had to open your chest to resuscitate you. I see a wad of bandages mounded on your chest and I can only imagine the gash beneath it. I'm glad you are not aware of what has happened to you.

The doctors performed a fast rewarming technique. Apparently a slow rewarming was tried unsuccessfully on the three children who died earlier and because that procedure hadn't worked, you were treated differently. You tolerated the surgery well and your core temperature rose to thirty-eight degrees Centigrade in the first hour. Now you are off the bypass machine and breathing on the respirator. You are young; big and strong, you come from good stock and the doctors expect you to be out of the hospital in ten days. They say it's too soon to tell what the outcome will be for your feet, but there are signs of frostbite and you may lose some toes…. A small price to pay, my darling.

I followed a nurse to the coronary care unit (CCU). She was tall and slender and had shoulder-length hair which swayed back and forth as she walked and was highlighted by the bright fluorescent lighting overhead. She bounced along ahead of us, as we entered the CCU she turned and said it was a miracle. I realize it is a miracle. A priest was with me and I clung onto his arm as we marched along the corridor. I didn't know what to expect, I didn't even think about it, I was just grateful that at last I was going to see you.

*Giles! Can you hear me?* Based on what the doctors told me, Giles, I thought you might be sitting up in bed. I cannot believe my eyes; I am shocked. Whatever it was that I expected, I wasn't prepared for this. The Red Cross supervisor described your condition as "guardedly optimistic." I did not know what that meant until seeing you now.

"He looks awful," I said, when I first saw you. "Just awful. He's such a dreadful color."

The priest squeezed my arm and reminded me that you are alive. I have blinded myself with illusion for so long, Giles, kidding myself that nothing could happen to you. I cannot see clearly any longer.

The priest's voice echoed in your room:

*"Our Father, which art in heaven; hallowed be Thy name, Thy kingdom come, Thy will be done, on Earth, as it is in heaven. Give us this day our daily bread, forgive us our trespasses, as we forgive those who trespass against us. Lead us not into temptation, deliver us from evil, for Thine is the kingdom, the power and the glory for ever and ever…AMEN."*

God is with us, I must not forget. But where has God been over the last three days? Why did He wait so long?

It is almost midnight. I haven't slept for three nights in a row, and yet I don't feel tired. My body aches, my brain is numb, but sleep would take me away from you. There is a dormitory in the hospital which is available for families. I have been offered a room there, but I don't want to leave you.

### *Friday, May 16th.*

Your body has been severely damaged by the cold, your limbs have been frozen for several days and the doctors don't know what the future holds. Dr. Bietz rang me at the crack of dawn this morning, to tell me that you had a good night. He said he had to operate because the muscles in your arms and legs ballooned in the membrane as your circulation was re-established. It is like cellophane and was stretched to the limit. The procedure is called a fasciotomy.

I see the blood-drenched bandages which swaddle your limbs. I cannot see the incisions, but already blood and serum are seeping through the flimsy cloth. The surgeons have opened your chest and you have gashes on your forearms and calves—surely they won't operate anymore.

What is happening? I hardly recognize you. Your face is puffed and your skin gray, but perhaps not quite as ashen as when I saw you last night. Your body is swollen and deformed by edema.

There are countless doctors surrounding you—measuring this and titrating that. There are tubes everywhere, Giles: some are red and some are clear; some carry fluids into your body; others take them away. I wish I had more understanding, but I can only guess what they all mean. The rhythm of the respirator pounds out its beat unrelentingly and can be heard far away from your room. The sounds of the respirator and the drone of helicopters are my lullaby now.

I slept soundly last night; I had almost forgotten what it is like to sleep. I stayed in the hospital dormitory, but it was too far away. Jo, the Red Cross nurse, took me there after I left you last night. We wandered through the labyrinth of hospital corridors and found ourselves in the inky darkness far away from the coronary care unit. Jo seemed to know her way around, and soon found my room. It's a small room with a single bed, a table and a telephone. It's like the room I had in Manchester, with the same vague odor of starch and disinfectant, and a simple brown cover over the bed. I noticed a crucifix over the door, and I grabbed it. I will keep it with me to remind us that God is here. As long as He is present, you will be safe. Remember that, Giles. Even though you may not hear me in your transcendent state, I tell you—He is here with us.

You will never know how grateful I am that Jo was there. She was so kind, quietly efficient, giving me confidence and strength. She promised to return today. I don't know her, but I sense she will be my crutch in the days to come.

My room must be on the top floor of the hospital, and I think we are close to a busy highway because I heard the roar of traffic below. I don't know where this hospital is and Bill doesn't know either, but he said he would find out and come in later today. I hope he brings me a change of clothing...I am still wearing Joanne's jumpsuit.

I forgot to tell you that Pat Doran called from Texas early this morning. I couldn't believe it when I answered the phone and she was on the line. Heaven knows how she found me. Remember her from Puerto Rico? She said your name is all over the news and she didn't think there could be many Giles Thompsons, especially in the Portland area.

I saw Jack and Ross in the dormitory and I sense they are as baffled as I am. What *could* have happened up there? Nine people dead! All those children! Marion! Father Tom! You came very close, my precious. How easily life is taken away.

It's nine o'clock and you have been in the hospital for over twelve hours. I met Dr. Bietz earlier, one of the doctors who opened up your chest to resuscitate you. He is such a nice, unpretentious person—a huge man with dark, bushy hair and a voice which is deep, soft and comforting. He told me that your body was frozen when you arrived last night, and he was surprised at how well-dressed you were, in your thick wool pants and rain pants on top of those. You were wearing thermal underwear, Bill's wool shirt, a sweater and a coat. The doctors were led to believe that the climbers didn't have proper equipment, but you were certainly appropriately dressed. He is convinced that your clothing saved your life.

He really can't explain why you and Brittany are the only two alive. Maybe you survived because you were at the top of the pile and had air through the tunnel to the surface; perhaps Brittany survived because she was lying beneath you and protected by your body. They really don't know. You are here; that's all that matters.

Dr. Bietz explained that they have never treated a patient as cold as you. Most hypothermic patients are alcoholics who have to sleep on the street through the night. Alcohol provides protection to the body as it is a vasodilator, and this type of patient usually comes around after a short time in the hospital. He also explained that, in heart surgery, the body temperature is taken down to similar levels quite often, but it is done in a controlled environment, and doesn't last long enough for the limbs to freeze. In cases of prolonged exposure, such as yours, the circulation centers around the trunk as the heart slows down, and the blood flow is cut off to the extremities. Your arms and legs were out in the ice and were frozen hard. Despite this grim report, the doctors are hopeful that you will do well.

You have been placed on dialysis because your kidneys shut down as soon as circulation was reestablished, but I understand that eventually your kidneys will function on their own.

My mind is assaulted by so many facts and new terms, and I can hardly grasp the reality of your condition. Perhaps it will become clear to me soon. Even with my strong medical background and training, I am confused by this; it is beyond my comprehension.

Dr. Cameron Bangs is here; he is an expert in hypothermia and is assisting in the management of both you and Brittany. He is a small, unassuming person, dressed in outdoor clothing. His hair is rather disheveled and he looks ready to go hiking at any moment. I hope it won't be long before you meet him.

It's like Piccadilly Circus in your room, Giles. There's a nurse taking readings and making notes; X-ray technicians trying to slip a film under your chest and an endless array of intravenous lines passing in and out of indescribable mechanisms—some drip, some pump—but they all beep incessantly. The green line on the screen of the heart monitor peaks and undulates with your heart beat. I watch it mesmerized, not fully understanding what it signifies, but each beep means you're alive. I know that.

I am working hard to memorize the names and faces of the doctors who play such an important role in your care, but it's difficult to keep them straight. Dr. Asaph seems to be the senior physician. He is a cardiac surgeon and was one of the doctors who operated on you. I met Dr. Hikes, an orthopedic surgeon, who did the fasciotomies this morning. He told me your muscles were markedly swollen and they had to relieve the pressure by surgical incision. How awful. The damage inflicted on your body by the cold is beyond my imagination.

Dr. Dreisin, a pulmonologist, is managing your lung condition. He is concerned about pneumonia developing and is watching your lungs carefully. He showed me your chest X-ray and pointed out dark shadows. You were cold for such a long time that fluid built up in your chest (pneumothorax) and in addition, he observed a collapse of the lung (atelectisis). It appears that the left lung is much worse than the right. Dr. Dreisin is a kind man and I know you will like him. His dark eyes exude a deep compassion and speak much louder than his words.

Dr. Long is the trauma specialist from Emanuel Hospital. He has been instrumental in the management of all the cases, and is helping the physicians at Providence to make appropriate decisions on you. There is a woman studying your chart. I only ever see her from the back; she is small with dark shoulder-length hair and I'm told her name is Dr. Orwoll. She is a hematologist. She monitors the barrage of blood tests which indicate how your body attempts to return to its normal state. They tell me your blood chemistry is grossly abnormal and you are receiving continuous transfusions of blood and blood products.

Jack came to see you earlier after visiting Brittany at Emanuel. She is about the same as you it seems, but they didn't have to open her chest or do fasciotomies, maybe because she is a girl and doesn't have as much muscle mass as you. I don't know.

Robindra is waiting outside, curled up in a chair with your leather jacket around her shoulders. I remember her from school as her name is so distinctive. I used to watch her gazing intently at you, but you were always in another world and hardly seemed to notice her. She may have a crush on you, Giles. She waited outside the CCU all night, bewildered and lost like the rest of us. Jack tried to persuade her to go back to school, but she wants to stay here with you.

Sergeant Harder from the 304th. Search and Rescue Air Force Reserve appeared this afternoon, dressed in full uniform, nervously playing with his cap. I only saw him from a distance at the mountain and I didn't realize what a tall, broad-shouldered man he is, and much younger than I thought. With tears in his eyes he struggled to explain, "I'm so sorry! All those kids! We tried and tried, we should have found them earlier."

It seemed strange to see such a strong, forceful man in tears. As a man in the military, he must have been trained to be tough, but this tragedy is above and beyond his experience and much too close to home.

I touched his arm. "It's not your fault; I know you did your best. I was there and saw everything. You mustn't blame yourself." We attempted to comfort each other, but there weren't any words to express our pain.

"I have children of my own," he cried. "I know what it must be like for the parents. I wish I could explain, but I don't know what went wrong." He was terribly distraught. I pray he can forgive himself.

There is already a lot of mail waiting for you, Giles. Some Portland schoolchildren wrote notes to you and drew pictures. I amused myself studying them today. Lovely flowers arrived also which I have taken up to my room because we can't have them in here. There are many people pulling for you, my love.

Bill drove to the hospital from Longview this evening. I haven't seen him for days; he looks tired but is eternally optimistic, even in this dark tunnel of uncertainty through which we are traveling. He loves you, Giles, even though he may not always show it. I know he loves us all. He brought me some clothes, but they are not quite what I had in mind. I'm going to look pretty glamorous around the hospital from now on, in my pink shoes and a turquoise dress, however I am grateful to be able to change. I can't stand myself in this jumpsuit a minute longer.

Bill told me the phone rang at 4:00 this morning and when he answered it he realized it was a reporter who had somehow found our name and number. He asked Bill questions about you, about the Climb and the rescue. Bill listened in silence and then interrupted by saying, "Do you realize what time it is here?" Apparently the reporter was calling from Washington, D.C. "It's the middle of the night and you have woken me up to ask me questions which I don't intend to answer even if I could."

"I don't care what time it is," said the reporter, "I just want a story."

Bill went to the *Daily News* later and asked if they would take charge of inquires from the press. He installed an answering machine at the house so that we can screen our telephone calls from now on.

R oss, Joanne and your aunt Elizabeth were here earlier. Elizabeth said that last night was like winning the lottery. She was alone in Joanne's apartment watching the television when the program was interrupted with news of the rescue. The list of victims seemed to take forever to announce with long pauses between the names. Your name was listed at the end as one of the survivors. We are extremely fortunate.

Ross says it's awful at school, everyone is crying and walking around like zombies. No one can believe what has happened. Who would! It's a nightmare which lingers on.

T he day has gone by somehow. The family left this evening and I am staying close to you. The doctors don't tell me anything, but I can see for myself that your condition is becoming progressively worse as the day draws on. Every minute seems like an eternity, watching your body heaving against the respirator. Your breathing is labored; each breath more of a struggle than the one before, as though your life is draining away. You seem to be drifting further from my reach. Hold on! I am with you. Don't cross the abyss; stay here with us.

How I wish I could take your place. I have had my days, albeit frittered them away, and now it is time for you to live. Oh God, you do not need this sixteen-year-old in your fold, he belongs here on Earth to give back the spirit to those who connect with him. Take me. I am no longer needed here.

I wish there was something I could do…I feel helpless and in the way just standing here, I will go to the waiting room to wait for news, although I'm not quite sure what I should expect. The nurse has given me a pillow and a blanket; I will sleep on the floor. I won't be away for long; I am close to you if you need me. It is after midnight.

## Saturday, May 17th.

Last night I had a dream, Giles. I dreamt that you were a little boy again and we were running together through the surf in Puerto Rico. We were surrounded by palm trees and balmy breezes caressed us. The water was cool and refreshing on our feet, we kicked at the foam as we ran with the wind playing in our hair. We gamboled like lambs in spring along the tropical shore. You were giggling infectiously, your little flaxen head bobbing beside me. We stood in a tide-pool pushing our toes into the sand and you laughed as your feet disappeared into the murky water. We ran on, jumping over clouds and skipping through rainbows when you let go of my hand and vanished into the darkness. Suddenly the air turned cold and I couldn't see you; you disappeared into the blizzard before me. I screamed out loud, groping frantically in the blinding snow, my tears mingling with the freezing rain. "Where are you my child!" I cried. Then I heard you; a faint voice beyond the gloom.

"I'm okay, Mom! I'm okay!"

There are five lines running into your body: one into each jugular vein in your neck, one into each femoral vein in your groin and a line going into your abdomen, straight into the vena cava. Some lines are pumping blood and blood products, others are for dialysis.

Your body is even more misshapen today, grotesquely distorted by the fluid in your tissues. You look enormous lying before me, your body entirely covering the bed. The nurses and doctors are working on you constantly, testing blood, changing dressings, measuring this and that, and every now and again a machine is rolled into your room for one purpose or another.

Dr. Asaph has just explained what is going on. Apparently, enormous quantities of blood and coagulation factors are being transfused into your body. You have already received almost three hundred units. Your condition is called disseminated introvascular coagulopathy (DIC) when the body voraciously consumes platelets. It is a reaction to the dead muscle cells in your system now that circulation has been reestablished. There are enzymes in the dead muscle called endotoxins which the body reacts to as though it were an injury, and therefore uses platelets as a defense. Your body's clotting mechanism is completely overwhelmed, resulting in massive internal bleeding of the tissues. Dr. Asaph said it's quite a common condition; but never like this. The doctors are using a test, creatine kinase (CPK), to measure the enzymes. Normally, doctors are concerned about CPK readings of 1,000—yours was 18,000 on admission and has been rising ever since.

The nurses have taken the dressings off your arms and I am shocked at what I see. Your muscles are totally bared. The entire formation of the muscle reminds me of a drawing in an anatomy book, except that your muscles are huge, swollen several inches beyond the skin. It would fascinate me were you not my own son. The grotesque spectacle alarms me and I have to leave the room.

Nan and Pop came to see you earlier. My mother is confused by all this with no concept of how critically ill you are. Your body has changed so much she hardly recognizes you. They have just flown in from England and are trying to understand the foreign medical system in which you are trapped. They stare blankly at the tubes and wires and at you unable to breathe by yourself. They don't realize you are fighting for your life. Did you know they were here? What goes through your mind? All I see is the whites of your eyes through the slim slits of your eyelids.

Ross is playing his guitar for you. I want him to play until you wake up and hope you recognize the soothing sounds of his music. I'm sure you hear him because your eyes roll back and your head turns towards the familiar melodies of your brother. Do you recognize it, or is it just a coincidence? Sometimes Ross plays in the stairwell and his music echoes through the vents; the doctors and nurses have become accustomed to the mystical sounds drifting through this unlikely place.

R oss' friend Anastasia brought her mother Victoria to see you. She says she is a mystic and has spiritual powers. I hope you approve, Giles; I was skeptical at first, but who am I to judge? Certainly we need all the help we can get. She stuck out like a sore thumb in the cardiac intensive care amongst the white-coated figures. She wore a long, flowing skirt and a shawl around her shoulders. Her hair hung in a cascade of curly braids down her back and her long earrings jingled when she moved her head. Her soft velvet voice calmed the frantic atmosphere and I felt her strong spiritual aura.

"I believe in prayer," she said. "Not conventional, religious prayer, but in prayer to the God within me. I want to pray over Giles."

She handed me two crystals which look like pieces of clear, thick glass about the size of a large bean. "These are healing crystals," she explained softly. "I would like to give them to Giles." She stood by your bed for a long time, her head lowered in prayer. Finally she looked up. "He's going to be alright: he will do well." Then her eyes focused on your feet. "I don't know about the legs though," she added solemnly, "I don't see them in his future. I think he might lose them."

I have taped the crystals to the underside of your bed otherwise they would surely disappear with all the activity around you. Victoria has given me hope that the crystals will do their work.

A number of your friends from school were here this afternoon. Some of them I know, others I don't. They appeared out of nowhere and congregated in the sitting room at the dormitory where we are staying. They wanted to see you, but the doctors won't allow anyone except the family to come into your room.

A football game was playing on the television, but no one was interested in it. Their minds were far away, trying to come to terms with the Tragedy. Robindra hovered in the background, still wearing your jacket, her face searching mine for news. A foreign exchange student who has just arrived from Spain was with them. He must have been suffering from jet lag because he slept most of the time. He hardly speaks any English and looked quite baffled — I wonder what he thinks about all this.

Bill joined us later and I pleaded with him to interpret the bizarre reports that the doctors are giving me, to shed some light on the dim prospect that I see.

"He's sixteen," he said, "that's what will save him. He will be fine. I saw cases like this in the military when you can do practically anything with youth on your side." I know he hasn't told me everything, but maybe I don't need to know.

When I returned, the hospital administrator, Sister Karin, asked to see me. She has an apartment where your grandparents can stay and has kindly offered us the use of a little waiting room on the other side of the CCU, only seconds away from your side. Family and friends from school can visit us, I can be closer to your room at all times and when your condition improves, perhaps you will see your visitors there. It will be so much better for us. It is a pleasant room with big couches and large comfortable chairs, it has windows and at last we can see outside. We even have a bathroom with a shower. I do hope that Sister Karin's reasoning isn't because we are making a nuisance of ourselves. We're trying to stay out of the way, but we need to be as close to you as possible.

I wander the endless labyrinth of corridors in this building of perpetual light and busy people. Ghostly silhouettes disappear down unknown passages, their footsteps muffled by the carpeted floor. I have been lost in this maze, just as my soul is lost with you, but there are guides to show me the path. Mary Magdalene silently guards the corner where I must turn—shrouded in white porcelain she reaches her upturned hands to support me. I turn right at Saint Francis of Assisi, surrounded by his birds and animals; he shows me the way. There is a long wide corridor where I linger to study photographs of faces with similar smiles, images of important people looking back at me through transparent eyes. These are my companions who listen to my pain as I pace the unrelenting tunnels to your room.

Dr. Asaph has been with you all night snatching odd winks of sleep on a cot set up for him in an empty room close by. I spend most of the dark hours, sitting on the floor outside your room, listening to the terrifying roaring in your chest. He looks exhausted, gaunt and unshaven, still wearing his green operating room scrub suit. I'm sure he hasn't slept since you arrived here three days ago. We have been as one through these dreadful nights. Sometimes I sense his despondency, when your condition appears to be out of control. "He's going to make it," I tell him. "He's going to be fine."

It was 4:00 in the morning and there were just the two of us in your room with the life-support systems. Your breathing was shallow and belabored. I appealed to you. "Come on, Giles! Come on! We have come this far! Come on...you must fight!" I spoke with all the fervor that I could muster. I clutched the crucifix in my pocket and I prayed to God...I beseeched Him to listen to me. What will He do with you? Where will all this end? Your life seemed to be hanging on a thread, dangling your soul across the chasm between heaven and earth. You appeared to fade away and I felt you must be dying.

I found Dr. Asaph sitting amongst the array of monitors and charts. "I'm not so sure any more," I said, my eyes blurred with tears. "I am beside myself with worry. Giles' breathing has changed and he seems so much weaker. What do you think?"

"He'll make it," he replied wearily. "He has to make it. Try not to worry."

This was the only time I truly doubted, thinking that you might not pull through. Up until then I had been determined, confident in your strength, but in that instant, I gave up hope. I must never allow myself to do it again.

### *Sunday, May 18th.*

I ventured outside today, to a world which has continued to live on despite our despair in this house of pain and wanderings. It was the first time in over three days that I have felt the cool air on my face, heard the birds singing or seen the fresh clarity of daylight. Bill took Elizabeth and me out for lunch to a little hamburger place close by, but I was too far away from you. I was assaulted by fiendish images wrenching at my soul. I couldn't eat…all I could do was weep. My body was soaked with perspiration and I trembled with fear. I had to return to your bedside. I was only gone a few minutes, my darling. Forgive me…I shouldn't have left you.

While we were away, you were taken to another part of the hospital where the doctors wanted to try a hyperbaric treatment. You were disconnected from the life-support systems, except for oxygen, a few IVs and a portable respirator. I saw you lying on a stretcher outside your room, you were much worse than when I left. Dr. Asaph and Dr. Hikes explained how important it is to try this treatment and apparently Providence has the only unit in the Portland area. I was introduced to Dr. Henry, the hyperbaric expert, and he explained that you were put into a sealed chamber which was pressurized using oxygen. They often use a hyperbaric chamber to treat the bends, but in your case, they used it to force oxygen into your dead muscles, hoping the tissue would be revitalized. Dr. Summers, an ear, nose and throat (ENT) specialist put "buttons" in your ears (myringotomy) before the procedure. Without these buttons, your eardrums could burst due to the extraordinary pressure in the chamber. Normally, a hyperbaric treatment takes an hour, but because you were off the respirator, you couldn't tolerate it for very long.

"Any amount of time will help," Dr. Hikes assured me. "We must keep trying, we must get oxygen into the tissues and save as much as we can."

I sensed the panic surrounding you. We could have lost you in the chamber. I am frantic with worry; I hope they don't try it again. I fear they may be risking your fragile existence by taking you off life-support and putting you in this sealed compartment.

Y ou have fresh bandages today after the surgeons took you to the operating room before dawn to remove dead muscle from your legs and arms (debridement). All that picking away must be a terrible shock to your body. Your lungs continue to fill with fluid and the doctors have to tap it off as often as they can.

Father Roy was standing beside me, staring vacantly at your static form. He looked at me, and saw my despair. He opened his attaché case and took out two small cups, laid a corporal on the bed, opened a little flask and poured wine into the goblets. The blood of Christ. He put out crackers. The body of Christ. We had communion at your bedside. I clutched the crucifix close to my heart as we prayed, "Lord hear our prayers!" Roy's exaltations echoed through your cell as I prayed silently. "Please, God, be with Giles! Please help him through this crisis."

I feel inadequate, paralyzed by helplessness. Your fate is in the hands of God and I pray He will guide the doctors.

Roy has been with us through this interminable day as I have watched the clock…hour after hour. One more hour! Another hour gone by! If you breathe for another hour, then I pray you will get through the next hour! You were born at 11 Curlew Drive: your hospital room number is eleven: you were the eleventh climber: Mother's Day was May 11th. Perhaps eleven is a lucky number. This is how I pass the time; praying desperately; willing you to hang on; frantically searching for evidence of your future.

Your feet are terribly swollen, Giles. Each time I look at them, I realize they are rapidly turning black as gangrene destroys them. The nurses have put cotton wool between your toes because serum is seeping through the skin. Your calves are wrapped in bandages, soaked in blood where they have carved the skin to allow the muscle to expand. I am afraid to ask the doctors, I try not to think the worst, but grim realization stares at me. There are so many other critical things going on with your body, but I know in my heart that your feet are severely damaged, and it may not be possible to save them.

Bill and I were invited by Dr. Long to join him for an interview. When we entered the office he offered us a seat in front of a huge oak desk. He sat behind it and Dr. Hikes sat off to one side. The atmosphere was electric in the dark and dingy room and I knew they were about to pass sentence on your future.

Dr. Long is a tall, distinguished man about forty-five years old. He has a round, young face with a stock of brown, bushy hair. His voice is soft and reassuring, exuding the self-assurance of an American accent. Images of our travels in the Caribbean flashed before me when I remembered how much safer I felt in the aircraft when I heard a deep American drawl coming from the cockpit.

Dr. Hikes appears to be much younger, in fact he seems too young to be an orthopedic surgeon at all, but the nurses tell me he is well trained and competent. I hope so. He has a ruddy complexion, thin fair hair and a friendly smile. He is a big, burly man with huge shoulders which he probably needs to push dislocated hips and shoulders back into place.

"Giles is very critical," Dr. Long began, peering over his glasses. "The DIC is completely out of control; the CPK readings are 192,200 and we are in danger of losing him. We are faced with the decision to amputate his legs. We have taken away as much dead muscle as we can by debridement, but there is still a great deal being absorbed by his body. This dead tissue is toxic to the system and the reason he is in this critical condition. I don't want to go into all the minute details of how this happens, but suffice it to say, his body is now overwhelmed…we are very concerned."

He fidgeted with a piece of paper looking over his glasses at me, then at Bill, then at Dr. Hikes. I looked at Bill hoping to get the answer I wanted to hear, but he stared straight ahead.

"There is something else we could try," he continued. "We could inject a vasodilator into his spine in the hope that it may stimulate more circulation and perhaps revive more of the muscles. We have never tried it before in a case like this, although we use the drug quite frequently, so we don't know just how effective it will be." This sounded more hopeful, perhaps this was the answer.

"However, there is something you should know. There is a certain amount of risk associated with the use of these drugs in this way. There is the possibility that we could damage the spinal cord, and if that happens, he would be permanently paralyzed from the waist down." He peered at us like a judge casting a sentence.

There was a long and heavy pause, the air was tense. Dr. Hikes pretended to read a magazine, his hand trembled as he turned the pages.

"What are the chances of that happening?" I asked.

"Oh! The risk is quite high. Although we really don't know for certain in Giles' case," said Dr. Long. "According to the literature, there's a thirty, maybe forty percent probability of spinal cord damage. Of course, there is no guarantee either that it will work, but we will try it if you want us to, and we are willing to take the risk."

"It sounds too risky especially if, as you say, there may be a chance that it won't make any difference."

"That's true," he replied.

"What do you think?" I looked at Bill. He shrugged his shoulders, but I knew he understood much more than he was admitting to me. He is a pathologist and knows the significance of the spurious lab reports.

"Just how critical is the boy?" Bill asked Dr. Long.

"I fear that we might lose him if we don't do something soon."

"It sounds to me as though we really don't have a choice." I spoke decisively. "We can't ask Giles, of course, but I'm sure he would rather be without his legs than be paralyzed and confined to a wheelchair. It appears that, even if you do use this drug, there is still a chance that he might lose his legs.

"I don't think you should do the injection." I tried to sound confident in my decision, but I wasn't sure at all. "It sounds much too risky; I would rather leave his body to stabilize without it."

"Do we have your permission to amputate if we have to?" Dr. Hikes spoke at last.

"Well, yes of course," I said. "You must do what you have to do. I know you will make the right decision when the time comes."

They both looked relieved, and I felt that they too were ambivalent about using the injection. "We are obligated to tell you about alternative treatments," Dr. Long concluded.

"I know that," I answered. "The important thing is to save his life, and I can see for myself how critical he is."

Dr. Long stood up. He was even taller than he appeared behind the desk and towered over us. He held out his hand and smiled gently. "Thank you for everything," I said.

We shook hands vigorously and said goodbye.

Father Roy was with you when I returned. "They are going to amputate Giles' legs," I told him. "I think tonight." Dismay crept over Roy's face. "They have to, it is the only thing that will save him."

I am here, close to you, Giles. Hold on, Giles! Hold tight! I am here to lift you high above the clouds as you drift in oblivion.

It is obvious that your condition is extremely critical and continues to deteriorate. Your breathing is labored which is partly related to pneumonia—but there is more. I don't understand the meaning of the blood tests, but I do realize the results are highly abnormal. There is no sign of improvement and your body is losing the battle. The doctors are backed against the wall, something has to be done.

It's eerie in the CCU, just the beeping of the monitors, the rhythm of the respirators and the occasional whisper of a nurse. The doctors all look the same, like ghosts in their green scrub-suits. They wear masks, green hats and even green covers over their shoes, and I can't tell who is who. They forget that their faces are covered and talk to me, assuming I know who they are. They are like leprechauns flitting around the hospital performing miracles day after day.

It was after nine o'clock when you were taken to the operating room. I thought I was prepared.

I was in our room with Nan waiting for your return. My mother didn't fully understand what we were facing. She tried to act normally, but she was obviously apprehensive. She went on and on about the loss of legs and what an awful thing it would be not to be able to walk or run, never to feel the exhilaration of the wind in your face as you run along the beach. "At least he won't get 'called up' to fight in a war," she whispered. She rambled on, but it was comforting really.

It was so quiet. I looked around at the red velvet furniture. Whatever possessed them to choose such a color? I suppose they thought that red would be warm and cozy. It does seem to conjure up the right atmosphere, especially with the flowers filling the air with their intoxicating perfume.

The eerie silence was too much. I decided to listen to some music...something you like. I fumbled through the tapes which your friends have brought in, and found one by Peter Tosh. I have listened to reggae many times before. It has an air of optimism about it, soothing and rhythmical. It has a calming effect on me, and gives me hope...hope for the future. As the music played, I looked up. The surgery suite is on the floor above the waiting room, perhaps your subconscious could hear the beat, perhaps you could feel our presence.

I prayed, "Please, God. I don't deserve your consideration, but please be with the doctors. Please help them make the right decisions. Please, God, be with Giles. Don't let him be alone in his suffering."

I wondered if God likes music, I wondered if God has time for things like that. In olden days music was really important in religion: hymns, requiems and such, but modern, popular music doesn't seem appropriate somehow, even gospel music seems inadequate.

My mind wandered, I wasn't listening to the words at all, just feeling the rhythm. What an uncanny situation this is! This time last week I was waiting for Bill to come back from Los Angeles, getting ready to go to work, thinking about the Climb, wondering about the weather. If only I had known then what I know now, I could have done something to prevent all this.

The music played on. *He's a mystic man...I'm a mystic man. Walking in the future...stepping in the future.*

The rhythm was slow and methodical. I realize the song is about drugs, but the words are so poignant. Could it be a message for us? "Walking in the future!" The song is about the oppression of black people and their fight for a reasonable life. There are many parallels and the words seem to be directed at us. Will there be a future? Could I face the future if anything happened to you, Giles?

The time dragged by painfully slowly as we watched the hands on the clock tick around its face. They seemed to torment us. Hour after hour went by in a timeless state, with the clock ticking relentlessly.

It was just after midnight when there was movement in the hall outside; we could hear the elevator doors opening and the quiet murmur of voices. I was frozen in my chair, staring at the door. Soon a stretcher appeared under the bright light in the hallway; a nurse was pulling it feet first. There wasn't a mound under the sheet where your feet would be. "They have taken his feet," I whispered to my mother. She paled in the dim light of the room fidgeting with her skirt, and I heard her sobbing.

"They had to do it...they didn't have a choice." I tried to console her.

Although I was overcome with sadness, at the same time I had a sense of relief. What does it mean? Will you be confined to a wheelchair? Sixteen years old! Why did it have to happen to you? I look at my own feet. If only they could have taken mine to save yours, I would give them gladly.

Dr. Hikes soon appeared, still wearing his green scrub-suit and hat, his mask dangling around his neck. He looked grim and seemed uncomfortable as he sat down. I could see by his expression that he was dreading the meeting.

"There wasn't any hope," he said, "we kept taking away dead muscle until there was nothing left. We couldn't save his legs. We have left about six inches below the knee on both the right and the left. That is enough of a stump to fit a prosthesis. He will walk. In fact he will ski, play basketball and probably wear out his prostheses every month or so."

He lifted his head and we stared at one another, his eyes and mine full of tears. "I'm so sorry," he said softly. "Sixteen! I wish we didn't have to do it. In orthopedics, amputations are considered a failure because they are a last resort. We did everything we could."

"I understand that there was no choice. You mustn't blame yourself."

"The right leg is much worse," he continued. "The tissue is dark above the amputation, which means there isn't a good blood supply. We will have to work to save the right knee by continuing the hyperbaric treatments until we can see some viable tissue there. There is a strong possibility that we won't be able to save it. Knees are so important for walking and physical activities, even more important than feet really...but we will have to wait and see."

I turned away. "When will we have some good news?" I wondered.

"Do you think he will stabilize now?" I asked Dr. Hikes. "Will the amputations be enough to stop the internal bleeding?"

"I hope so," he replied. "We should start to see some improvement right away. I'm glad we didn't wait any longer. I had a patient when I was a resident who was young and athletic like Giles. He had a knee injury which damaged an artery and there was a lack of circulation in the leg. We debated about amputating; in the end, we decided against it and lost the patient. I'm sure we have made the right decision here. It's just very difficult when a person is so young, but his legs were too far gone to be saved."

"I'm sure it was the right thing to do," I responded.

At that moment a nurse popped her head around the door. "You can come and see him now if you like." She said cheerfully.

You were already hooked up to your lifelines, Giles. I watched the undulating line on the heart monitor wavering before me. You were back on the respirator which rhythmically forced air into your lungs. It was odd not to see your feet sticking up under the sheet, but I couldn't think about that…it's a small price to pay to save your life. Your breathing was still labored but, even so, you seem better, more tranquil. It's going to be alright now, I know it is.

As I looked at the empty space under the sheet where your feet used to be, I was suddenly struck by the irony of it all and how I have taken feet for granted. I thought about the importance of feet and what a critical role they play in almost every movement. Shoes are important too, a part of a person's personality. I remember your father wore down the left heel of his shoes, and after he died, it was as though he were still in them. They were his signature.

When you were two years old you developed tiny blisters on the ball of your foot and between your toes. Each day the blisters grew larger and spread from one foot to the other. We were living in Puerto Rico at the time and you hardly ever wore shoes around the house and garden. I thought it was a healthy thing to do, but I noticed that the locals did not run around barefoot as we did. I took you to an American doctor, Dr. Thompson, strangely enough. He decided that you had a fungus and gave me instructions on how to take care of it. I was to apply an ointment regularly and keep your feet bandaged. I religiously complied, but the condition did not improve, in fact it appeared on top of your feet, on your hands and I even noticed it developing on Ross' skin. It was an odd infection, the blisters seemed to heal, but then became re-infected. I was concerned and took both you and Ross back to Dr. Thompson. He was upset with the lack of progress and told me in no uncertain terms, that if I didn't take care of this condition, and if it continued to become reinfected, there was a strong possibility that your foot would have to be amputated.

I was appalled at the idea and redoubled my efforts at the prescribed treatment. However, the infection continued to get worse, spreading repeatedly to other areas of your body and from one child to the other. My neighbor suggested that I get a second opinion from a Puerto Rican doctor who might understand this condition, and suggested a dermatologist in San Juan. The doctor took one look at the blisters and said it was impetigo. He recommended that you and Ross soak your feet in soapy water three or four times a day and then leave them to the air. I was to disinfect the floors and let you run around indoors without shoes. This treatment was completely opposite to what Dr. Thompson had prescribed. It took some imagination to get you to sit still long enough to soak your feet. I put buckets of soapy water under the table at mealtimes, and the blisters cleared up in no time at all.

Living outdoors in Puerto Rico was such a treat. Almost every weekend we went to the beach with other *gringos*, although the beaches nearby were hardly as one imagines them to be in the Caribbean. Parties at the beach were carefree with plenty of food and drink. We didn't worry about sun damage in those days and romped freely wearing very little clothing. You spent hours playing in the sand and surf. One day, someone dumped hot charcoal from a barbecue onto the beach, buried it in the sand and, as we were leaving, you walked through the red hot ashes. You had severe burns on your little feet and I remember you crying incessantly with pain. On the drive home, all we could do to relieve you was to cover your feet with ice. I felt your agony as I do now, and wished I could suffer for you.

S hoes were very important when I was growing up. I only had one or two pairs, but I had to look after them diligently every evening, when I was expected to clean them for school. It was considered to be very slovenly to have dirty shoes, and I was often sent home from school with a note to my parents saying I must clean mine. In contrast, in America today, people don't seem to care about shoes, or maybe it's just a sign of the times. It was also considered very important to have properly fitting shoes in those days. I distinctly remember the X-ray machines in the shoe shops, which allowed us to look at our feet in new shoes, to make sure there was enough room to move our toes. We had Oxford brogues for the winter, Clark sandals in the summer, and buying shoes was quite an occasion.

When I was thirteen, my father took me out to buy my first pair of high-heeled shoes. Cuban heels were fashionable then and we selected a brown pair. They were court shoes and had a sensible heel; not too high, broad enough for my toes and enough room for my feet to grow. I thought I had arrived in those shoes. Whatever happened to those shoe styles? We had the illusion heel, the Louis heel, winkle pickers, and clodhoppers, but stiletto heels have lived on.

A couple of years later, I had my first pair of really high heels. By then my parents had given up worrying about my shoes, or maybe they just got fed up of fighting about it. My first pair of stiletto heels were enough to put my back out. I remember clearly how uncomfortable they were, I could hardly walk. My toes were so cramped; it's a wonder I wasn't crippled for life.

There was constant fighting about shoes at our house. In the winter, my mother insisted that I wear something warm on my feet, and bought me a pair of sheepskin-lined boots. Looking back, those boots were fabulous and I wish I could afford a pair now, but at the time, I thought they were quite awful. When I looked down and saw my awkward shoes, I knew I couldn't go out dressed like that. My boyfriend, who was your father, would meet me at the bus stop at the end of the road where I lived. I couldn't possibly let him see me in those boots, although I don't think he could have cared less about what I had on my feet. I had a pair of pink shoes which I liked very much and was allowed to wear on special occasions. I devised a plan to wear my nice pink shoes and to keep my mother happy, or rather to avoid another fight, by wearing my boots. It was impossible to sneak in or out of the house without my mother noticing my shoes and I wasn't allowed to have a key. She saw me to the door when I was leaving and gave me specific instructions, such as "Look both ways before you cross the road," and "Don't talk to any strangers." She would be at the door waiting for me when I came home.

I would leave the house in my boots, and she would look at them and say, "Aren't those smart?" I found it difficult to agree, but I always did. She didn't know that I had my pink shoes hidden underneath a neighbor's bush. I had to time my actions carefully so that I could change into my pink shoes and get the boots hidden before my boyfriend arrived. Coming back was also difficult as I didn't want your father to know what I was doing. I didn't get away with it though, I was caught in the rain in my nice pink shoes which left water marks on them. My mother knew they hadn't just been in the wardrobe.

These long forgotten memories crowd into my mind as I reflect on my life. My feet are still attached to my body despite all the abuse inflicted on them. Yet you, in your innocence, have sacrificed yours in order to return to life.

We are rarely in conflict, Giles, but we do argue about shoes. You always insist on wearing jogging shoes without socks, and wearing them until they are despicable. I want you to wear something more sensible. Do you remember having athlete's foot and an in-growing toenail which had to be surgically removed? I reminded you then it was because of wearing those dreadful shoes without socks.

Just a couple of years ago you broke your leg, while fooling around with Jay, your stepbrother.

Last weekend, before the last performance of the play, I thought my worries were over when you came to Longview and we shopped for three pairs of shoes. A pair for the senior prom which would have been held last Friday, a pair of rain shoes and a pair of sneakers to replace those deplorable jogging shoes. Never in your life have you owned so many shoes.

It is as though your feet have been condemned by fate since the beginning of your short life. Now they are gone and you have a new set of problems to address. My frivolous concerns about shoes as a teenager are nothing to what you have to face. Shoes will be very important to you from now on and will probably be at the forefront of your worries in the years to come.

## *Monday, May 19th.*

W here are you, Giles? Are you running in your dreams? Are you skiing in your mind? Do you see moguls before you challenging your heart?

Your legs have disappeared to an unknown place in the hospital; I know not where. Maybe they will be studied before they are incinerated and a medical article written about the effects of extreme freezing on human tissue. Who knows? They are gone — gone from your life. Your life is forever changed. No longer can you jump over sofas and break your leg, no longer will you feel the warm sand oozing up between your toes; those days have gone. It gives me solace to know that you do not understand what has happened to you; God protects you by keeping you asleep. Maybe your subconscious will absorb the harsh reality of the amputations, so that it won't be such a shock to you when you wake up.

I have been with you most of the night, Giles. I may have snatched an hour or two of sleep in the waiting room, but I don't leave you for very long. It is still dark outside, but dawn will break soon and begin another day of perpetual routines.

The doctors are trying to be positive about the amputations, but it is sad for them as it is for us all. Dr. Hikes talks continuously, nervously rambling on about modern prostheses and how clever they are. He knows more about it than I do, but it seems unlikely that artificial limbs can be all that wonderful. He almost makes me feel as though I should have a pair myself. He talks about a zippy new wheelchair designed for young people and how much you will like it. He says you will ski again, maybe play basketball and predicts that you will wear out your prostheses faster than you wore out shoes. I only listen; I am quite bewildered.

Anyway, we have to face up to it regardless of how we feel— prostheses, wheelchairs and stumps are part of our future. I have so many questions and new terms to learn. They call your legs "stumps" now. I don't like that expression, there must be a better word to describe amputated legs. The staff keeps on referring to "AK" and "BK". "What is that?" I asked and they explained that it means "above the knee" and "below the knee". It's odd to abbreviate simple words like that when there is so much complicated terminology in medicine which needs to be abbreviated. It's all most confusing, even more than before you had the surgery.

I was telling Dr. Asaph about our buying three pairs of shoes last Saturday. He assured me you will wear them, but I said, now you will wear them out from the inside. He looked at me aghast as though I had lost my mind. This thing hinders my thinking, Giles— I cannot rationalize any more.

I met Dr. Andrews, a plastic surgeon who assisted Dr. Hikes in the surgery last night. He said he took sections of viable skin from the amputated legs and grafted them over the exposed muscles in your arms. He tells me it will take about a year for the muscles to return to their normal size during which time they must not be exposed. He told me you can always have the grafts removed later; they don't have to be permanent.

The doctors are genuinely concerned about infection and we have to take extreme precautions—"reverse isolation" is the term used. Anyone who comes into your room has to wear a gown, a mask, a hat and surgical gloves. Everything has to stay in this room and be autoclaved or disposed of separately—it's quite a performance. The trouble is, we all look the same, menacing silhouettes in green costumes, busying ourselves around your bed. Now I really don't know who is who. There are so many doctors involved in your care, we have made up nicknames for them. Dr. Dreisin is Bow Tie, that's him over there because I can see his tie against his green-shrouded chest. That person looks like a nurse, and that figure sounds like Dr. Asaph. Our tragicomedy must look odd—like marionettes in a sterile theater.

At a particularly crucial moment when all the doctors and nurses were frantically working on you, Dr. Dreisin took off his bow tie and handed it to me. He gave me a sign that he knows you are going to come out of this. I believe him.

Another doctor is leaning against the door outside; I don't know his name, but we have christened him Controlled Beard. He is there day and night, like a sentry standing guard over your fate. I think he is an internist, watching…waiting…reporting on your condition. He must be a distinctly important player on your team.

They tell me that the DIC is coming under control. Although the readings are still alarmingly high, there is evidence that your body is stabilizing. Perhaps we can begin to hope, Giles…maybe you will be *walking in the future*.

Your body continues to be the recipient of every test in the world and you have the use of every machine in the hospital. You have chest X-rays every few hours, electrocardiograms (EKGs) two or three times a day, continuous dialysis and infusions of blood and blood products. The doctors are amazed, even they don't understand where all the blood is going. You have already received in excess of three hundred units, not all of which is whole blood, some of it platelets and other blood products. The accident has depleted resources of blood locally, and blood is being brought in from California. The Red Cross is on the alert and is running short of O-negative—your blood type, Giles. I have the same blood type as you, my darling, and I asked if I could donate my blood directly to you. Perhaps the blood which gave you life will bring your life back. However, the Red Cross will not allow it. There isn't a system in place for families to donate directly. I'm sorry, I would do it gladly. I wish I could give you my blood, then I would be doing something and perhaps I wouldn't feel quite so helpless.

Twice a day you are placed in the hyperbaric chamber. I was allowed to come with you today, but it pained me to see you in the sealed coffin-like cylinder. I was overcome with fear when you were taken off life support. If they had to remove you in an emergency, it couldn't be done immediately because it takes ten minutes to depressurize the chamber. You were trapped in there.

G iles! I wonder if you will remember your life before this dreadful event. Will you know who you are or will your mind wander forever through the annals of oblivion? Perhaps if I tell you about yourself you will not feel so lost when you wake up, and if ever you are taken away from me again, you will know about your family.

Y ou were born in March a little over sixteen years ago; in England, far away from here. We had a little house in Hampshire where we painted our bedroom purple in preparation for your birth. The room looked over the Solent and we could see Southampton in the far distance. Huge ocean liners sailed by our window on their way to America and other far-off lands. I remember waving goodbye to the Queen Mary when she left her home in Southampton to be laid to rest on American shores.

You were my third child, Giles. My friend said that having the third is like falling off a log, and although your passage into the world was relatively easy, my body felt as though it was being wrenched apart. My bones turned to ashes when my hips opened instinctively, ready for your inevitable journey.

Your father sat behind me, gripping my hands as the contractile force pushed you into the world. All I had learned in the books and classes—when to breathe and when not to breathe—was forgotten in a feeling of profound amazement when everything culminated in the procreation of a new soul. The midwife picked your blood-washed form from the bed and marveled at our extraordinary gift.

"Ach, what a beautiful wee boy!" she exclaimed, in her broad Scottish brogue, wiping your tiny head. She placed you onto her scales and weighed you. "Eight pounds, ten ounces," she announced. "What big shoulders he has, it's a wonder you didn't tear."

She swaddled you tightly and handed your little body to me which felt strong and resilient beneath the sheet. I folded my arms about you and I offered you my breast, the most basic of human gestures since man has roamed the earth. "We will leave him to sleep," the nurse said softly. "It's the way nowadays, we don't believe in slapping or bathing the baby right away, it's too much of a shock for him. We will bathe him later."

It was a long time before you woke up, and when you did you hardly cried, you were a placid child. Your sturdy little form was covered with fine, downy, blond fuzz at first which soon disappeared. You had quite a head of hair which was so blond that it could hardly be seen as it blended with the color of your soft fair skin. Your eyes seemed to know me right from the beginning, as you watched me through deep, midnight-blue sapphires. The nurse remarked. "All babies have eyes that color, but they won't stay that way." Yours did, and are as blue as the day you were born. I still remember those quiet, restful hours nursing you, although it's long ago in a far-off land so foreign from where we are now.

Born in a hospital in the North of England, your sister, Joanne, was five years old when you arrived. Ross, your brother, was two years old and was born in the tangerine room next to yours. All of you looked like peas in a pod when you were first born, but now you hardly look related. Joanne has silky golden hair and fair skin and her features are a mixture of your father and me, although people say she looks like me. Ross' hair is straight and much darker, and as he gets older he resembles your father whereas you were like Colin when you were small, but now I see similarities to my family.

The days when you were small were happy and carefree, although I didn't realize it at the time. My mother used to say, "It's the best time of your life." But I didn't believe her. We didn't have much of anything, but it didn't matter. We spent most of our time outdoors, mainly because we couldn't afford to heat the house and I took you for long walks in the pram—to the park, the library and the shops. In the summer we went to the beach. Although it was stony and the weather was usually cloudy, we didn't care. We took off our clothes and swam in the icy water anyway.

Our whirlwind social life filled our calendar. Each week, I would sew furiously to make a new outfit for a suburban party on Saturday night. In the sixties, it was important to keep up with fashion; we had to be in the "groove". The "Mersey sound" emerged and the Beatles took us by storm; we were in the thick of it and loved very minute. Life was much simpler then. We didn't have to worry about education, whether you would ever learn to read and write. Your father and I had a sound English education; Daddy was a professional engineer with a good job, and I was trained in radiotherapy. We felt secure and were confident in the future. The world was our oyster.

When you were born, your father had already accepted a position with an oil company in Puerto Rico. We had to become "aliens" to emigrate to America, and waited for months for the official papers to be processed. It was a torturous time because at first I wanted to emigrate; I wanted adventure and to see the world while the children were small. However, as time went on and as we waited, I changed my mind. I didn't want to leave my homeland and all that was familiar. I didn't want to leave my family and go to an unknown place so far away. Yet, English people have done it for centuries without hope of ever returning. At least we could always go back.

People said, "Everything is bigger over there…and you can't just have one. It's a consumer society."

We were going to Puerto Rico. "It will be different," I thought.

"Everyone has a gun over there," they said. "They'll shoot you for anything."

Puerto Rico will be different—besides we can always return home.

You were ten months old when the packers came and wrapped our meager worldly goods in a profusion of paper and cardboard which was worth more than our belongings themselves. I cut your hair the night we left and put it in a basket. The packers carefully packed our garbage and your curls were shipped with our other things. Months later, your beautiful blond hair arrived safely in Puerto Rico. I still have those locks, Giles.

I choked back my tears throughout the long flight across the Atlantic as I visualized the faces of our parents when we said goodbye. They were confused by the decision which took their little family to the other side of the world. On arriving at the Miami airport, we were herded like sheep by policemen whose behavior shocked me. They strutted aggressively as though we were criminals, their hands poised over their guns ready to draw should one of us do something wrong. They put us in a stark, cell-like room like inmates, awaiting our fate—for someone to say it was alright for us to come to the United States.

I held you tightly in my arms as we waited on a hard bench with Ross and Joanne fearfully clinging to me. I fought back my tears and tried to convince myself we were doing the right thing, but homesickness engulfed me and tore me apart. You slept innocently in my arms, not understanding the enormity of the changes we had made, but you were content as long as you were fed, warm and dry, and as long as we were with you—nothing had altered for you.

Everything did seem bigger in America, just as we had been told. We flew from Miami to Puerto Rico and arrived in the early hours of the evening. A taxi drove us from the airport which was huge, bigger than anything I had ever seen before. We seemed to float on its suspension and it could have carried two or three other families. I was amazed at its size after the tiny cars we had left behind in England. The plastic seats stuck to our skin because of the heat, and you skidded on the slippery surface as the car swayed and turned corners. I gazed wistfully out of the window at the concrete, one-storey houses with iron bars on the windows and doors giving them a prison-like appearance. The car bumped over potholes in the road and there weren't any proper sidewalks. Mangy dogs scavenged in piles of rubbish strewn over the landscape. I could see wooden shacks and falling-down fences—a far cry from the manicured countryside of home. "What have I done by coming to this God-forsaken place?" I asked myself.

"We can always go back," was my only consolation.

Colin unlocked the gate to our iron-clad concrete box which was to be our new home. We dubiously peeped inside and surveyed the plastic furniture and stone floors. The dim blue lights were forbidding and the house was so much bigger than anything I had been accustomed to before. I couldn't get over the size of the refrigerator, it was enormous and I couldn't imagine ever having enough food to fill it. There we were; we had moved and we had to make the best of it.

The first two years in Puerto Rico seemed endless. I felt like a cuckoo in a sparrow's nest, especially as we didn't speak the language. However, the locals were very kind. They were fascinated by your fair skin and blond hair, so different from the swarthy complexions of their babies. They would stroke your golden head in awe and say, *"Ah, que lindo!"* They would laugh and stare at us as though we were from another planet, which we were—after all we were aliens.

We soon settled in as strangers in a strange land, and England faded into a distant memory. I busied myself with the family and relished the thought of returning home in two years. The South American way of life was extraordinarily different from life in England. Time meant nothing, tropical breezes banished my English inhibitions, and sounds of salsa and merengue heralded fun and laughter. People drank all day long, unlike the restricted pub-hours which I had been used to, when a couple of beers on a Saturday night was all we could afford. We were introduced to rum-soaked drinks, which tasted and looked so benign, but were terribly potent. Before long, I was out of my depth, experimenting with *Cuba libres,* long green things and drinks called "planters punch". It wasn't unusual to find me drinking in the middle of the day and collapsed in a stupor at four in the afternoon.

The weather was always beautiful. The temperature hardly varied between seventy and eighty degrees, with balmy breezes constantly blowing off the ocean. At first, I was entranced by the weather, after the cold dampness of England, but the lack of seasons soon became monotonous. No blossoms or bulbs in the springtime, no changing of leaves in the autumn; it was summer, day after day, but the abundance of tropical flowers more than compensated. Poinsettias grew wild by the roadside, hibiscus grew the size of saucers, and bougainvillea in a vast variety of colors adorned every garden both rich and poor. Every evening the crickets serenaded us along with the *coquis*, which are claimed to be the smallest frogs in the world and unique to Puerto Rico.

It was enchanting, and soon we felt an integral part of the island. The local people were charming and their strong family structure impressed me. They accepted us without reservation and included us in their parties which they had any time, any day. All generations were present, from the very young to the very old with everyone enjoying each other.

I attended classes at the local university to learn Spanish, but it didn't come easy to me. I had never been good at languages and I thought I was too old to start. However, I soon learnt to nod and laugh at the right time, fling my arms just as the locals did, and no one realized that I didn't have a clue as to what was being said—until of course, they expected an answer. Spanish came naturally to you, Ross and Joanne, whereas your father and I struggled to make ourselves understood with our limited vocabulary.

Instead of taking our long walks to the park with the pram, we went to the swimming pool every day after school. You were still a toddler when you fell into a cactus by the pool. You must have had twenty spines sticking out of your face, making you look like a porcupine. It was a miracle you didn't lose your eye. When you were three, I almost lost you at the pool. You fell in when my back was turned, but mercifully someone saw you and pulled you out by your hair before it was too late.

I couldn't keep any clothes on you when you were small. At the drop of a hat you would strip them off and toddle away in the nude. Once I caught you pushing a toy down the street without a stitch on—no wonder you picked up an infection on your feet because you never would wear shoes. Even then it seemed that you were accident-prone, but you were fearless and adventurous. Soon my golden-haired baby disappeared, and a little boy emerged.

When I emigrated, Giles, I lost the crutches that had been my support. I had to start all over again because the past was erased with a single stroke, and no one understood where I came from or who I was. The guidelines under which I had been brought up didn't exist in Puerto Rico, and I drifted away from the family. I lost my sense of belonging, the sense of comfort of being around my own people. I think it's easier for men to move to a new and different world, perhaps because they have a job which must give them a feeling of belonging. I only had my family to take care of, my sense of identity was gone and I felt terribly lost. I started drinking heavily and roaming more and more until one day, I came home, and your father's closet was empty. Daddy couldn't take any more and had moved out.

Soon we were divorced. My father was shocked when I told him. "How could it happen so fast, one minute married, the next minute not," he said. "Always remember, in the eyes of The Church it is 'till death do us part'." In England, at that time, a couple had to be separated for two years before they could even file for a divorce, and it was only granted under extreme circumstances. My parents were appalled that our divorce was settled so quickly and that no attempt had been made to reconcile our differences.

We lived apart for a year. That year was perhaps the most chaotic period of my life. Between clandestine meetings with new-found lovers, children problems and troubles with my car, I lost track of time and who I really was. It seemed as though it would be idyllic to be single living on a tropical island, but it soon got old. My boyfriends didn't want to acknowledge my children, my invitations did not include you. It wasn't long before I missed the family life which we had worked so hard for and which was so fragile as to be crushed by a brisk sweep of a pen. Separation didn't work for either of us, Daddy wanted his children; perhaps we were both searching for something—something which we had all the time—family and our children.

That year was particularly difficult for you, your brother and your sister. The foundation of your entire world had been placed in jeopardy, and at the same time, I came close to losing you over my desire to have a final fling. I was convinced that at thirty-four, I was possibly on the verge of decrepitude.

Daddy, whose staunch ideals never flinched throughout the havoc which had cleaved our family apart, felt that if we left Puerto Rico, we could wipe the slate clean and start all over again. He believed our marriage could be as before, if only he could whisk us away to a new place.

You were seven years old when your father moved us from the tropical island to the mainland of America where we joined the "rat race" in Texas. We threw away our flip-flops, forced our feet into sensible shoes, said goodbye to the land of *mañana*, set our watches and started to live by the clock again.

We bought a huge house which had everything I had ever dreamed about in England: bedrooms for everyone, three bathrooms, formal this and electrical that. It was more than the mind could absorb at first; an example of a standard of living which I had only heard about. I even had a car of my own and at last I was independent. I could go where I wanted, when I wanted. Soon you became typical American children, you discovered "the snack" and American television, both of which we had been spared in the tropics.

Joanne went to the local high school, you and Ross went to an Episcopal school. You were a fine student, Giles, good at all subjects. You became involved in athletics in which you excelled and your urge to construct things became evident.

Soon after we settled in, I was offered a full-time job as a technical manager at the local cancer center. I couldn't turn it down. I believed financial independence would give me the freedom which I had always yearned for, but I soon learnt I would pay a big price for that freedom.

I worked all the hours God made and discovered it wasn't easy to juggle a full-time job, maintain a big house and bring up three children. I was determined to foster my career so that if ever I was left alone, I would always qualify for a good job, and wouldn't have to depend on anyone.

You were sorely neglected, Giles. I was unable to participate in many of your activities, but at least your father had the kind of job which he could leave to pick you up from school. I often came home late from work and hardly had time to say goodbye in the morning and weekends were spent catching up on household chores. Your formative years were barren as far as family life was concerned, but at least you three children were close to one another. Ross and Joanne were able to fill the void that my absence created. I was always torn between work and home, home and work, but work always came first.

It's easy to be wise after the fact, Giles. I have spent many hours looking back over those years, now that you have left home and the house is empty. I regret taking so much time away from your childhood, time which can never be retrieved. As I look at you now and realize that you could be taken away from me in a single stroke, I fear that I may never have the chance to make it up to you. I want you to know that it was never worth the sacrifices I made, even the satisfaction of having had a successful career never outweighed the guilt I experienced for not being there for you as a child.

You were a bright little boy and we loved you dearly. Colin gave our family stability and security, and I provided the entertainment. Long distances separated you from the ongoing influences of your grandparents, yet another price we paid for living abroad. We saw them whenever we went back to England, and even though they came to stay with us frequently for extended periods, it wasn't the same as having them nearby as a part of our everyday lives. You were deprived of that unique relationship with your grandparents, learning woodwork from your grandfather, Joanne being taught to sew by Nan, and Ross learning music from them. Grandparents should play an important role in a child's upbringing. They are a link to the past, a reminder of where you came from—an extended family to share in the decisions of your young life. Nan, especially, was saddened by our leaving England. She had never had a family life of her own and wanted to be a part of ours, but because we were so far away, she felt deprived of her grandchildren.

Our house was constantly buzzing with activity. Ross has always been musically inclined, and started out on his career by beating on his homemade drum sets. He progressed to a flute and musical sounds were perpetually coming from his room. Joanne, in her own creative way, kept herself busy making some last-minute gift for someone. The three of you were good at entertaining yourselves, playing soldiers in the garden, dressing up in make-believe uniforms and building traps out of garbage can lids to catch some unsuspecting beast. Ross loved to hurl his toy soldiers out of the bedroom window hoping that their tiny parachutes would break their fall. Even in those early days, you were all creative and artistically inclined and would often put on drama performances to entertain your grandparents through those interminable hours when I was working. Ross would dress up as Rosanne, you as a pirate and Joanne would play a supporting role. You liked to construct things and made an endless succession of model airplanes and cars, and there was always a fortress somewhere in the neighborhood which you and your friends had made. You were athletically inclined and became interested in sports. You played in Little League, football and basketball. I was so busy, I didn't have time to come to your games and there were many activities in which you couldn't become involved, because I wasn't available to take you or pick you up. But I want you to know that I always encouraged you in what you wanted to do. Even so, those were happy days, when the innocence of childhood overshadowed the problems which surrounded you.

You were a remarkable swimmer, even when you were very small. With inflatable armbands, you would jump in and out of the pool without fear. Eventually, you no longer needed the bands and you swam like a fish down to the bottom, propelling yourself through the water with the greatest of ease. Swimming was never my forte, I still remember struggling to swim a length in the icy cold water of the pools in England. Just thinking about it makes me shiver.

Do you remember Patra, the dog we acquired in Puerto Rico within a few days of arriving there? It wasn't difficult to have a dog, because strays lined the streets and all we had to do was reach under a hedgerow to pull out a puppy. Patra was a scrawny spectacle really, but we loved her; she was part of our family. Now we have Rufus and Smoky—such a terrible pair. They are waiting for you, Giles, they know that something is wrong. Bill tells me that they waited and waited on the doorstep when you were on the mountain, but he says they have relaxed now. Your dogs know you will come back.

Our lives took on a dizzy, hectic pace and through it all I was oblivious to the fact that your father was losing weight, and the significance of his sleepless nights never alerted me that he was ill. When you were ten years old, your father went to the hospital for a barrage of tests which determined a diagnosis of cancer of the pancreas. The lapidary prognosis spelt doom with, at best, a year left to live.

When we moved to Texas the relationship between your father and me was never the same; something was irrevocably broken. We were strangers under the same roof, unable to talk about the painful nuances which had driven us apart, hoping that silence and time would heal our wounds. Although our relationship was far from perfect, I never, ever would have wished this to happen to him. The news broke my heart one more time. There was no consolation, there was no turning back, all we could do was look forward and do the best we could to get through this dreadful episode in our lives.

Daddy's suffering was awful; the excruciating pain which racked his body was totally out of control. Often Ross was the only one at home to inject him with the futile medicine which was prescribed. His body deteriorated in no time at all. The strong, virile man who was the stalwart of our life turned into a frail, cachectic form, a mere shadow of his former self. I was grateful that you were too young to fully appreciate the seriousness of his disease, but I'm certain, whatever you sensed about your father's illness must have affected you deeply.

It was a warm Texas spring day when Colin died. He had slipped into a coma on Friday morning and it was Monday. Joanne said goodbye to him as she left for school and even in a coma, he heard her and seemed to wave. Ross stayed home from school that day, perhaps he sensed that something was about to happen. He quietly went upstairs and took refuge in his music. He still finds solace in playing, even now he loses himself in it, especially when he has something on his mind. The muffled sounds of his guitar, blended with the songs of the mockingbirds outside, provided the background to our scene.

After three days of being suspended in time waiting by your father's bedside, it was as though our vigil would go on forever, but death came quickly at the end. About eleven-thirty in the morning, Colin became agitated. I went to get him a drink of warm, sweet tea to moisten his parched lips, and when I returned he was restless. I thought perhaps he was in pain, so I gave him a morphine injection which seemed to calm him. I lay on the bed beside him in a timeless transition between life and death and waited, not knowing what to expect, but realizing that his sufferings would soon be over—that paradise awaited. Again he became agitated, and there erupted a distinctive rattling from the depths of his being. I had heard of "death rattles", but had never experienced this mysterious orchestra which plays the overture to death. It didn't last very long but it seemed like a lifetime, and I knew the end was near. His lips trembled and he mouthed the words "I love you," as he departed.

I gripped his hands as his body was rocked by a final spasm, and his soul passed into paradise. That last exhalation ended his suffering, and the grotesque countenance of death stared back at me.

A vacant stillness and silence engulfed us with only the music of the mockingbirds singing his requiem. His spirit rose from his sickbed and hovered above me looking down from his ethereal passage, out of reach and beyond life's torment and human sufferings. I called out to him, "I will see you in Paradise! Godspeed!"

For a moment we were suspended in space, connected by our lives together, but "death do us part" as he transcended beyond me. The beginning and end of life happen in absolute silence. Life in the womb is in silence, just the feeling that there is life, and here at the end…deathly silence again.

The moment was broken by the harsh ringing of the telephone. It was Joanne saying she would pick you up from school and bring you home. Ross and I held vigil by your father's side. Ross said he had never seen a dead person before.

Colin's face was translucent, like alabaster, and his body was cold. I noticed he still had a scar on his neck where he had cut himself shaving the week before. His hands were those of a different person, no longer able to reach out, nor to grip a pencil, but stiff and rigid through metamorphosis.

I had rehearsed my part in the event of Colin's death and, like a programmed robot, I reached for the phone to call the funeral home. About half an hour later a policeman came to question me about the circumstances of your father's death. Supposedly it had to be done, but the interview seemed callous, lacking the delicacy of the moment and breaking the trance of our journey forever.

When I went back to your father he had passed across the chasm to eternity and left a tenuous fragrance of death which permeated the air, and was all he left behind. Even when he was taken away in a body-bag to prepare him for viewing, the distinctive odor persisted. I burnt scented candles in his room which danced gently with his spirit, but the smell of death remained for many days.

His body was carried away to an elegant place, unlike anything he had been used to in life. They dressed him like a navy captain and made his face up like a movie-star with a smile which he never wore in real life. You came to the parlor and sat in the Chippendale chair and said that you weren't going to cry, but I could see you valiantly fighting back your tears. We rarely went to the funeral parlor and Daddy spent the last few days on this earth alone. It seems odd to put people in places like that for the few remaining hours they have on this earth. Instead we had flowers to remind us of his passing, just like the flowers we have now. I find them overpowering, Giles. I know there is a meaning behind them, and I am grateful to the many people who remember us, but I wish I could throw them away. All they do is remind me of death and suffering.

On the surface we seemed to deal with our experience admirably, but underneath we suffered our grief in silence, and put that day of painful memories into our past. To this day, Giles, when I think of your father it is his dying moment which is the most vivid thought. I would miss your father. I had been prepared for his death for some time, but not for the grief that I would suffer. I had known him most of my life; he was my friend and now he was gone. I had no one to talk to about England, about our family and our friends over there. No one to share the little nuances of life which only he could remember. The father of my children and the only other person who loved them as I did was gone from our lives forever.

Soon after your father's death, Bill came into your life. You hardly knew him when he helped us to pack our belongings one more time, loaded us into the van and drove us north to Washington. You didn't accept him at first, Giles, and showed your resentment openly. I don't blame you for that. It couldn't have been easy to have your father gone and see your mother with another man. He came into my life unexpectedly, I certainly wasn't looking for a relationship at the time when we met at the cancer center where I worked. I love Bill dearly. Our love isn't an infatuation which comes and goes, but the kind that began with a casual acquaintance which grew and flourished into a strong relationship until we were bonded and committed to each other for life. I realized it was too soon for my children, but I couldn't let it go. Besides, I doubt whether we could have survived in the jungle in which we found ourselves.

Bill had been a pathologist and later in his life changed his career to become a cancer physician. He had come to a crossroads in his life just as I had, wanted to leave Texas, and when the opportunity arose to start a new cancer center in Washington state, we decided to take it and leave the vale of tears behind us.

Remember when Bill and I were married, Giles? We stopped in Nevada on the never-ending journey to the Pacific Northwest, Bill stood in front of the van with his hands on his hips and said, "How about it?" It's a blur in my memory now, but I know I was apprehensive about it. I wanted everything to work out and, more than anything, for us to be a family. Although we can't see into the future, I was determined to do the right thing—not only for myself, but I wanted assurances for your future also.

We stopped at a "wedding shop" and asked the receptionist about the procedure to get married. She beeped the preacher and, within minutes, we were ready. I hadn't given any thought to what I should wear until I rummaged in the back of the van and found an old Mexican dress which still had paint on the bottom from the time when I decorated our house in Texas before we left. We could have rented everything from the shop, a dress and tuxedo (just to the waist, enough for the pictures), a plastic bouquet of flowers, even the rings. We had bought wedding rings at a Texas fair, and we didn't need any frills.

I cried through the ceremony as the booming voice of the preacher echoed throughout the simple little chapel, and his piercing stare seemed to pass judgment on our motive for marriage. You three children were our witnesses, bewildered at what must have been a comical scene. Nevertheless we did it; the whole thing was over in an hour, including a call to England. We bought a bottle of champagne, checked into a motel and you played in the swimming pool while we toasted to our future—that was our wedding reception. We never looked back after that and pressed on to Longview.

Remember the CB radios, Giles? We each had our own "handle". You were the "Nacho Kid", Ross was the "Wave Master", Joanne was "Bomber Beak", I was "Queen Ann" and Bill was "Quincey", after the pathologist. It was a difficult trip, filled with mixed emotions, but somehow we made it. We laughed and we cried on the way, but I still have happy memories of that adventurous journey across the United States.

Longview is a pretty little place, snuggled in the Columbia River valley, approximately fifty miles north of Portland, Oregon. Lake Sacajawea (named after the Indian squaw who traveled with explorers Lewis and Clark) is the focal point of the town where people congregate to exercise and play. The tall fir trees surrounding the lake are mature and beautiful and their massive branches watch over the many children who play there. In the spring, the gardens suddenly burst into life with a rainbow of vibrant color as rhododendrons, azaleas and flowering trees open their blossoms.

I was immediately attracted to Longview; it reminds me of home with its neat manicured gardens, incessant rain, and it appeared to be a safe place to bring up my children. The locals talk about the weather as they do in England, which is something that Texans hardly ever mention.

We found a suitable house built in Pacific Northwest style tucked into one of the many hills which encompass the town. I have always missed England, longed for the familiar ties to my people, to laugh at their silly jokes and engage in familiar conversation. Perhaps this is as close as I will ever come to being home again.

We soon made friends and had a happy life in this small unpretentious town which gave us an opportunity for a new beginning and a place to grow. We set up a cancer treatment practice and were soon an integral part of the community. Bill is held in high regard as the cancer doctor who lives on the hill. He is a good stepfather, a wonderful doctor and someone whom we can respect and love. After everything we have been through, I finally feel at peace; at last we have found our place in life. How lucky we are to have each other. Our families have joined together, not without problems, but on the whole it has been a successful union.

Giles, you were eleven years old and still a little boy when we moved to Longview, with a strong will and moodiness which comes with early adolescence. Your body grew at different rates; like a Labrador puppy's, your feet seemed too big for your legs and your nose appeared to dominate your entire face. Your straight, silky golden hair turned, almost overnight, wiry and curly and faded to an ashen blond. You settled in well, you liked your new school, made new friends and it wasn't long before you were playing football and basketball. Soon the house was filled with sports equipment of every type.

Ross continued to be passionate about his music and soon after arriving in Longview he discovered the classical guitar. Before long he outgrew his music teacher, and felt there might be other opportunities in Portland, so he enrolled in Oregon Episcopal School (OES) only fifty miles away from home.

OES was a positive move for Ross, it provided him with a safe, tranquil environment as he dealt with the uncertainties which come with teenage years. He was intellectually challenged through in-depth discussions about philosophy and religion. I was pleased with the influence it had on him. He traveled to Longview by train almost every weekend at first, but his visits became less frequent as time passed. He learnt how to get around Portland on his own, and it wasn't long before he gained his independence.

Joanne didn't stay with us for very long. Her heart was still in Texas and she went back to college there. She was my first child to leave home and I missed her desperately at first. I felt guilty that I couldn't keep her close to me, but she was determined to go her own way. I thought I would have her forever, keep her a little girl close to my heart, but it was time for her to go away. I supported her in her endeavors, but I prayed that she would come back to the family one day.

Our new family became interested in skiing and we bought the cabin near Mount Hood. We spend many long, happy days up there. I often stay there when you are skiing to catch up on my hobbies which have taken a back seat with my working all the time. I have time to myself again and an opportunity to contemplate our good fortune.

The cabin was the scene of my worst foreboding, Giles. I waited there on that dreadful night when you were still lost on the mountain. It was then that I heard you calling: "I'm okay, Mom! I'm okay!"

I will never forget that night as long as I live.

Here you are on the brink of consciousness. Call to me, Giles! Tell me again that you are alright.

## *Tuesday, May 20th.*

It has been a long and sleepless night, and I am still here by your side through our long vigil together. I wonder what you are thinking as you drift in your somnolent state. I cannot tell whether your mental powers are conscious of us, or whether you are far away in some never-never land. I search for signs of recognition, but you look back at me with a blank stare. You seem to be more restless today, as though fighting the forces of the machines which sustain your life. Through it all, your indomitable person shines from beyond the capricious green lines on the monitors and I sense your tenacious spirit conquering the condition which invades your body. Will you get well, Giles? Will you be the same as before? What meaning do these days hold for you? Have you returned to that place of innocence, to the purple room in England where you were born?

Your friends and teachers from school were here to see you last night. The atmosphere in our little waiting room was vibrant with chatter and laughter. At last, we have reason to hope, a glimmer of light is appearing after this week of darkness. Two have survived the icy tomb. It could be worse...not much, but it's something.

Ralph was here too. I hardly recognized him from when I last saw him, less than a week ago on the mountain. He is a slightly-built person anyway, but he looks as though he hasn't eaten or slept since then. I wonder if he will be familiar to you when you wake up. He and Sam, the Basecamp Program director, explained how the Climb was structured and who was in charge. They too are baffled as to how this accident could have occurred.

The Basecamp Program is part of the curriculum. Climb leaders from the school and hired guides have taken sophomore students up Mount Hood on many occasions and they consider themselves to be experienced.

The Sophomore Climb is a day hike. The group sets off in the early hours of the morning and attempts to go as far as possible if conditions are favorable. It isn't a mandatory expedition, nor is the object to get to the summit. Sam explained that you were not prepared to spend the night on the mountain, nor did you take any out-of-the-ordinary equipment. Obviously students vary in their physical ability, and indeed, the south face of Mount Hood is a relatively easy ten-hour climb. Thousands of people have ascended this mountain, ranging in age from seven to seventy, including inexperienced climbers and the physically impaired.

When Ross went on the Climb two years ago he did complain about the bright sunlight and heat, but when it came time for you to go I really wasn't concerned, because I was confident in the guidelines set forth by the Basecamp Program. I have since found out though, that Mount Hood has the highest accident rate of any mountain in the lower forty-eight States, and in bad weather or in poor conditions, can be a serious environment requiring skill and experience for survival. Ralph told me you almost walked out with him, but you were exhausted after working on the cave entrance. How I wish all the climbers had tried to walk out with him. Perhaps he is right when he says he couldn't have done anything differently under the dreadful conditions you were in. If only we could put the clock back, Giles, but time marches on.

You would be excited to hear that there is talk about making a movie. A Hollywood film company was at the school yesterday, and it looks as though they plan to do it. I was quite flabbergasted because I wouldn't have thought this incident was interesting enough to make a film—but then what do I know about such things. For a moment we were distracted from all the horrifying events of the last week, and speculated about being film stars. I think I would like Meryl Streep to play my part, and Sam wants Robert Redford to play his. We laughed at our tragedian parts for a brief moment, but I have already put such things out of my mind. The thought of a movie appalls me.

No one ever told me how difficult being a parent would be, but even as I understand it now, I wouldn't have it any other way. There are many things which I regret in my life, but parenthood has never been one of them. All the joy and happiness you have brought to me far outweigh the turmoil which we have experienced. Nothing in my past has prepared me for this last week, Giles. Waiting hour after hour, first on the mountain and now at your side, aching for a promise from whomever is in charge of your destiny to tell me you will be alright.

Your adolescent years have been particularly anguished for me. You are so remote now, the little boy who followed me everywhere has gone forever. No longer do you want me to read you a story and you don't want to come to the pool with me anymore. You have your own way now. Your clothes are like a ragamuffin's, you never bother to iron them. It is the fashion to have a rip in your knee and even across your behind. To have your underwear showing appears to be quite acceptable. Even though you spend hours in the shower, you always look as though you have just fallen out of bed and your hair has become so unruly, I can't tell whether you're coming or going. I can't identify with your music, it's alien to me. Just as my mother was confused by the different world into which I drifted as a teen, I find myself feeling the same.

Your friends left you some tapes, but I have already thrown them away. They were by The Grateful Dead. I have never heard of them, Giles, but I'm revolted by the title. I'm sure your friends didn't even think about the significance of their name, but I can't have that name associated here. I have no idea what it means, but I don't want any part of it. Forgive me. I hope you will understand.

I read about dreadful things happening to teenagers these days. Will you stay strong my darling? Will you be able to avoid adverse influences which could destroy your life? Will your prudent and astute character resist them, and lead you towards a fulfilling future? I pray every day that you will stay on the right path. I cannot lead you anymore, my parenting can only guide you and offer you opportunities, but it's up to you to decide.

It doesn't seem long since I was sixteen. I was wild and adventurous too, although I think you are more conservative than I was, more like your father. I remember that time as though it were yesterday.

Our lives were quite different to yours where school and homework were our entire existence. The educational system in England was strikingly different to that of America. My school was "all girls" and your father's "all boys". I notice that several of your teachers are also your friends. It was never like that for me. My teachers were spinsters, because in those days, government employees had to leave their professions if they got married. Many at my school were of marriageable age during the First World War when almost a whole generation of men were wiped out.

Discipline was stifling, there were rules and regulations for everything. The theory that childhood is a period of placid innocence did not exist in those days. School was a test of endurance, and the more stringent the test the child survived, the better prepared he would be to face the demands of adulthood. We had to wear uniforms which were designed to make us look as "uniform" as possible. We weren't allowed to wear makeup or jewelry; tidy hair had to be off the face and collar; we had to wear regulation shoes, socks and even underwear. There was no doubt as to why we were at school: we were there to be educated…not to have fun. We didn't have time for anything but study—five hours a day and all day Sunday was our weekly routine for homework—even with that I barely kept up. The pressure of exams always loomed over us and the only time for recreation and trouble was Saturday night.

Your father and I were already sweethearts and passionately in love. My mother said it couldn't be love at such a young age and did everything possible to discourage us. Colin was the first real boyfriend I ever had. I was fourteen and he was seventeen when we met. I was flattered to think an older boy would be interested in me. He was far ahead of me academically; on the football and cricket teams; he was a prefect at school and heading for university. I was nothing.

We dated for years, but we only saw each other one night a week. The hours of petting left me exhausted and even though Daddy tried to get me home on time, we were always late. There were incessant arguments with my parents, always having to explain and long lonely silences were my punishment for crimes which I didn't know I had committed.

Fashion was the big thing: hooped skirts that popped up at the front when we sat down, back-breaking shoes which were impossible to walk in and "can-can" underskirts which made us look like a top-heavy lamp. Bouffant hairstyles which we were afraid to wash lest the beehive should collapse into an unrecognizable heap, and stockings with suspenders which created a cold gap on the thigh.

The boys, not "out of the top drawer", as my mother would say, had their fashions too: drainpipe trousers, string ties and shirts with frills down the front. They wore crepe "bumper" shoes which made them look like puppets as they stood on street corners whistling at the girls. American music bellowed from the juke boxes in the coffee shops. Bill Haley and the Comets caused riots in the cinemas where teenagers ripped up the seats. Elvis the Pelvis came along with pelvic gyrations which titillated older women to giggle, but they would never explain why. I remember going to a concert and screaming through the show, not caring about what was being played; it was just the thing to do. Colin went off to Liverpool University and saw the Beatles at the Cavern long before they were heard of in England or America.

My being sixteen was different again to your grandmother's upbringing in Wales. Practically her entire family died of tuberculosis and her mother passed away when she was a teenager. Being the youngest, she was left to look after her father at home and wasn't able to complete her education. Your grandparents met when they were very young and married when my mother was in her early twenties. When the Second World War came, her life was rocked by uncertainties. I was born during the war and spent my infancy in air-raid shelters while my father was fighting in some faraway place. My mother often told me about those days: how the sirens would go off in the middle of the night; how they wore gas masks and put the babies inside gas masks to go to the shelter for the night.

Married women of my mother's generation rarely worked, but were expected to look after the home and take care of the children. Although my mother always encouraged us to have an education and be qualified in something, for herself, her children were her entire life. I think the experiences of your grandmother's youth, and the war, had a profound effect on her. Perhaps the constant feeling of insecurity, not knowing from one day to the next what the future held, made her overprotective. Maybe not having a life outside the home made her neurotic about her own children.

I was a rebellious teenager, as probably all teenagers are, and all I wanted to do was run with the boys. There weren't as many adverse influences then as there are for you, Giles, such as drugs, alcohol and violence. We were allowed to go into pubs at eighteen and some children experimented with cigarettes, but nothing else was available. Nowadays, you see more on television advertisements than we even dared to think about.

Even so, there was enough adverse influence for my mother, and there were always terrible conflicts at home. If and when I was allowed to go out, she was there to say goodbye as I left the house, and was waiting for me when I got home. She would drill me as to where I had been and what I had been doing.

"You don't understand!" I would say. The problem was, my parents did understand. They knew we had been "necking" and what that could lead to. If I got pregnant I would have to get married at a young age and my education would be ruined. They knew I could associate with the wrong crowd and get into trouble. They had struggled for what they had, and they knew the importance of an education in order to succeed in a civilized world. They did understand, but they could only communicate in conflict. I was lonely and unhappy and I couldn't wait to leave home, which I did when I was seventeen. I went to the city to train in the medical field.

My mother desperately missed her own mother, and would tell me how lucky I was to have a mother, and that I should be grateful for all the things my parents did for me. She often talked about the "old country" and about the customs in Wales. She longed for that life again, for the close communities where everyone knew one another and looked out for each other, and of course, knew everybody's business.

When I grew up, I vowed that I would never be dependent on a man, the way my mother was. I vowed I would always have a life of my own separate from my children and, although I stayed at home with you when you were small, I always wanted to pursue my own profession. It wasn't easy, there was always a conflict within me. I wanted to work, but at the same time I wanted to be at home. There was no doubt you wanted me there, there was no substitute for me. I encouraged you to be independent—perhaps too much so.

When Joanne reached adolescence, I relived the same clashes with her as I had with my own parents, and I often heard myself saying the same things as my mother used to say. Joanne would go out at night, not say where she was going and would rarely be home on time. I would pace the floor waiting for her, getting more and more anxious. By the time she came home, I would be frantic with worry and of course, we would argue; just as my mother and I used to argue. I didn't like Joanne's friends just as my mother disliked mine. Joanne called me a snob like I had called my mother a snob. She would often lie to me, just as I had lied to my parents and would say: "You don't understand." Just as I had said.

What went wrong? I hadn't planned it that way. My mother seemed to have the ideal attributes of a mother, and yet those years of growing up were by far the most difficult of my life and here I was doing it to my own children. Even though I thought I knew the traps of parenting and believed I had done everything to prevent the problems—history repeated itself.

I often think of adolescence as the "forgotten age". In more primitive societies, young people are nurtured through puberty by a number of adults, different generations mix with one another and the young learn from their elders about being an adult. However, in Western society, parents and children are left alone to cope with the changes with little structure to support them. As a result, the rift between parent and child is often impossible to bridge. There is very little mingling of different age groups, as there was in Puerto Rico, and few communities feel responsible for providing safe places where teens can be allowed to grow up with the unthreatening nurturing of adults.

My adolescent years were difficult years for me, but different again from those of my parents. My generation marked the first wave of change—"rock and roll" became popular; television was invented, although it had very little impact on our lives, and the idea of women's liberation was emerging. We were branching out in a new direction, but there were no models to emulate, no society to support us in our rebellion. Even so, it was nothing compared to the pressures you are under.

My upbringing didn't do me any harm, and I am grateful that we were pressured to become educated which took up most of our energy and time as teens. I admit, that if I could conform to those traditions with my own children—I would gladly have made martyrs out of them.

There are many teenagers around you, Giles, I am becoming part of their world in this complex maze of feelings. Robindra stays with me day and night in our waiting room, with your leather jacket pulled around her shoulders. She is a constant comfort to me. I don't know her at all, but it doesn't seem to matter. We hardly talk, but our hearts are focused on you—nothing else occupies our minds. Your friends are bewildered by the deaths of so many of their school-friends and teachers, and are in awe over your present condition. They are deeply affected and I watch them gazing intently into space, trying to make sense of it all.

I think I am gaining a better understanding of your generation; being close to your friends is helping me to bridge the gap between us. It is just as difficult for you as it is for me. We need to understand each other and take more time to communicate. Today, the real meaning of motherhood occupies my heart—you could leave me at any moment and even if you come back, your mind could be separated from us. I want to hold back the time, spare myself this torture and wake up from this nightmare which haunts me.

Giles, you were fourteen when you went to OES. You were reluctant to go at first, but you soon settled in. You live in the dormitories and have made friends easily. You rarely come home at the weekend, and suddenly I have an empty nest. I am happy for you because I know you are content; OES is a good place for you.

I have been surprised by your developing interest in drama, and your admiration for your art teacher. Jack has an interest in both you and Ross and has influenced you to become interested in set design and construction. Ross is involved in theater too and is quite an actor. He has performed in several school plays, often playing a leading role. I was impressed and somewhat surprised at his talent, and found your passion for the creative side of drama even more surprising. You have often worked with Jack long into the night, building remarkable sets for one play or another.

It is only a week since I came to see you in the play—*You Can't Take It with You*. It's ironical really, almost all the cast were scheduled to be on this Climb, or were in some way connected to the climbers. All of the climbers were exceptionally gifted children, especially in the arts. Perhaps that was what brought you together to challenge the mountain last weekend.

The atmosphere in the Great Hall was exciting and exuberant, both in the audience and on stage. It was the last performance and the cast was relaxed even when the antlers collapsed when Ross slammed the door. I was enthralled by the play, never having seen it before, and moved by the subtle message which it conveyed. The play was about an eccentric family who preferred to live their lives the way they wanted and to spend their time with each other. They were not concerned about material things and keeping up with convention. It was lighthearted, and yet its message was clear.

I waited in the car to see you after the performance. The rain was coming down in torrents and in just a few minutes the grounds were flooded, the drains unable to cope with the volume of water from the sudden downpour. It was exceptionally cold for May, although the inclement weather in this part of the world never ceases to amaze me.

You jumped in the car and said you couldn't stay, that you had homework to do, and had to get some sleep before the Climb. "Surely the weather must be very bad on the mountain if it's like this in Portland, and surely you won't go in conditions like this," I thought.

"I don't really want to go," you said. "Hiking isn't my thing."

That was the last time I saw you.

Why did I let you go on that ill-fated climb? I didn't feel good about your going at all—I can't explain why. It may have been a premonition, I don't know. Why didn't I listen to the voices which screamed from within my soul? I kept hoping that the Climb would be canceled, which isn't like me at all. I have always wanted you to explore new horizons and challenge yourself at every opportunity. I have never been an overanxious parent, especially when I know you are in good hands, but I was apprehensive about this climb. I have had many hours to think about it here at your bedside, pacing the floors of the hospital and Timberline Lodge, wishing that something had intervened to stop you from going. Perhaps if you had been sick or injured, or even moved to a different climb for some reason, you wouldn't have been in that dreadful storm. If I had been more forceful or if I had remotely recognized the danger, I could have stopped you. Forgive me for not acting on my instincts.

I was in the elevator on my way to your room early this morning when I recognized the two men in the carriage with me as reporters. They were talking loudly to one another about the news of your amputations.

"Can you imagine what it must feel like to wake up to find your legs gone?" one said.

"Man…" said the other and shook his head. They obviously didn't know who I was, nor did they care. They got out of the elevator laughing and joking—just doing their job I suppose. I am devastated, Giles, to hear strangers talking about you in such a flippant way. Surely part of their job is to respect human dignity. Is it their job to discuss your surgery in public without any regard for whomever might be listening? I wish Bill were here, the incident has left me feeling lost at sea, without a soul who cares about what it means to have a son who may never return to consciousness or walk again.

The nurses continue to pursue their predictable routines hour after hour and don't seem to notice me anymore; I think they feel comfortable knowing you have a watchdog beside you. They tell me you are stronger, that the tests reveal more positive results. Perhaps you will regain consciousness soon—maybe later today.

Dr. Asaph explained the terms intubate and extubate to me. Intubate is when you were placed on the respirator and extubate is when you are taken off. You have been intubated for four and a half days and the doctors feel you might be able to breathe on your own. Apparently you won't regain consciousness until you are extubated. There is a name for everything here and sometimes I think they try to blind me with science, but I struggle to keep up. Words cannot express how grateful I am that these kind and competent people are taking care of you.

The doctors quoted a case in which a young girl, who had drowned in icy water, suffered brain damage during rewarming when blood vessels burst in her brain. I pray that this hasn't happened to you, it would be the final blow for you to have come this far, only to suffer brain damage. I am full of mixed feelings, Giles. On the one hand, I am confident that your circumstances are different to those described and you will pick up your life almost as before. On the other hand, I am beset with doubt. Suppose an obscure vessel in your brain has been irrevocably damaged by all these procedures? What mystery do you hide from us, my child? Only you can calm the troubled waters in this intensive care unit, by recognizing us and talking to us.

In a way, I wish they didn't have to take you off the respirator, but could keep you alive in this state so that we wouldn't have to face what might be ahead. I sat outside your room, my eyes fixed on the floor. I wanted to be closer, but I felt in the way. There wasn't any space inside, especially with so many doctors and nurses all anticipating your awakening.

I prayed once more, "Oh, God! Please let Giles be alright. We have come this far." I wonder if God can hear me. I have been imploring Him for a week. How can I ask Him for one more favor? Will He hear my prayers?

# PART II

I waited for what seemed like an eternity. Then there was some movement in Giles' room; the doctors were leaving and a nurse ran past me. I caught sight of Bow Tie and stood up to block his path. He smiled jubilantly. "He's fine," he said, "he's breathing on his own! He's doing fine. He isn't conscious yet, but he will be soon."

"Thank God! Thank God for another miracle!"

Returning to the waiting room again, I sank into the soft red velvet chair and stared at the door. Within a few minutes my sister Elizabeth and Ross arrived, after having been out for breakfast. They looked refreshed and in relatively high spirits. I explained that Giles had been taken off the respirator and I was waiting for news of his mental status, waiting for the words that would determine his future prognosis.

We sat together in silence and waited, as each minute ticked by...slowly but surely. I wondered what could be taking the doctors such a long time. Perhaps Giles wasn't awakening after all; maybe it was a mistake. I felt agitated and wanted to hear the news whether it be good or bad, but at the same time wanted to hold back the clock and keep myself oblivious.

At least an hour passed by, and unable to stand the suspense a moment longer I was preparing to go back to the CCU to find out for myself, when Dr. Bietz appeared in the doorway. His face was beaming with pleasure and his eyes shone brightly. "Could it be good news?" I thought.

"He is conscious," he said cautiously, "and there doesn't seem to be any neurological damage at all. He is responding normally."

I stared at him, my eyes filled with tears of relief. What a blessing! Giles will be alright! At last there is hope. Ross and Elizabeth hugged one another, and Ross shook Dr. Bietz's hand until I thought it would come loose. We laughed nervously and then almost hysterically as the news we had awaited, for so long, finally came to fruition. We cheered, "Hurrah!" Ross and Elizabeth danced. What a miracle! It was almost too good to be true.

Dr. Bietz tried to maintain some decorum in the frivolity of the moment as he said, "I have told him everything, even though he isn't fully conscious. I have told him about the amputations, about the death of his friends and teachers in the cave. He is heavily sedated and is drifting in and out, but this is the best time for his mind to absorb this terrifying information. As he regains consciousness, the realization will dawn on him and he will begin to deal with it immediately."

I mulled over in my mind the rationale which he explained. Perhaps he was right; maybe Giles should know right away. I didn't have any opinions on the best way to approach a situation like this. I had to trust his experience.

"Several years ago my wife and I were in a traffic accident," Dr. Bietz continued. "My wife was killed and I suffered severe injuries. As soon as I regained consciousness, my doctor told me about her death. Later, I felt it was a good thing to be told in that way, in a semi-conscious state I mean, because I digested it mentally and came to terms with my loss gradually. I think Giles will do the same."

We looked at each other, and his sad eyes reflected the pain of his past, and the strength he conveyed to our family. I prayed to myself, thanking God for our good fortune to be blessed with such dedicated professionals.

"I am so anxious to see him," I said breaking the silent connection between us. "I want to speak to him and be reassured he is alright."

Dr. Bietz led the way back to Giles' room. I gingerly approached the bedside and watched Giles lying on his sickbed. It was odd not to have the rhythmical pounding of the respirator and there was an emptiness which was almost haunting with only the muted beeps of the heart monitors. I looked at the green line forming repetitious patterns on the screen. The nurse had removed the tracheal tube from Giles' throat, but there was still an array of translucent tubes entering various parts of his fragile body. He looked rested and his color had almost returned to normal.

I waited patiently for him to stir and give me a sign of recognition. After a while, he began to move and the nurses, who had been unobtrusively caring for him, left us alone. His head turned towards me and he opened his eyes.

"What are you doing here?" he mumbled. His eyes were wide open as though startled to see me. "Aren't you supposed to be working?"

I laughed nervously, realizing that Yes! Dr. Bietz was right. Giles recognized me and was responding normally.

"I have been here since they brought you in last Thursday and now it's Tuesday morning, nine days after you left for the Climb," I replied.

Giles turned his head and gazed up at the ceiling. "We shouldn't have gone. The weather was awful. The wind was blowing a gale and it was so cold—you have no idea."

I had spent countless hours imagining the conditions which the climbers faced, picturing them building a snow cave and hiking down the mountain. In our conversations we have speculated about what they should and should not have done. I am beginning to understand the severity of the storm, and it is becoming clear to me that the situation was one in which even experienced climbers could not have managed, let alone a party of day hikers.

"Why did you let me go?" Giles murmured after a while. "Why didn't you stop me from going?"

I stared at him, but didn't reply. Why did I let him go? Why didn't I question thoroughly the rules associated with this climb? Would it have made any difference if I had? He would have laughed at me had I said I was apprehensive and wouldn't allow him to go. Besides, I was confident that there was no danger and that everyone involved with their supervision was competent. After all Giles is sixteen. Surely I should allow him to go on school outings.

"I didn't mean that," Giles said, "...it's not your fault."

I know that—but I *am* partly to blame. If I hadn't insisted that he go to OES; if we hadn't moved to Washington; if we hadn't come to America in the first place he wouldn't have been up there during that dreadful storm. It's too late to change it and mulling over the "what ifs" won't help now.

"I didn't want to go," Giles said sadly, "and I wish I hadn't gone."

"I wish you hadn't gone too, but you did, and we can't put the clock back. At least you are here, alive and safe. The rescuers couldn't find the cave. They searched and searched for three days with no clues at all. They had helicopters and ground crews combing the mountainside. It was only by chance and at the very last minute that they happened to strike the tarp near the cave."

Giles turned away and lay in silence trying to piece the puzzle together, his expression twisted by the anguish in his heart. If only I could change places with him. It doesn't seem fair for such a young and vital person to be in his position. I want to take it all away.

His eyes closed and he drifted off to sleep, the drugs protecting him from his mental pain. I quietly slipped out of the room to find Dr. Asaph waiting outside. He looked like a different person, relaxed and rested as though his life was returning to normal again. He smiled warmly when he saw me, and asked if Giles remembered much about the Climb, and how he had reacted to the news of the amputations.

"He appears to be thinking about it, but it is so enormous I'm sure it will take a long time for him to absorb it all," I told him.

"I think we need to bring in a psychiatrist right away, there are many difficult issues here and I think it would be wise to have professional help as soon as possible. Dr. Eastman is on duty this week. I will ask him to talk to Giles right away."

## *Wednesday, May 21st. to Tuesday, May 27th.*

R oy is with us every day. What would I do without him? He listens to my perpetual ramblings and tries to keep our spirits up by talking about the outside world. As soon as Giles saw Roy he said, "Hi, Roy!" Roy laughed, he has waited a long time to hear that. The students apparently call him Roy, but he doesn't seem to mind.

> *One night a man had a dream. He dreamt that he was walking along the beach with the Lord. Across the sky flashed scenes of his life. For each scene, he noticed two sets of footprints in the sand, one belonging to him and the other to the Lord.*
>
> *When the last scene of his life flashed before him, he looked back in the sand. He noticed that many times along the path of his life there was only one set of footprints. He also noticed that it happened at the very lowest and saddest times in his life.*
>
> *This really bothered him and he questioned the Lord about it, "Lord, you said that once I decided to follow you, you would walk with me all the way. But I have noticed that during the most troublesome times in my life there is only one set of footprints. I don't understand why, when I needed you most, you would leave me."*
>
> *The Lord replied, "My precious child, I love you and I would never leave you. During your times of trial and suffering, when you see only one set of footprints, it was then that I carried you."*
>
> —Anonymous

I read these poignant words repeatedly and I am comforted to know that God is with us. I am glad Providence is a Catholic hospital, because religion has such a strong presence here and I feel His aura around us. There are a number of nuns here and a couple of them have become my friends. They have a calming influence over my tormented mind and I feel secure in their presence. I wander the maze of passages every evening to have some time alone. At about eight o'clock, a nun broadcasts a prayer over the loudspeaker. I stop in my tracks to listen and even though it is difficult to hear the words—just to realize a prayer is being said, comforts me.

A continuous flow of letters is arriving from all over the country, and in my quiet moments I read them. Some of the letters come from religious groups who talk about the power of prayer, and say they are praying for Giles. Others suggest Giles has been saved for a reason and God has a plan for him. Many people understand what we are going through.

N ow that Giles is conscious, his awareness of the injuries and the horror of the experience on the mountain have added to the complexity of his condition. The long hours of darkness are the worst time of all. He is in so much pain and discomfort and so exhausted and on so much medication, his mind cannot rest, and sleep rarely allows him to escape from his agony.

He sometimes drifts into a drugged sleep, but then a nurse will disturb him to give him medication, take a reading, hook him up to a machine, change a bag or something. I stay with him most of the night helping him to turn, moistening his parched lips and stroking his fevered brow. He seems to want my maternal comforting, just as he did as a baby when only my attention would appease him.

Dr. Rogers has started "hyperalimentation", which is a complete nutrition given intravenously. Giles is able to eat a small amount of light food; a little Jell-O or an egg here and there, but he can't eat enough to regain his loss of weight and strength. He is receiving fluids intravenously in an attempt to replace the enormous amounts of water he has lost. He is able to drink minimal amounts and it is my job to coax him to take liquids. He can't sit up or even hold his head up so we have devised a long convoluted straw to allow him to drink lying down.

This week Giles has been gravely ill. His daylight hours are filled with procedures: transfusions, hemodialysis, X-rays, echocardiograms and electrocardiograms. Twice a day he is taken to the hyperbaric chamber where he experiences severe claustrophobia now that he is conscious. Perhaps it brings back a memory deeply hidden in his mind, a fear of being trapped and unable to get out. It gets stiflingly hot inside the compartment which fits tightly around his shoulders. He is most uncomfortable and unable to move by himself anyway. Dr. Henry, the hypothermia specialist, sedates Giles before he is put in there and the medication allows him to sleep for a short time, but it soon wears off and he lies in excruciating pain. To gain the full benefit of the treatment he is supposed to stay in for an hour, but after half an hour he is pleading to get out. We try to persuade him to stay in there a little longer, just five more minutes, until finally he insists that he can't stand it. Even then he has to stay in an extra ten minutes to depressurize the chamber. It is agonizing for me to watch him.

Dr. Hikes continues to hope that the oxygen forced into Giles' damaged muscles will ultimately revive them. He takes him to the operating room every day to remove dead tissue from his arms and legs. On Friday, he had to admit that the right leg could not be saved. The tissues have not shown any sign of improvement and he had no choice except to remove the knee and the remaining part of the lower right leg (knee disarticulation).

Giles' hands are of great concern. Because of all the surgery, the tendons will shorten as they heal resulting in a "curling" of the fingers. He started physical therapy this week although he is so weak he can hardly move. The therapist has made splints for each of his hands which keep the tendons and the muscles stretched out. They don't hurt him and they aren't uncomfortable, but they are cumbersome and get in the way. The physical therapist tried to get

Giles to sit on the edge of the bed. It was an awful struggle and suddenly Giles realized how terribly weak he is, and began to cry. He flopped back against his pillow, I held him in my arms and our tears mingled, but there was nothing I could say to comfort him. The therapist's eyes were filled with tears and she left us alone in our grief.

D r. Eastman, the psychiatrist, met with Bill and me soon after he had talked to Giles. He is a soft-spoken, unassuming man, dressed in a Harris tweed sports jacket. He said he felt quite nervous talking to such a celebrity, because Giles' name is all over the newspapers and reports of his condition are televised every day. He laughed self-consciously when he realized what he had said, because after all, Giles is just a sixteen-year-old boy and isn't even aware of his fame.

He spent some time with us, trying to paint a picture of Giles' family background—where he came from and the relationships which are important to him. Dr. Eastman's eyes glazed over as we unveiled our lives to him: Giles' father's death, coming to live in Washington and the adjustments Giles has had to overcome in his short life.

"How do *you* feel about Giles?" Dr. Eastman asked Bill.

"It has been very difficult to take on a family, especially so soon after their father's death. I couldn't fill his shoes, and neither did I want to. However, Giles and I have been forming a closer relationship lately, and I think things are much better. When I drove him to school the other week he told me about his studies and his dreams for the future. He told me about wanting to be an engineer like his dad. He is growing into a fine young man and I am learning to accept him."

Dr. Eastman shuffled in his chair. "We must encourage Giles to talk about the loss of his legs as much as possible," he said. "It will take a while for him to accept it. It is important for him to express his feelings. How does he seem to you? Is he the same as before?"

"He is very sick of course," I replied, "but yesterday some friends of ours came in to see him. They are from Peru and he carried on a normal conversation with them in Spanish."

"Really!" Dr. Eastman seemed surprised. "Did he speak Spanish before?"

I realized that he was serious and laughed nervously. "Well, yes of course he did."

He looked embarrassed and smiled when he realized what a silly comment he had made. Maybe not! Perhaps people do wake up from comas speaking a new language, but it seems highly unlikely.

"Does he have any siblings?"

"He has a brother, Ross, who is two years older; and a sister, Joanne, who is five years older; they are close to one another. He also has four stepsisters, but he really hardly knows them, and he has Jay, his stepbrother. He is quite close to Jay I think. Isn't he, Bill?"

"Oh yes, they get along fine."

"How are you two doing through all this?" Dr. Eastman asked.

"Fine," Bill replied.

I know that my absence is particularly hard on Bill. He comes to the hospital every day and he has to keep the clinic going on his own. He must be lonely at home by himself.

"You must allow some time for yourselves." Dr. Eastman peered over his glasses as he spoke.

Bill looked at me as I held his hand.

"We will do alright I think," I said. "It's difficult for you, I know—Giles isn't your child."

"I will see Giles every day this week," Dr. Eastman continued, "but then I am going on vacation. I will ask Dr. Philips to fill in for me. I think you will like him."

This week Ross went to almost all of the nine memorial services held at the school; one for each lost climber. On some days, there were as many as four services and he was asked to play his guitar at most of them. After three days he is emotionally drained. To give of himself in this way and then to come to the hospital and to see his brother suffering, is having a profound effect on him. The family tends to lean on Ross and look to him for strength and support, but this week has been too much. I am worried about him.

Elizabeth and Joanne attended some of the services also and I was invited, but I couldn't bring myself to go. Not that I didn't want to, nor that I didn't care, but it is more than my mind can absorb. On Wednesday, I realized that I am hardly coping at all when students brought flowers from one of the services. The image of the flowers, a reminder of the magnitude of the Tragedy, was too much for me. I became hysterical when I saw them, and completely broke down. How am I going to hold myself together through this? But I must—I don't have a choice.

On Thursday, there was a memorial service for the climbers at the Episcopal cathedral in Portland. It was held at eleven o'clock in the morning. There were several hundred people there: students and staff from the school, the rescue teams, personnel from the hospitals involved, families and friends of the climbers. Dozens of reporters and television cameramen were waiting outside, and they even came inside the church to film the service which was broadcast live on a Portland channel.

The families of the victims sat together at the front of the cathedral, and I recognized many of them from the interminable hours of waiting at the mountain. There we were again gathered together in a corner of the church. I thought I saw the deputy sheriff and other rescuers. Familiar faces, now appearing as ghosts in my nightmare.

Stan sat behind me and we held each other's hand the way we had done at the mountain. In a daze I watched Roy drifting in front of the altar and going through his rituals. I listened to the headmaster giving his sermon, but I didn't hear a word. I relived those three tragic days on Mount Hood with the people who had become my companions. Some sobbed uncontrollably, others sat with blank, stunned expressions, staring into space, numbed by the pain of their experience.

All I could think about was Giles at the hospital and how close he had come to having his name on the long list of victims. Fear engulfed me when I realized his name could still be added and that he was barely alive. I was relieved when the service was over and slipped out of the church without acknowledging anyone. I hurried back to the hospital as quickly as I could.

We heard that Brittany was doing well. Joanne and Elizabeth visited her at Emanuel Hospital on Friday. She too is off the ventilator and responding normally. She hasn't suffered as much tissue damage as Giles, hasn't had amputations nor as many invasive procedures and is progressing much faster. It will take Giles longer, but he will make it in the end. I must believe that.

A father of one of the children who died came to see me after the memorial service. We became close through the long hours of waiting on the mountain and the grief which we share connects us. He is like a brother to me even though we have only known each other a short time.

"I want you to know, I am glad that Giles survived," he said sadly. "I don't feel any grudges, or wish it were my son in hospital, and I don't want you to feel guilty that Giles made it and my son didn't."

There was nothing I could say to comfort this fine, unselfish man.

"We are very fortunate I know, but Giles has paid a big price for survival and it isn't over for him; he has a long, long way to go. I don't feel guilty," I told him. "In fact, I am fighting for him. He *must* survive—even if it's only for the others."

We talked for a long time, and I realized that he didn't understand how critically ill Giles is and that we still could lose him at any time. He has miraculously survived, but his life still hangs on a fragile thread.

I was sorting flowers when Jo, the Red Cross nurse, came to see me. I was thrilled to see her, she has become an important part of my life; a place for me to unburden my fears and anxieties. "What can I do for you?" she asked. I hesitated and then I remembered. "There is one thing. I feel such a wreck in here. Do you know where I could get my hair done?" Jo looked startled. I don't think she expected a request like that, but as always, she rallied.

"I don't know anywhere around here," she said thoughtfully, "but I do have a neighbor who I'm sure would come over and do it for you here. She is quite good."

I didn't care how it would be done as long as it felt cleaner and less unruly. Jo went off and in no time at all returned with a young lady who washed and cut my hair. Any other time it would have been a small thing, but it was wonderful and I feel like a new person.

Jo comes to see me every day without fail. She always has a little story about her life to tell me and keeps me in touch with a world outside from which I now am totally detached.

A hospital volunteer put together a scrapbook of newspaper clippings and she gave it to Giles. I can hardly believe it. The papers are full of the events of the past two weeks, and we are in the midst of a media frenzy without even knowing it.

The next day, I was with Giles helping the nurses with their daily routines. The television was on and the morning news was being aired. Suddenly a daily report on Giles' medical condition came on. Giles' eyes were wide open and he jerked his head off the pillow. Although he is weak he found the strength to look at the screen. He was startled to see himself, and it is a novelty for him to realize he is in the limelight.

On Saturday night Bill went home early, Elizabeth and my parents went back to their apartment. Ross and Joanne rented a movie and we asked the nurse if we could use the video player in Giles' room. It was the first time that the four of us had been alone together to just relax, and Giles was feeling quite perky that evening.

The film, *Top Secret*, was a silly English farce about the Second World War, certainly a serious subject turned into a comedy in a way that only the English can do. It was a hilarious film and we were soon engrossed in it. We started to laugh and once we got going, it seemed that we couldn't stop. As the film progressed, we became louder and louder until we were creating quite a disturbance.

The coronary care unit is silent at night except for the beeping of the monitors and the occasional whisper of a nurse or a visitor. It must have been strange to hear raucous laughter in such a somber place. A nurse popped her head around the door, wondering what on earth was going on. She asked Giles if he felt alright, obviously worried that perhaps so much laughter might upset him or cause pain in his many wounds. He laughed along with us and indeed, it seemed to do him a lot of good. For a brief moment, we were able to forget where we were and the circumstances which had brought us to this unlikely place. Laughing together will hold us together, especially as we need each other so desperately. It was a wonderful release of built-up tension, and I realized, as long as we can enjoy each other like this we will stay together.

It is Memorial Day, and I have been thinking about families today. I think about them gathering up their children, getting their things together to go on a picnic, go to the park or just stay at home and play in the garden. I think about the other parents who had made plans for this Memorial Day, but because of the accident had to cancel everything. I think about the plans we had made. We were going to the cabin; I have already bought the material for the curtains I had planned to make this weekend. My parents were to come up and spend a few days with us and probably Joanne, Ross and Giles would have come also. There will be other days, but they will never be the same.

## *Wednesday, May 28th. to Tuesday, June 3rd.*

A nurse handed me a note and waited a moment for me to respond.

"It's Magic Johnson," she said excitedly. "Magic Johnson—he's on the phone."

"Who's that?" I said. "I don't know anyone by that name."

"You know," she sounded exasperated, "he's a basketball player."

"Oh! I don't know him."

I took the note from her. "I'll tell Giles."

She looked taken aback, but didn't say anything.

Later, I gave the note to Giles. "It was a Magic…Johnson…" I said hesitantly.

Giles sat up. "Really! Did he call *me?*"

"Yes. Who is he? What kind of a name is Magic anyway?"

"That's his nickname. They just call him that because of his playing."

"Well, I'm sorry. I didn't know."

Giles lay back and rolled his eyes in disgust.


M y heart breaks a little more each day as I watch Giles suffer.

One day this week, he rolled over to look at me fidgeting as he fought pain and discomfort. "Pray for me!" he said. I clutched the crucifix in my pocket and squeezed his hand as I leaned over to kiss his forehead. I hadn't realized that Giles prayed, but I am comforted to know that he does. It is important for him to pray to his God as he walks this uncertain path to recovery.


A nurse suggested that people could donate blood in Giles' name and told me the Red Cross would defer some of the cost as a donation. It probably won't be a lot of money, but it would help. I can't imagine what the hospital costs are mounting to, but I can't think about it now. I do have good health insurance, but that won't take away the costs; someone has to pay. The idea of people donating blood, instead of sending flowers, appeals to me. Our room is full of arrangements and it's impossible to appreciate them all and besides we can't have them in Giles' room anyway.

I mentioned the idea to Bill. "Especially as there has been so much publicity, I'm sure the *Daily News* would help out. We could have a blood drive in Giles' name which would help the Red Cross to replenish their blood supply."

Bill immediately made arrangements to have a blood drive at St. John's Hospital in Longview. He contacted the newspaper and the radio stations to solicit their help in giving it publicity.

No one could have been prepared for what actually happened. The Red Cross anticipated about two hundred and fifty donors and were prepared for that number, but more than five hundred people came. There were all ages; among them students who remembered Giles from his school days in Longview. Long queues of people lined the corridors of St. John's and there was a wait of over two hours to give blood. Many couldn't wait and others were unable to give blood for some reason. I heard that the atmosphere was vibrant. "I want to do something," an elderly lady told the press. "It could have been one of my children or grandchildren who needed blood."

"I just want him to know we are thinking about him," a burly workman told a reporter.

The Red Cross finally ran out of bags and had to turn people away. Who would have thought there would be such a response? The Red Cross notified us of those who gave blood. Some of the names are familiar, but many I didn't know. I am moved and comforted when I realize so many people are pulling for Giles, and this is such a positive way of showing it.

D r. Philips is a different type of person than Dr. Eastman. He is a small, slightly built man, who wears a big sweater, cotton trousers rolled up at the bottom and loafers. He never fails to have a little purse and a notebook with him. He looks comfortable and ready to sit down to chat at any time; I feel at ease with him.

I haven't had anything to do with a psychiatrist before, except for Dr. Eastman of course, so I don't have any expectations. Dr. Philips and Giles bonded instantly. He was like an old friend and nodded enthusiastically as I recounted the events of the last two weeks. When I had finished, I realized he was crying also. He is with us almost all the time and already we are referring to him as Dick. He often stays late into the night when he drops in to see Giles after doing rounds at the hospital.

Dr. Asaph explained that Christine, a lady from the school, arranged for a group of parents to prepare meals for us. Each evening wonderful baskets of food are brought in which are really delicious. Even though I hardly eat, the dishes always disappear and there is enough to offer our visitors. Bill has a meal when he comes each evening and I save some for Dick when he visits us late at night, because he is always hungry. Although he is a small person and doesn't carry an ounce of extra weight, it is surprising how much he can eat.

Giles has been making satisfactory progress and at last I feel there is hope for his recovery. The DIC, manifested by uncontrollable internal bleeding, appears to have settled down and the blood transfusions have been cut back dramatically. Dialysis and hyperbaric treatments are twice a day and he goes to surgery almost every day. Before and after each dialysis, the nurses weigh him to measure the amount of fluid removed from his blood. They use a canvas sling which is kept underneath him at all times making it easy to simply attach it to the frame of the scales to lift him up. It is impossible for Giles to wear anything in bed, every part of his body is attached to something or covered with a dressing. He just has a sheet draped over him which the nurses remove to get an accurate weight. When they were weighing him one morning this week, I rushed over to Giles with a towel to cover him.

"He is a person you know, not just a piece of meat," I said.

It is evident that Giles is in the midst of a terrible situation. We are hearing rumors of lawsuits and investigations, and nomenclature which we don't understand. Bill suggested that we look for a suitable lawyer for Giles as soon as possible. We haven't had much to do with lawyers before, but we know a young attorney in Longview named Paul Roasch who has helped me with classes at the cancer center. I was impressed by his integrity and his ability to communicate with people. Bill asked him to represent Giles.

Paul came to the hospital this week. Giles is heavily medicated, but is a little more alert in the mornings and the day Paul came to see him, he seemed ready to talk and there was a slot of time between procedures. Paul arrived just after nine o'clock on Tuesday when Jack happened to be in Giles' room. I almost asked Jack to leave as I thought it might not be advisable for a school representative to be present. But then I decided he would be support for Giles. Paul is a tall, athletic man, probably about thirty-five or forty, although he could be older than he appears. I hope Giles will identify with him, their relationship is important. Paul is so tall, he had trouble in navigating himself in the small hospital room and around the equipment surrounding the bed. Eventually he perched on a small stool, and took out a pad and pencil as he introduced himself.

Apart from our brief talk immediately after Giles regained consciousness, we have not discussed the Climb. Giles is quite bewildered by the circumstances in which he has found himself and hasn't mentioned anything.

Paul didn't waste any time getting to the point of his visit. "Tell me what happened on the mountain. Take your time and tell me what you can remember. Start from the beginning." He had his notebook ready, and gestured to Giles reassuringly.

"We were a couple of hours late getting started," Giles began, slowly and thoughtfully. "We should have left the lodge by three o'clock in the morning, but I think it was closer to five before we got going. Climbing was very slow, the snow was deep and heavy. Marion was breaking trail with Father Tom. I couldn't understand why, because she was obviously weaker than the rest of us and showed signs of exhaustion early on.

"We got to the top of the Palmer chair. John and one or two others were complaining about feeling sick and they wanted to turn back. Ralph asked the group if anyone else wanted to go down and I thought Marion would have gone, but she wanted to go a bit further. Mike walked back to the lodge with John."

"What was the weather like then?" Paul asked.

"It was alright. It was snowing and cold, but I didn't feel it. In fact, I felt quite hot and stopped a couple of times to take clothes off." Giles paused. "Finally we reached Crater Rock and sat down to rest. I was talking to Erik, we discussed how late it was getting and that we wanted to turn back. The weather was starting to deteriorate and we couldn't understand why we were continuing. Marion was really tired, but Father Tom kept pushing her saying it was good for her, and that she had to keep moving as we were almost at the top. We asked Ralph if it was time to turn around. He went to ask Father Tom, who said there wasn't much further to go and he wanted to make an effort to reach the summit.

"It didn't make sense. It was obviously late, although we didn't have any idea what the time was, but we must have been climbing for at least twelve hours, and conditions were deteriorating rapidly. Father Tom was determined to get to the top and wanted to go on. In the end, Ralph told us we were turning back— we were relieved.

"We hadn't gone far when the storm closed in on us in full force. It seemed to come from nowhere. One minute it was calm, the next the wind was howling and we were in the midst of a blizzard. It was unbelievable. We couldn't tell where the ground was. We were completely engulfed in snow, a gale-force wind was blowing and it was very very cold.

"We had put down marker flags on the way up so that we could trace our way down. We did find one, but the others were completely buried in the snow. Pat was feeling sick and acting disoriented; I think he must have been hypothermic. We warmed up some water and Susan got into the sleeping bag with him to try to warm him. We stopped about an hour, during which time we stood around in the storm that was by then a complete whiteout, and tried to keep ourselves warm. When we started walking again the conditions were still awful and we couldn't see a thing. I lost my footing at one point and fell into a crevasse; but I managed to save myself with my ice ax and pull myself back onto the trail."

Giles paused. "Go on," said Paul.

"Shortly after, Ralph took over leadership of the group when it became obvious Father Tom was getting sick and disoriented also. Pat was staggering around; Ralph wrapped him in the sleeping bag and dragged him along like a sack of potatoes. I carried Ralph's pack and took the lead. I was wearing a yellow raincoat so I stood out like a beacon at the front for the others to follow. Susan was behind me with the compass and she called out the direction. That was how we went; she called out and we stepped as she instructed. Father Tom told us to veer to the left in order to miss Zig-Zag Canyon which we knew was dangerous in a whiteout. Progress was very slow and it was getting later and later."

"Are you feeling okay?" Paul asked. "Do you want to continue?"

"I'm alright," Giles said. "We decided to dig in because the snow and wind made it impossible to go any further. Ralph dug a snow cave with the only shovel we had, which must have taken about an hour to do. We huddled together and waited until he finished it. I felt useless and wanted to do something, so I got the tarp and put that over us. We had left our packs on another tarp nearby. I thought about putting my skies up on end in the snow. If only I had done that—they would have found us right away." His voice drifted off and he lay silently for a moment before he continued.

"Eventually, the cave was ready and we all got in, but it was too small. It was like having eleven people on a single bed; if you can imagine that. I went over to get the packs, but there must have been at least two feet of snow on them and I couldn't move the tarp underneath. During the night, we had to take turns to go out into the blizzard, because there wasn't enough room in the cave. I heard Father Tom shivering and screaming outside. We had to struggle to keep the cave entrance open because the snow was piling up so quickly. The snow melted inside the cave with the heat of our bodies and before long we were lying in a pool of water.

"In the morning, Ralph said he was going to get help. I was glad that something was finally being done instead of just sitting there waiting. He asked me to go, but I had just finished digging the entrance and I was breathless, so Molly went with him. 'We will keep walking until we find help or until we die,' Ralph said as they left."

Giles stopped and looked at Paul. "Do you know where the cave was?"

Paul took his pen and drew the mountain. He sketched the Palmer chair and roughly pointed out where the cave had been found. Giles sat up as much as he could, obviously startled:

*"Man...! Over there...! What were we doing over there?* We were lost. *How could we have been so far over?* How on earth could that have happened?"

Giles was on the brink of tears, but he pulled himself together and continued.

"We waited and waited all day while the storm continued. The cave entrance changed as the snow built up and it became harder and harder to keep it open. Allison pushed her way through the entrance to the outside because she was smaller, and we hoped she would open it up. Then Erik went outside and must have tried to get back inside the cave because I remember hitting his foot with my ice ax. All I could see was his foot through a long narrow telescope which was now the entrance to the cave."

There was a long silence, just the incessant sounds of the machines which echoed in the hollowness of the room. "I think that will be enough for today," said Paul, and changed the subject to everyday chit-chat.

I could hardly contain myself. My initial response was one of overwhelming fear which turned to anger. I had to leave the room. We didn't discuss the Climb again until much later, but—I was beginning to understand.

The day of Paul's visit was just about the last that Giles felt reasonably well. Each day since then has brought a new set of crises as one complication after another has developed. I first noticed his raging temperature when he came back from a hyperbaric treatment.

"It has happened," said Bow Tie. "This is our worst fear. We must find out what is causing his fever because he may have developed an infection somewhere. We are very concerned."

"Oh no!" I cradled my face in my hands. What else can go wrong? He has been doing so well. "Perhaps it's pneumonia...or perhaps the flu," I argued, unwilling to accept that Giles might have another setback.

"That could be part of it, but from the blood tests there appear to be gram-negative bacteria present. Gram-negative bacteria are in the bowel which means that during the internal bleeding caused by the DIC, bacteria from the bowel found their way into the bloodstream. This is what we feared the most. It is very serious indeed. We are bringing in specialists from the university who will culture the bacteria and help us to select the most effective antibiotics to fight them."

Within the hour two more doctors appeared on the scene: Dr. Gilbert, a tall, balding man probably in his fifties and his assistant, Dr. Woods, who didn't look old enough to be out on his own, never mind being involved in such a complicated case. We have christened them the Bug Brothers as we struggle to memorize everyone's name. They took cultures, returned to their lab and immediately started Giles on a continuous infusion of antibiotics. They hovered around every day checking on his response, taking more blood samples and doing more tests. There was obviously grave concern that the infection may be close to the heart or even in the heart itself.

Dr. Asaph requested another computerized axial tomography (CAT) scan, to ensure that there wasn't any evidence of infection in Giles' chest. I objected at first because Giles has already had four CAT scans and I know there are five rads of radiation exposure with each procedure, plus he has had umpteen chest X-rays. I am concerned because the amount of radiation is becoming significant, especially to the chest, i.e. to the thymus gland of a young person; furthermore radiation has an accumulative effect. I felt obliged to point out my concern to the doctors, but Dr. Asaph explained that they can't take any risks at this stage. The infection is far more critical.

Dr. Marx reported later that a shadow on the CAT scan indicated that yes indeed, there was something under the sternum. He thought it could be a blood clot from the heart surgery, but his main concern was that it might be an abscess, and if the infection got into Giles' heart, it would be fatal. He said they should take Giles to surgery immediately, open his chest again to let the pus drain out, put a tube in to irrigate the cavity and leave the wound open to the air. The surgery will give them the opportunity to take cultures of the suspicious area to find out what it is on the CAT scan. At the same time, they want to change the clips holding the sternum, from a fabric material to metal, because the clips may be causing the infection. They intend to leave the wound open to allow it to drain, and heal from the inside.

The procedure sounded awful, almost barbaric and I was again skeptical. Giles is so incredibly weak. In all my experience of working with cancer patients, I can't recall ever having seen anyone as feeble as him. He doesn't even have enough strength to lift his head off the pillow. He was a big, stocky boy before the accident, weighing about 180 pounds. Now he is only 125—a mere shadow of his former self. The doctors say his legs weighed about thirty pounds, and that of course accounts for some of the weight, but even so, he has lost a tremendous amount in just two weeks. The edema (swelling) has subsided and it is now obvious how much weight he has really lost.

"Are you sure that this is really necessary?" I asked warily. "There have been so many procedures and Giles has no strength left. I don't see how he can tolerate any more. He isn't the boy who came in here. He needs time to recover before you do any more."

"We can't take the risk," Dr. Asaph assured me. "It sounds like a radical procedure to you I know, but it really isn't. We do it all the time, and the patients, even elderly, weak patients, tolerate it well. Don't worry."

I can't help but worry. Giles' condition is extremely fragile. He doesn't have any reserves and his strength wanes with each surgery. Surely the doctors can see his condition. For a moment I think they were concerned that I might not give permission for them to proceed. I wouldn't do that...I trust their judgment. Giles' fate is entirely in their hands.

Despite my concerns, Giles tolerated the surgery well and Dr. Asaph was visibly relieved that they took this precaution. Although they didn't tell me at the time, it turned out that there were indeed gram-negative bacteria under the sternum, so Giles was at serious risk of developing pericarditis, an infection of the heart membrane which could well have led to his death.

My mind spins at these prospects and has become numb with all the information I have to sort through on a daily basis. I feel my energy draining away. My nights are consumed by anxiety and I only sleep from total exhaustion when my brain simply can't take any more. I have tried to sleep when Giles is resting, but I am afraid to leave him for very long. My days are filled with conversation, either with the doctors and nurses or with people in and out. My parents visit me every day to give me support, but they really need me more than I need them. I feel guilty because I can't give them the attention they search for with their eyes. I sense they want me to spend more time with them, to visit them in their apartment to have tea, but I dare not leave. Suppose the doctors have a question which they can't answer without me? What if Giles needs a drink and the nurse is too busy to get one for him? This is a lonely journey, one which I have to travel with Giles and the closest members of my family. What little energy I have left is completely focused on Giles, and my emotions are entirely directed towards his survival. All I think about is him.

Giles' friends from OES and old school friends from Longview are always nearby. I feel comfortable with them as they seem to accept me and understand what I'm going through. We rarely speak to each other, but it doesn't seem to matter.

Giles' close friend John comes almost every day to sit with him. Giles is groggy almost all of the time, falling in and out of sleep while they talk. It doesn't make any difference to John; he stays for hours on end. Jack religiously visits us. He is particularly dismayed by the clothes which Bill brought in for me, he thinks they are much too loud for a mother to be wearing around the hospital. He is especially concerned about my pink shoes, or pumps, as he calls them. He says I am about the same size as his wife and he is going to bring in some of her clothes for me. At this rate I will have more clothes than I can possibly wear, even more than I have at home, but at least I won't have to wear the jumpsuit again…I can't even look at that thing.

Al, one of Giles' close friends, is often here. He has an enormous amount of hair cascading about his shoulders in a wild mass of curls, almost down to his waist. He isn't very big and his hair dominates his entire person. He is the silent type, but I sense he is moved and doesn't know what to say. I remember Al's father telling me about the time Al interviewed for OES and the headmaster said the education would make a man out of his son. A few years later, Al followed an African native fashion when he wore sandals, a sarong wrapped around his waist, and grew his hair. His father took him back to the school and asked the headmaster what kind of a man his son was, who was now wearing a skirt and long flowing hair.

Al's parents came to visit us this week after a particularly stressful day of surgeries, and the usual barrage of tests and procedures. I was exhausted and emotionally drained and so when they asked me how Giles was, it was the last straw. "I wonder if all this is worth it," I wailed. "It's one procedure after another all day long. He is in so much pain, and so weak; I can't stand to see him suffer like this. I sometimes wonder if he wouldn't have been better off going with the others." They looked uncomfortable with my outburst and made an excuse to leave and then asked if Bill and I would join them for dinner. I was feeling awful and the thought of going out in public seemed ludicrous. "We'll have to take a rain check, but thank you for thinking of us," I replied.

## *June 4th. to 10th.*

*THE WHITE HOUSE*
*WASHINGTON*
*May 23, 1986*

*Dear Giles:*
*Mrs. Reagan and I have you in our thoughts and prayers. You are faced with an extremely difficult personal challenge, but I believe Our Lord always gives us the courage and determination we need to face these problems. While the future may not look too bright right now, as each day passes, hope will grow in your heart and your spirit will strengthen. Please know that we are part of the love and concern that surround you.*
*Take care and God bless you.*
*Sincerely,*
*Ronald Reagan*

A pparently, news has spread far beyond the shores of the United States. A letter arrived from New Zealand addressed to: Giles Thompson, Religious School, USA.

People have sent me newspaper cuttings from all over the world. One report from the *London Times* was totally inaccurate, stating that rescuers had found the climbers wrapped in blankets. The number of people found was wrong and there was other misinformation. It surprises me that newspapers aren't more careful about what they print.

D espite the surgery to Giles' chest, the fever continues, and the doctors are baffled as to what can be causing it. They have been speculating that something may have ruptured in his abdomen, but further tests and X-rays show nothing. They decided to use a radioactive tracer test—a radioactive substance injected into the bloodstream attaches to the white cells. After an hour or so a Geiger counter is used to scan the body to determine where the white cells are clustered. Obviously they cluster at the site of an infection as they congregate to eradicate it.

I was skeptical again because this procedure would mean more radiation, but the doctors assured me that the doses are insignificant; so I had to go along with it. The scan was exhausting for Giles. It took over an hour to survey his body, and was done in nuclear medicine, located in another part of the hospital. He had to lie still on a hard, narrow table for the duration of the procedure. It took a lot of persuasion on my part for him to tolerate the discomfort.

The scan showed clusters of activity around the heart where he had the surgery and around the surgical sites in his legs and arms—which is to be expected. However, the test is inconclusive. Giles had a scan every day this week, and each test is more agonizing for him than the one before. In the end, I had to ask Dr. Asaph if they were really necessary. He agreed that it is yet another test added to the endless routine of procedures and he canceled further scans. I am relieved. At least, Giles doesn't have to go through that particular torture any more.

D r. Philips is part of our family now. When it was time for Dr. Eastman to come back from his vacation, we asked if Dick could continue to be our psychiatrist. Nothing is too much trouble for him, he stays with Giles well into the night, helping him to face up to his circumstances and talk about his losses openly. At first, I didn't understand why we needed a psychiatrist, surely we have enough physicians, but Dick is helping Giles through this painful process. I believe it is a necessary one—one which will pay dividends later when Giles has only himself to rely on.

Ross is normally a gregarious person, but I have noticed a big change in him lately. He mopes around the hospital and plays his guitar all the time and I know that, when he plays as much as this, he is withdrawing into himself. It's understandable, but neverthe-less I am worried about him. His girlfriend Rachel is a sad, deep person by nature. She is a beautiful, tiny little girl with a pale complexion and large, dark, sunken eyes. She is very dramatic and in fact wants to be an actress, which isn't surprising as she is always on stage, but she hardly says a word. I don't think I have ever met anyone as taciturn as she. We forget that Rachel is there, except that you can't ignore Rachel, she is so striking. She seems quite comfortable to be present in silence, but I wonder how she will get by as an actress with so little to say.

I asked Dick to talk to Ross and Rachel together; there is something worrisome going on which I can't quite put my finger on, and I hope he can sort it out. "He is dealing with a great deal," Dick told me after talking to them, "but he has a normal reaction to it. He is verbalizing his anger, which is healthy, but we must encourage him to keep talking and give him time to heal. He will be alright."

Jack is a tower of strength for Ross. Even though Jack is their teacher, he has a peer relationship with his students. He is a gifted mentor and takes a keen interest in his pupils as people, as well as students. I have been impressed with the results of his teachings, especially in Ross, who is not particularly artistic except in music. Jack finds a way to bring out an artistic flare in all of the students, even when they don't seem to have any. He and Ross spend hours together waiting at the hospital. They were sitting behind some bushes in the grounds of the hospital having a discussion this week when suddenly the sprinklers came on and the two of them were drenched. They didn't tell me what they were talking about, but because of the spiritual experiences I have had since this episode began, I can't help thinking it may have been a message from above.

The doctors go to great lengths to ensure that I am fully informed about Giles' condition. They either talk to me in the CCU or they come to my waiting room after they have seen him. It is becoming clear that their opinions differ and I am confused in my attempts to decide what is fact and what is merely opinion.

The younger of the Bug Brothers came to see us one morning. I think he either is an intern or has recently qualified because he was obviously trying to impress us with his knowledge. He gave a long recitation about AK and BK. Ross was fascinated with the terminology and commented, "It could be used in many instances—BE (below the elbow)—and BN (below the neck). That would be a decapitation." We giggled and continued with the joke, but the Bug Brother was trying to be serious and obviously didn't think it funny at all.

Giles is worried about the infection and has been asking the doctors questions. They take great pains to explain to him what is going on in a way that he can understand. However, I was horrified one day this week, when I overheard him asking a doctor if he could die from this infection and the answer was yes. Not perhaps or maybe, but "Yes!" I was mortified to hear such a thing, but relieved that Dick was with Giles to reassure him.

Giles has an inordinate amount to put up with as one doctor after another parades through his room to examine him. Dr. Asaph was delighted the other day when Giles responded angrily and used a four-letter word. He said it was a healthy reaction and a sign that he was recovering. He was quite apologetic when he said: "You probably don't think so, do you? After you have spent all these years teaching him manners." We shared the relief of Giles demonstrating a normal reaction to his plight, at last his spirit is recovering. Although I'm not so sure about the four-letter words.

The doctors tell me they have a press conference every day and I sense they are feeling the pressure of the whole world watching them. I happened to see a television report, and was appalled about the intricate details of Giles' medical status being talked about so openly. Later, I challenged the doctor whom I had seen on the news and asked why it was necessary to give so much detail to the public. Is it really anybody's business? He told me, if an accident occurs in a public place, such as the mountain, then medical reports are public domain. I am confused, knowing how important medical confidentiality is today. How can they release such personal information to the public without our permission? I am so consumed with the day-to-day survival of Giles I will not question it further, but the idea bothers me.

D ick was quite excited when he told me Giles looked at himself in the mirror. After studying his image for a long time, he said, "Mmm! I don't have zits any more." Dick chuckled in his infectious way and said the antibiotics must have cleared up Giles' skin. Something in his treatment has affected his hair also. He has always had curly hair, but now it is a mass of uncontrollable tight blond curls.

Dr. Asaph was telling me, because Giles is such a high-profile case, several medical equipment and drug companies have offered new products to use on him. One company has donated an air bed. The mattress is constructed in deep sections which can be inflated independently so that the bed will adjust to the patient's position. This week the bed was installed, complete with a new frame, and Giles was lying on it before I knew what was happening. I suddenly remembered the healing crystals which Victoria had given to us and which I had taped to the frame of the old bed. Panic-stricken, I looked everywhere for the bed, but it had gone with the crystals taped to it. At first I was distressed when I realized a token of healing had disappeared, but now I feel better about it. Perhaps it is a sign that Giles is healed and he doesn't need them any more.

The air bed is quite impressive and, because Giles is unable to roll over or turn by himself, he finds it very comfortable. However, the other day the middle section deflated unexpectedly, and Giles disappeared into the center of the mattress. Each section is about two feet in depth and for a while, he was almost smothered and unable to lift himself up. Fortunately, there were nurses nearby to pull him out.

D r. Hikes thinks it is important for Giles to meet young people who have been through a similar experience. He arranged for Hugh, a young man from the East Coast, to visit him. Hugh was in a similar mountain accident where he lost both of his legs below the knee. He told us about the things that he likes to do. He is interested in rock climbing and has become quite well known in those circles. He wears special prostheses which have a means of attaching to the rock. In a competition which he won, the able-bodied competitors complained because they felt he had an advantage and shouldn't be allowed to compete. I'm sure they wouldn't be willing to go without legs to gain that kind of edge.

Thursday was Ross' graduation from OES; the class of '86. Prior to the accident, we had made plans to have parties with friends and family, but everything had to be canceled in the wake of the Tragedy and the preoccupation with Giles and Brittany. Susan, who died on the mountain, was a senior also and would have graduated with Ross. Giles had planned to go to the senior prom to be held the day after the cave was found, but the dance was canceled. His tuxedo still hangs in my car.

The graduation ceremony was held at the Episcopal cathedral in Portland. The usual reporters and photographers were outside when I arrived. The church was filled with friends and families and there were only a few places left to sit. The atmosphere in the church was tense. It seemed inappropriate to be celebrating anything so soon after such a dreadful tragedy. I think Ross would have preferred to avoid it altogether, and I certainly would rather have been somewhere else—anywhere.

Despair and anguish were still fresh in our hearts as we went through the motions of closing one chapter and opening another. The service was long and somber, and Ross, whose surname begins with T, was one of the last at the podium. The audience clapped and cheered in an automatic response to the achievements of their loved ones.

After the ceremony, the students filed out of the cathedral in a long procession led by the church entourage. The students forced a smile at their friends as they marched out, but looked uncomfortable. Outside, a big cheer and a whistle sounded, but it was oddly strained.

There had been some discussion about canceling the traditional graduation celebrations in recognition of the Climb. Some parents felt life should go on as usual and saw no reason for the Tragedy to affect their children's fun. I wonder how they would feel if they had lost a child or if they had a son or daughter in the hospital.

A dance was held afterwards, with a band and trimmings for a big celebration. I went to support Ross, and noticed other involved parents looking as lost and bewildered as I felt, but putting their best foot forward.

A class party was planned to be in a secret place after the dance. The parents were assured it would be chaperoned and that alcohol would not be allowed. Transportation to and from the party was arranged so the students wouldn't have a means of driving. Everything had been thought of, but nevertheless I was sick with anxiety. What was I to do? Say no? I thought of the reports about the deaths of young people at graduation time. Had we had our quota? Surely lightening couldn't strike the same place twice. Or could it? The cold hand of fear gripped my heart again and I fought an irresistible urge to bring Ross back to the hospital with me. I wanted to listen to the premonitions which I had ignored in the past.

I followed Ross around the dance floor, not wanting to let him out of my sight. It was ridiculous really and I knew it, but I couldn't help myself. Life must go on. It was important for the class to be together and Ross needed the support of his peers.

Jack persuaded me to venture out of the hospital at lunchtime on Friday. I was skeptical at first, unable to leave Giles' side for a moment in case anything should happen. Finally, I pulled myself together and dragged myself out. Once outside I felt rejuvenated to be away from the constant noises, the odor of medicine and the perpetual light of the CCU. When we were driving along the road, I noticed a high-pitched whistle coming off the macadam as the cars passed over a section about two miles long outside Providence

Hospital. I asked Jack if he could hear it, but neither he nor anyone else is aware of it. It is strange that only I can hear the whistle.

I haven't been home to Longview for almost a month. Bill drives the fifty miles to Portland every day to see us. This week he asked me if I would go to the clinic and help him to plan the treatment on a particularly difficult case.

The patient was a seventeen-year-old girl, the same age as Giles and the children who lost their lives. She had Hodgkin's disease, a type of cancer which is effectively treated with radiation in the early stages. It is a particularly complicated treatment for reasons which far exceed the capacity of the pages of my diary. Her family were beset with worry and apprehension; their daughter had cancer and they were fearful of the treatment. Under normal circumstances, my biggest strength is to be a pillar of support for patients and their families facing these horrifying prospects, but in this case, I couldn't detach myself from my own grief. Their conversations echoed my anguish and I was unable to become involved with their concerns because I am so consumed by my own.

Before returning to the hospital, I went alone to our house on the hill. It was strange to be home again after the events of the past few weeks. It felt as though I had been away for years— perhaps how a soldier must feel when he returns from a war. I stepped cautiously over the threshold, almost afraid to enter a world which has persisted despite my absence. Like a ghost looking back at a life which has involved me, but now seems strangely unfamiliar, I crept from one room to another. I stroked the furniture, feasting my eyes on a dream which came so close to being broken. One step at a time, I went to Giles' bedroom and opened the door. There were posters of football and rock stars just as he had left them. His football helmet and boots sat in a prominent place on a shelf, gear which he will never use again. There were his skis and his ski boots, books and mounds of stuff which are a part of his personality.

Would I ever have been able to face all this had Giles not survived? Could I have come back to all these memories? This must be like coming home to the nursery without the new baby. There are so many things to remind us. I knelt down by the bed and prayed for the other parents who have already suffered through this experience. I prayed to God to give them the courage to face the future without their children.

As I wandered back up the stairs, my trance was broken by the telephone. When I answered it, I realized it was a reporter. Being caught off guard, I didn't think quickly enough. He began to question me: "What is it like for you? How are you feeling?" I could hear the monotonous clicking of a transcriber, in the background.

"I am living the life that every mother dreads daily," I said slowly.

"I don't know what you mean."

"When your children go off on their own and you expect them back at a certain time. You wait and you wait for them to come home and you dare not imagine that perhaps they won't come back. The fear is always there. In my nightmare, my child didn't return."

"No, I don't know," he said calmly.

"You don't have any children do you?"

"No, I don't."

"You wait—you will find out one day when you have children of your own."

As I put the phone down, I remembered our dogs, but then I realized a neighbor had offered to look after them for us. I felt compelled to see them, a living reminder of our fragile family life, an emblem of consistency. I found them in a dog pen behind my neighbor's house. They howled and wagged their tails with delight when they saw me. They jumped up and down with excitement at the thought of a romp on the beach like we used to, with no cares other than to have dinner and go to bed early in time for school. Those days are gone, at least for now.

Suddenly, I became anxious to return to the hospital. On arriving, I found Giles in a terrifying condition. He was complaining of severe pain on the right side of his chest and his body was shaking in uncontrollable spasms. His face was completely drained of blood leaving a grayish pallor. It was most alarming! In a panic I found a nurse and asked her if she could give me a reason for such a change. "Nothing that I know of," she said, "he went to surgery earlier and the doctors put in a catheter for dialysis. He came out of the anesthetic just a short time ago."

I was aware that the doctors would be inserting a catheter while I was away. The catheter was for dialysis and was put into the subclavian vein, just below the clavicle. Every few days they alternated right and left sides. It had been done several times before and was a relatively simple procedure, except that he had to have an anesthetic.

"I can't breathe," Giles said weakly. "It really hurts."

I felt even more concerned and asked the nurse to look at him. She took his blood pressure and temperature and told me everything appeared to be normal.

"But it isn't normal." I looked at her in amazement. "Look at him! Something terrible has happened. We need to find a doctor."

An X-ray was taken and the radiologist held up the film to show me that the right chest was completely blacked out. "It must be blood," he said, "he must have bled into his chest when we inserted the catheter. It's most unusual for this to happen." He shook his head as he stared at the film.

"What do you think we should do about it?" I asked. I was dismayed by his casual attitude towards what seemed to me a serious turn of events.

"There isn't much we can do. I think we should leave him alone for now and watch him carefully."

Bow Tie took some fluid off the chest and confirmed that it was indeed blood and it wasn't infected, but then decided to leave Giles alone.

The doctors seem remarkably unconcerned and say his body will absorb the blood in time, but I am convinced that this event is related to a marked change in his condition. Up to now he has been showing signs of improvement, eating minimal amounts and regaining some strength, but since this episode he can't hold down any food at all. It is another puzzle for the doctors. They can't understand what is causing him to vomit all the time.

G iles continues to have dialysis twice a day and has progressed sufficiently to have the treatment in the dialysis unit with other patients. The procedure takes over an hour and I go with him to help pass the time. I always carry the crucifix with me, sometimes tucked in my belt, sometimes in my pocket, but I don't go anywhere without it. I went to the bathroom on the dialysis unit and the crucifix fell out of my pocket, crashing onto the hard floor. Dismayed, I realized the little statue of Jesus had come off the cross. "Oh! No!" I cried to myself. What does this mean? Then a calm came over me. Perhaps it is another sign that Giles doesn't need Him any more?

### June 11th. to 17th.

*Dear Mr. Thompson:*
*Mrs. Ford and I wish to send you our very best wishes for a speedy recovery after your recent surgery. We hope your hospital stay and your recuperation period will pass quickly to enable you to return to a full and rewarding life.*
*Warmest, best wishes,*
*Gerald R. Ford*

T he letters of support continue to pour in from Portland, from Longview, and from far and wide. Literally hundreds of people, not just from the United States, but from overseas, have taken the time to send a card, a soft toy, or a long letter telling us about themselves and offering encouragement.

Many letters come from children and teenagers who often include a personal photograph. They ask to come in to see Giles or that he write or call them. It is impossible for him to respond, or even to read all of the letters, our days are consumed by other things. Dan Lagrande has offered to send out a form letter to acknowledge their kindness.

One man, who called himself the faith healer, wrote a long letter talking about his ailments and how he had overcome trials and tribulations in his own life. He obviously put a lot of time and thought into his letter, but after he received my acknowledgment, he wrote another long letter to say he couldn't remember writing to Giles.

Then there is Karen from Grand Rapids who writes almost every day begging for a reply. I am wondering if the media haven't quite got it across to the public as to how critical Giles is. He is just too sick and can't think about replying to his fan mail at this point.

I feel quite at home here and I am never alone. The hospital support staff—the kitchen staff, security staff, maintenance and housekeeping—regularly pop their respective heads around the door whenever they are passing our room, just to say "hello" and to ask how Giles is doing.

Our little waiting room has became a stopping off place for the staff, especially the doctors. They often drop in to report on Giles' condition and usually stay if they can. We talk and talk, and they tell me about their own families and the day-to-day gossip of the hospital.

Bow Tie comes almost every day. He has a little boy, Alex, about two years old and he loves to tell me about the developments in Alex's life; when he is off duty, we sometimes have a beer together. He and the other doctors are good to me. With endless patience, they make sure I understand the reasoning behind their actions before proceeding. I am eager to understand exactly what is going on and I realize they often look to me to help make decisions when they are in doubt. It makes life here easier to bear if I have information to rationalize. They have a lot to put up with in me, but always include me and make me feel part of the team. At the same time they are humble and never afraid to say they're not sure, or haven't run into this or that before. Obviously, Giles has affected their lives. I often find them in his room betting on a basketball or football game with him. Perhaps to help him pass the time or just to become his friend.

G iles has had twenty-four dialysis treatments in all. This week his kidneys began to function again. He had excruciating flank pain and his urine was almost black, apparently due to waste from the blood products. He may have a kidney infection, but the urologist feels the antibiotics, which are constantly infused, will take care of it. Giles is relieved to be free of this monotonous procedure twice a day.

He continues to have a low-grade fever and the doctors are baffled as to the cause. There has even been some speculation about the possibility of AIDS, as he has received so many blood transfusions. However, the doctors feel confident in the accuracy of the AIDS test which apparently has only been available for a short time. He still has blood transfusions, but only one or two a week now. This week he had a violent reaction to a transfusion. His symptoms were alarming when his body went into uncontrollable convulsions—his skin was clammy and he complained of being cold. The nurses and doctors were quite concerned until they realized that it was in fact an adverse reaction to a blood transfusion, which apparently sometimes happens.

I am anxious for Giles to be moved out of the CCU and onto one of the wards. We ask the doctors every day if he can go, but each day Dr. Asaph says it won't be much longer. We have heard that Brittany has already gone home and is taking active rehabilitation at Emanuel. When I look at Giles I feel sad. He has made a lot of progress, but has had to overcome many hurdles just to get to this point. I know the doctors are afraid to let him out of their sight and although it might be a small move out of the CCU, it would feel like a giant step towards being normal again—one more step towards being discharged and going home.

This week Dr. Asaph was about to give his permission for Giles to leave the CCU when Giles had yet another crisis. I awoke early one morning and ambled towards the CCU as usual, to find the nurses running here and there and a huge commotion surrounding Giles' room.

"His heart missed a few beats during the night when he was sleeping," the nurse cried. A lump rose in my throat as my own heart missed a beat. I searched frantically for a doctor to tell me what it meant, but Dr. Asaph couldn't give me an answer.

"We will have to keep him on the heart monitor for a few more days and watch him very closely. He must stay here in the CCU. If there is a problem with his heart, we dare not put him on one of the floors."

"Business as usual," I commented sullenly. Dr. Asaph nodded with a look as if to say, "We're not taking any chances."

The next night Giles' heart missed a beat again in his sleep.

"We are beginning to think it is a normal sinus arrhythmia," Dr. Asaph explained the next morning. "It probably happens all the time to teenage boys when they are sleeping. We are not aware of it, because we don't normally have teenage boys on a heart monitor. Giles' heart seems perfectly sound otherwise. It probably means that his sleep pattern is returning to normal."

Nevertheless they will keep him under alert in the CCU while they monitor his heart.


The weather is unbearably hot and there isn't any fresh air in the hospital. The nights are warm and still and Giles longs to go outside to feel the cool breeze on his face again. In the evenings, Dick and I take him outside in a wheelchair. There really isn't anywhere to go except the parking lot where there are a few trees and shrubs. One night Giles gazed up at the sky and studied the stars; he breathed in the fresh, cool, night air.

"I wonder what my friends are doing," he reflected.

I looked at him in his wheelchair wearing a hospital robe and a blanket tucked around his waist to cover up the remainder of his legs. He looks so frail, as though a gust of wind would blow him away, and his skin is sallow and blotchy. His arms lay lifeless beside his body, covered by pads of gauze and wadding. I feel completely powerless to change his state. I wonder what he is thinking and what irrevocable damage has been done to his strong character. The devastation to his body is easy to measure, but only time will show the damage to his heart.

"I wanted to learn to drive this summer," he said vacantly.

"You will." I gripped his shoulder, now just skin and bone, "There will be other summers. You will drive as soon as you are able."

I don't know whether he will be driving soon, it seems another world away, but it gives us something to look forward to — or something else to worry about.

D r. Hikes offered to show me around the hospital to pick out a suitable room for Giles. Apparently, there are several options open to us. First, he took me to the hospice floor which was fitted out with kitchens and has a place for the family to stay. It was a wonderful facility, but I don't like the idea of hospice.

We finally picked a room on the orthopedic floor — on the fifth floor at the far end of the corridor. Dr. Hikes feels we will be protected from the press there. Reporters are still milling around the hospital in the hope of getting an interview with Giles, but the hospital personnel are cognizant of the pressure for media attention, and do everything possible to protect us. They allow us to use back hallways to the CCU and to our rooms to avoid main corridors and entrances. I am oblivious of the media, their presence is inconsequential to me. Dan Lagrande, the hospital marketing director, visits me every day to ask me if I am ready to give a press conference. He warns me that reporters are everywhere and I should be careful. He said there were two very proper Englishmen to see me — clean cut and dressed in Saville Row suits.

"Don't be fooled by them," he said, "they are reporters from a tabloid looking for a sensational slant on the story. Don't talk to them whatever you do." How distasteful. Heaven knows what dreadful things a tabloid would do with this story.

At the end of this week, the doctors agreed to move Giles to the orthopedic floor. He has to continue to wear a heart monitor until they are convinced that the arrhythmia is not abnormal, but at last they feel he can be managed adequately on the floor. It was an exciting day as we said goodbye to the nurses. They have become attached to Giles and were sad to see him leave, but they promised to visit us in our new abode. It is unusual for them to have a patient as young as Giles in the CCU, especially for five weeks.

It took me almost a whole day to move the mounds of stuff which we have accumulated from the waiting room, including countless flower arrangements. The nurses soon converted "my room" back to an outpatient waiting room and there were already patients in there when I went back. It seemed odd to see strangers in "my room", but I am relieved to be leaving at last. That room has witnessed so many tears and seen all of our pain over the last weeks. I am glad to be leaving it behind.

I thank God to be going because Giles is getting well; circumstances could so easily have been different. I pray we will never have to come back. Reflecting over the past thirty-two days, I counted twenty physicians who have participated in Giles' care. He received four hundred units of blood and blood products, spent more than twenty-four hours in surgery, had twenty-four hemodialysis and thirteen hyperbaric treatments. I have lost count of the X-rays, CAT scans, minor surgeries, electrocardiograms, echocardiograms and tests for this that and the other. Giles had some physical and occupational therapy, but Dr. Hikes tells me it will be intensified when he goes on the orthopedic floor. What a medical record! I can only imagine the size of it. This severe case of hypothermia will go down in medical history, I'm sure.

## *June 18th. to July 9th.*

*Not since the death of John Kennedy (when I was 15), have I felt sorrow and pain to this degree. My thoughts and prayers are with you. I hope body and mind heal quickly.*
*Kathy Donohue*

We have received lots of letters written by schoolchildren as part of a class project, mostly a few simple words to say they are thinking of Giles. I think DJs at the radio stations must talk about him and put out an appeal for people to write.

Many letters are from amputees, people who write to tell us about their experience. They talk about the phases which they went through during recovery. Many write to say how hopeless it was for them in the beginning, but in the end they experienced few limitations. Some talk about their successful professions and how they have gone on to have families of their own.

A man who lost both of his legs at the knees (bilateral knee disarticulation) adjusted to a life without prostheses. He wore pads over the ends of his stumps and learnt to walk on them as they were. He included photographs of himself standing by his car, swimming and working in his garden. I was shocked to see these pictures; I don't think I will show them to Giles.

Their words of encouragement are inspiring: they tell us what is possible and that the loss of legs doesn't mean the loss of a future.

The nursing supervisor on the orthopedic floor has assigned a special nurse for Giles. Her name is Debbie. She is a sweet girl probably in her late twenties. Her pretty, round face and endearing smile welcomed Giles to his new surroundings; she immediately fussed over him in her kind and attentive way. She is on duty during the day and different nurses cover the evening and night shifts. Some nurses are young and attractive, and I expected Giles to want them to take care of him, but his favorite is an older nurse, Liz. She is an old-fashioned type who wears a little three-cornered cap held down with hair pins, heavy white stockings and a traditional, heavily-starched uniform. She is a dear person and Giles obviously respects her. She bosses him around in a loving way and won't let him get away with anything. She is a professional, he can see that.

Giles' room is light and airy with panoramic views of Portland. However, I didn't realize when I chose it that it faces west, and the sun shines squarely into the room in the afternoon. It is stiflingly hot and we can't open the windows. I feel for Giles, at least I can leave whenever I want to, but he is trapped in the stuffy atmosphere, unable to breathe the fresh liberating air outside.

I still have my dormitory room in the hospital, but I sleep in a chair in Giles' room which converts into a bed. Dick feels it's time for me to sleep in Longview and for Giles to be treated like a normal patient, but Giles seems to want me nearby. The night hours have improved tremendously. Giles sleeps for several hours at a time and the nursing staff don't disturb him. He wakes me up if he is thirsty or to help him turn, but otherwise we sleep until dawn. I still feel uncomfortable about leaving the hospital for long periods of time, but I often go home in the daytime. However, I want to be with him during the night when there aren't so many people around.

The doctors are still concerned about the cardiac arrhythmia so Giles continued to wear a heart monitor, but it is clear that whatever was causing his heart to miss a beat had nothing to do with his heart surgery. They reluctantly took the monitor away this week and have been waiting nervously to see what happens. He appears to be perfectly alright.

Dr. Rogers discontinued the hyperalimentation before Giles left the CCU; now the hospital dietitian is in charge of creating appealing meals for Giles. The hospital menu is designed around an average hospital stay of four or five days, and after six weeks in the hospital the fare is quite monotonous. Dick quickly saved the situation. He has a son who owns a German restaurant in Portland and he frequently brings in food from there. Giles really enjoys the delicious dishes which are such a welcomed change. He can only eat small portions, so we encourage him to eat a little and often. We have brought in a small refrigerator to store snacks and Dick brings in a tub of Häagen-Dazs ice cream almost every evening. Every calorie counts for Giles, but his weight hardly changes even though we try everything. My waistline, however, is disappearing by the day; but I will worry about that later. Dick must have noticed because he suggested that I join an exercise class in the hospital. It's a good idea, but I can't face an aerobics class. I feel guilty enough just walking around when Giles is unable to move.

Almost every day, Dan Lagrande asks me to talk to the press. He says they are still anxious to have an interview with me.

I am afraid of being put on the spot, or saying something unintentionally. I asked Dr. Asaph what he thought about it, and he encouraged me to do it. He tells me he talks to the press frequently and thinks they probably won't leave me alone until they have an interview with me.

"The community really wants to hear from you," Dan Lagrande said persuasively. "They want to know how Giles is coming along, and want to hear it from you."

"Alright!" I said decisively. "I'll do it!"

He made the arrangements for a press conference the next day.

What was I going to wear? I have never had a press conference held especially for me before and I wasn't sure. I don't have a lot of choices in what might be considered suitable, even though I have a fairly substantial wardrobe. Lounging pajamas probably wouldn't qualify.

I finally settled on a bright turquoise dress, one of the few things which I can still get into, and my pink shoes. I hoped Jack wouldn't notice.

Dr. Asaph met me in Giles' room and Dan Lagrande took us both downstairs. The press conference was to be held at 10:00 in the morning. Walking the long passages with Jim Asaph marching beside me, I began to feel sick with nerves and wondered whether I was doing the right thing. I told Jim I was nervous and thought maybe I should back out.

"Just say what you think and don't let them intimidate you," he said reassuringly.

"Do you think they will try?"

"They might, although they have been very sensitive in the interviews we have had."

"I hope they don't ask me about the Climb. I don't want to talk about that."

"You don't have to. This interview concerns Giles and his present condition."

We entered the conference room through a side door and immediately I was quite taken aback by the sight before me. I hadn't thought to ask how many people would be there; I expected to see perhaps five or six reporters and television news-casters hadn't occurred to me. The conference room was packed with people, at least sixty reporters were present. Some were carrying huge cameras and microphones such as I had never seen before. We sat down at a long conference table which was brightly lit like a stage, so we couldn't recognize the sea of faces beyond the glare. It was quite daunting. I suddenly had an urge to run away, but it was too late...I was committed. I took a couple of deep breaths to compose myself and tried to appear as though it was something I did every day. Then the questions began:

"How is Giles?" a voice without a face echoed from the back of the room.

"You take it," said Jim.

"He has been very sick indeed," I began; the lump in my throat felt like an apple choking me. "It has been a terrible episode. He is still extremely weak, but we are pleased with his progress."

A reporter shouted out saying he couldn't hear me, so I cleared my throat and repeated my response.

Jim, sensing my nervousness jumped in to give the medical explanation. He was articulate and blinded them with his knowledge. It was as though he had rehearsed his answers. I was envious and vowed to do the same. After his description, there was a pause as the reporters took notes.

"What happened on the mountain? Does Giles talk about it?" I dreaded this question and I thought quickly:

"Yes, he has talked about the Climb, but doesn't remember much about the cave."

"Are there going to be any lawsuits?" There it was! I knew this question would come up.

"I don't know. A committee has been set up by the school to investigate, and they will determine what happened on the Climb."

"Do you think the school Basecamp Program was responsible for the Tragedy?" There it was again, trying to get me to blame someone.

"One of the reasons I sent my children to OES was because of the Basecamp Program. My other son Ross went on the

Sophomore Climb two years ago and had a wonderful time. I had no reason to believe this climb would be any different. It is a good program for young people. OES is a good school and I support them." They probably didn't want to hear me say that.

A hush came over the room as they thought about more questions. I hoped they wouldn't pursue the subject.

"Will Giles go back to OES?"

"Yes, he intends to go back and we are hoping he will be ready for the beginning of school in September."

"How did he react to the loss of his legs?"

"He hasn't really dealt with that issue yet; he has had to concentrate on getting well. I don't think it will completely sink in until he begins serious rehabilitation."

Then.... "Do you have a message for the community? They would like to hear from you."

"Yes. I would like to thank the many people who have given their support. Thank them for the letters, gifts, flowers and calls. A special thank you to the people of Longview."

There was an uneasy silence and then Dan Lagrande stood up. "Are there any more questions?...Okay, that's all."

Jim and I got up to leave. "What did you think?" I asked him. "I could have done better, but I was tongue-tied and dodged most of the questions."

"You did fine," he said. "I liked the little plug you gave the school. That was positive and I know they will appreciate it."

"I hope so. It's hard to know the right thing to say. Reporters are so skilled at questioning and I had the impression they were trying to trick me into saying what they wanted to hear."

"Yes...that's right...but you did fine...don't worry."

The next day the article was on the front page of the *Oregonian* newspaper. In the photograph I had a smirk on my face and my eyes were screwed up. Elizabeth was reading the article when I came into Giles' room the next morning. She dropped the paper and thrust it into my hand. "Don't do that again," she said abruptly.

The headline read: "Mother Still Supports School Wilderness Program".

Oh dear! Why didn't they print the more positive aspects of the discussion?

I have decided I won't do it again. I can't think quickly enough to answer appropriately. They are probably going to print what they are going to print regardless of how I feel.

"Why did you say I couldn't remember?" Giles asked.

"I didn't want to get into a discussion about the Climb, so I avoided the question, but I did my best."

"You had probably better not do any more press conferences."

"Yes, you're right. Pity really…with more practice I could probably get quite good at it."

S ergeant Harder, the head of the rescue operation, visits us almost daily. He continues to struggle with the Tragedy, but I think it helps him to be close to the survivors. We cry together and wonder if life will ever return to normal. He tells me he has been spending time with Brittany at the pool at Emanuel helping her in her rehabilitation program. He has two little children of his own who watch *Sesame Street* and are enamored with the characters, particularly Bert and Ernie. Each day, he tells me about the latest episode. I am out of touch with children's programs, but it brings humor to our otherwise dreary hours in the hospital. He wants Giles to borrow the two dolls, one of Bert and one of Ernie, which belong to his children. He says they will bring him luck.

One morning this week we looked out of the window and saw a banner attached to the adjoining building. It read: "GET WELL, GILES!" The nurses were excited and wondered who could have done it and how did they get it up there. I looked closely and saw drawings of Bert and Ernie in the corner, so I knew who had done it, but I'm not sure anyone else guessed except perhaps Dr. Asaph. What a wonderful thought. It must have been quite a job to hoist it up, his crew must have helped him.

G iles' legs have healed sufficiently for the process of making prosthetic devices to begin. Dr. Hikes wants Giles to wear artificial legs while he is confined to bed so that he will get used to the idea of seeing legs and feet again.

Dr. Hikes knows a prosthetist in Portland—a German gentleman named Frank. Apparently, the prosthetic profession originated in Germany, evolving from the days when armor was made. Frank could easily be taken for a consulting physician with his pristine white coat and immaculate appearance. He and Dr. Hikes huddled together for hours planning the construction of the new legs. It is very exciting, we are elated with anticipation and it sounds remarkably easy. Frank soon got to work with his plaster of Paris and fussed around muttering about "Seattle feet" and hydraulic knees. The conversations were quite bizarre: like *Alice in Wonderland*. He took a mold of both the right and left legs, and then packed up his things and left.

A few days later, he returned with a pair of legs: an AK and a BK, and Dr. Hikes instructed Giles to wear them in bed for short periods of time. Giles has tried them on once or twice, but most of the time they stand in the corner of the room. They are like a person standing there and they even have size eight feet. We found a pair of socks and put on the running shoes I had bought for Giles before the accident. It seems odd to put your shoes on and stand your legs up in the corner.

Dr. Asaph and Dr. Hikes have decided it would make more sense to have a comprehensive approach to Giles' care. There are still dozens of medical specialists treating him, and there hasn't been any time to formulate a proper plan. They have put together a team who will work in unison to provide appropriate care for Giles and to prevent overlaps in services. The team consists of Dr. Asaph, Dr. Dreisin, Dr. Hikes, Dick, Debbie his nurse, physical therapists and occupational therapists. They arranged a daily plan-of-care meeting in which I am invited to participate. Each day, the main topics of conversation are Giles' continuous vomiting and his low-grade fever. The vomiting is a puzzle. We have tried adjusting his diet and the doctors have done numerous tests and X-rays, but there is no explanation for these complications. Typically, Giles eats in a reclining position, and when he sits up, his food comes up. It's worrisome and it's no wonder he can't gain weight. I feel helpless and frustrated by the lack of progress.

During a meeting, I took the bull by the horns and put forth my theory. "I think the vomiting has something to do with the blood in his chest. I can't explain it," I said, "but Giles was eating and progressing well until the day the catheter was changed. Whatever it was, something happened on that day which set him back."

"I think that's unlikely to be the cause," said Dr. Asaph patiently. "The bleeding was into the right lung, the opposite side to the stomach. However, we must solve this mystery. It isn't good at all to be throwing up all the time. It's bound to be weakening, especially as he has so few reserves."

"Perhaps it's the antibiotics," I added exasperated, "or maybe it's the fever." I was grasping at straws, but it doesn't make any difference. Giles continues to vomit many times a day.

A couple of days later Dr. Asaph ordered another CAT scan of the abdomen to see if perhaps anything had been overlooked. He and Dr. Hikes appeared soon after Giles returned from the procedure, looking quite pleased with the results.

"There are two things," Dr. Asaph said excitedly. "He has a lot of gas in the stomach, which is probably caused by drinking through a long straw. He must stop using that. The other thing is, his right chest cavity is full of blood and I think we should drain it off."

"I knew it," I said triumphantly. "I'm sure that is the problem."

Dr. Asaph immediately put a tube into Giles' chest and indeed, there was a great deal of blood which drained off. Giles stopped using the drinking straw and the vomiting slowed down, but didn't stop completely. Apparently, antibiotics, especially the strength of those given to Giles, destroy the bacteria in the stomach, and valuable bacteria for digestion are destroyed. Dick found the list of contra-indications for the antibiotics which said one side effect is a low-grade fever. Maybe the antibiotics are the cause of the vomiting and the fever. Maybe that's it.

The days are filled with activities—visitors in and out, physical therapy, occupational therapy, procedures and tests—but in the evenings there is more time to ponder. That is when the psychological effects of Giles' trauma become more evident. Dick spends hours with him, often late into the night. I'm not usually a part of these conversations, but one evening I couldn't help overhearing them talk. Dick was encouraging Giles to discuss the loss of his legs.

"What will I do if there is a fire?" Giles asked. A question that must be haunting him. "How will I get out?"

"There isn't anything you can do," Dick replied. "You are totally dependent in a case like that. Your legs are gone."

"What about skiing? Do you think I will ski again?"

"You might, but it won't be the same."

"I will probably never run again either, play football or soccer—no sports at all."

"No—that's all gone."

I am ignorant about psychology, but Dick's response sounded without hope and full of despair. "There will be things you can do," I interrupted. "I'm sure there will be sports you can play, you will be able to participate. You won't be able to run that's all, but you will walk again. Your new, artificial legs will work well for you I'm sure; you might be surprised."

"They won't be the same," Dick continued. "It's like giving a woman a doll after her baby has died and saying it will replace her child."

"Yes...but there must be some hope. Otherwise..." I shrugged and turned away swallowing my tears, frustration bursting inside of me. I do understand the process, but it was harsh treatment for me to witness. I want to protect Giles from the reality which he undoubtedly has to face, and pretend it really isn't there.

As the days drag on into weeks, Giles' psychological state deteriorates. He is sinking into a deep depression. Dick thought an antidepressant would be the answer, and although I'm not in favor of more drugs, I was willing to do anything that might help. The new medication has a horrible effect on Giles. He has dramatic, emotional outbursts, tears of anger pour from his soul, and one morning he cried out: "I hate this! Get me out of here!" He writhed from one side of the bed to the other, shouting and crying. It was awful. I couldn't bear to watch him. I felt compelled to ask Dick to discontinue the drug. It is too soon to bring so much to the surface, especially when Giles can do so little about his plight.

While he was under the influence of the drug, the team of investigators into the Climb were interviewing those involved. A committee made up of climbing experts, many of whom came to Portland from the East Coast to participate, interviewed the survivors. We had been informed that members of the committee were waiting as long as possible for Giles' condition to improve before they came to talk to him. We were all apprehensive about the interview, and for some unknown reason, I felt particularly uneasy about it. I knew it was necessary at some point, but I wasn't ready. Perhaps I will never be ready. I asked Paul, our attorney, to be present. Dick and I were in the room when Dr. Bangs and another investigator arrived.

It wasn't a good day for Giles; the anti-depressant was affecting him and he was also on medication for pain. He was heavily drugged and didn't feel inclined to talk to anyone. However, Dr. Bangs pressed on with his predetermined questioning.

"Start from the beginning," he began. "Tell me what happened."

Giles began his story, but after a sentence or two, he drifted off into a drugged sleep.

Dr. Bangs asked another question.

"I don't remember."

Soon it became clear that it was hopeless. Giles was in no condition to be interviewed and Dr. Bangs obviously realized it. But there was one question he had to have answered.

"You were at the front of the group....Were you not?"

"Yes."

"Susan was behind you with the compass. Was she not?"

"Yes."

"Do you remember the number that was called out? The number of degrees, I mean."

Giles looked up, exasperated. "No!"

"Was it 180?"

"I'm not sure."

"Was it 160?"

"I think it was."

"Are you sure?"

"Yes! I'm sure."

It was difficult to tell whether Giles was just saying that to get the interview over with, but it was obviously this question which needed to be answered.

Dr. Bangs asked him again, "Think back carefully."

This time Giles was more resolute in his answer and Dr. Bangs seemed satisfied.

"We will leave you alone now. We're sorry to have to do this. We will come back again when you are feeling better."

"I'm sorry," Giles said apologetically and promptly fell asleep.

They never did come back to finish the interview. They must have been satisfied.

E very day Giles goes to the physical therapy department. It is laborious for him and almost a waste of time. He tells me he lies on a mat and every once in a while a therapist comes over to do something with him, but it isn't a vigorous program. Giles doesn't have the strength or motivation for that. Occupational therapy is a little more interesting. He is in an "activities for daily living" program (ADL) where he learns to do simple everyday things all over again: dressing himself, cleaning his teeth, combing his hair and feeding himself. Meanwhile I am increasingly concerned about his hands and arms, particularly the right hand. He has almost no function or movement in it. Dr. Hikes isn't able to give me a convincing prognosis for it either.

"Only time will tell," he says. "It could take a year or so, or it may take a few months. There is a lot of damage there—that's all we know."

What if it doesn't come back at all? These thoughts haunt me. What then? He has lost both of his legs, and there is a strong possibility that his arms are useless, a prospect much more difficult for me to accept. If he can't use his arms and hands, how will he fill the day? No hobbies—unable to feed himself—unable to take care of himself. He will be totally dependent. There has been almost no visible progress in his hands. The damage to the nerves in his arms and hands is different to the other injuries he has suffered. I suppose we just have to be patient because the final outcome is unknown.

I drive to Longview almost every day. It is tiring and I am anxious for Giles to be discharged from the hospital. I am ready to get on with our lives again and return to normal…whatever normal is. I have almost forgotten.

Each day I try to convince the doctors that we can take care of him just as well at home, but they refuse to discharge him as long as he has a fever.

"Yes, but it isn't as though he would be returning to an average household," I pleaded. "There is a doctor in the house and I have medical experience. We would know what to do if anything happened."

They aren't convinced.

"What could happen?" I am beginning to think they want to keep Giles in the hospital, that he is somehow their possession. It is as though they can't let go of him. Which is an absurd idea.

"He has had so many setbacks…we must make sure," Dr. Hikes told me. "Longview…it's so far from here."

"I know, but we have a very strong medical community and a good hospital, you would be surprised. It's smaller of course, but they can do anything there that can be done here at this stage. We do have electricity and hot and cold running water."

"I know." He smiled, but didn't appreciate my sarcasm. "We'll wait a bit longer."

"What will he do at home all day?" Dick asked. "There won't be anyone of his own age. He will be very bored."

"He needs a chance to rest as much as possible," I insisted, "and to eat when and what he likes."

"What about the dressing on his chest?"

"The incision has almost healed and I can see to that. I understand sterile techniques, I have changed dressings before."

"He still has a suture to be taken out."

"We can deal with that…that isn't anything."

I wasn't getting anywhere. They weren't going to let him go home.

At last, Dr. Asaph announced his decision to discontinue the antibiotics. He was reluctant to do it because Giles still had a fever, but as there is no evidence of an infection, he felt it pointless to continue. I was relieved. One more treatment ended. One less thing to worry about.

The IV for the antibiotic was the last of the countless needles to be removed from Giles' body, and within no time at all, his temperature returned to normal. "That must have been it," said Dick. "It's a relief to know that nothing more serious was going on."

It wasn't necessary for Giles to be in the hospital once his temperature returned to normal. Dr. Asaph has told us, Giles could go home at the end of the week. It was music to our ears. Such a small thing, yet so long awaited and welcomed. At last!

Giles' thin, drawn face lit up with delight when I told him the good news.

"Really!" I'll be able to see my friends," he said smiling from ear to ear.

"You'll have to take it easy, or else they'll have you back in here," I warned.

Dr. Asaph left us to decide what day we wanted to leave. He gave instructions to the nurse to go over the dressing change procedures with me. We had to pick out a doctor in Longview and arrange home health services to help with bathing. Physical and occupational therapy would have to be done at home. I called Bill immediately to make the necessary arrangements; he uses home health services in Longview for his patients.

"Giles will need to have a chest X-ray done in Longview in about a week. Would you ask the radiologist to send us the results? We must make sure that his lungs are clear," Bow Tie added.

I was so excited, I could hardly contain myself. We decided to leave on Friday because it would take several days to get our stuff moved out of the hospital. There was no doubt that we made ourselves at home over the two-month period. Giles had one of everything, my room was packed with things and my parents had to evacuate their apartment. Short of hiring a moving company, we had a lot to do.

"I will take a load to Longview and bring the Triumph Spitfire back to take you home," I told Giles. "We can put the top down so it will be easier to get in and out. Joanne can take everyone else in her car."

I wanted to take Giles home in the Spitfire because the car had belonged to his father. He bought it barely six months before he died. He had always wanted an English sports car, but had never been able to afford one until the end of his life, and he had only driven it a few times. I kept the car for Giles, but now he probably will never be able to drive it because it has a manual shift. Colin would have liked to have known Giles went home from the hospital in his car. It's sporty and will lift his spirits—triumphant—just like its name.

Dan Lagrande met us in Giles' room to brief us on our exit.

"There will be a number of reporters waiting to see you leave," he said, "so I think we will take you out through the ER exit, where we won't interfere with the other patients."

"Alright," I agreed. "It sounds as though it's going to be quite an occasion."

"There was a big commotion when Giles came in here, so we expect it to be the same when he leaves," Dan laughed. Looking down he added, "We are all so happy you are finally going home. We will miss you of course, but we are glad for you."

Friday came and we were ready. Giles fixed up his hair and picked out something suitable to wear. Dr. Hikes arranged for a wheelchair and Debbie was to lead the procession pushing Giles. Dick, Dr. Hikes and several nurses planned to come too.

"The press will probably want to ask you questions," Dan warned Giles, "but you don't have to say anything to them if you don't wish to."

"No! I don't want to talk to them," Giles replied firmly.

The procession filed along the familiar corridors, past Mary Magdalene and St. Francis of Assisi, down the escalator to the ER where we had arrived fifty-five days earlier. The passage was lined with people: nurses from the coronary care unit and the orthopedic floor, the maintenance staff, kitchen staff, radiology, dialysis, nuclear medicine, hypothermia and surgery. Everyone was there. People who have become our family, in what had become our home. A huge banner stretched out before us which read, "WAY TO GO, GILES!" and there was a drawing of a skier in one corner. I think everyone in the hospital must have signed it.

As we had been warned, there was the usual mob of reporters with their cameras and microphones. When we got to the door, we stopped.

"No interviews please!" Dan shouted.

A hush descended, then a reporter stepped forward and put a microphone to Giles' mouth. "Are you glad to be going home?" he said.

"This a great place to stay; but I wouldn't want to live here," Giles commented with all the confidence and joy I remembered in his old self. He must have given it some thought before, because it just came out. All of our newfound friends laughed and cheered for Giles as Debbie wheeled him out. I fought back my tears as I realized these wonderful people were sorry to see him leave.

What a send-off!

I slipped out through a side door and started up the Spitfire, which I had previously parked in the ER parking, and drove to the entrance to wait for Giles. A guard from the hospital main parking lot was there to help me lift Giles into the car. He had become my friend during our stay at Providence, always waiting for me with a place to leave my car. "Good luck!" he said as he bent down to look through the window. "Be sure to come back and see us."

With that we left for Longview.

The sky was overcast as we followed Joanne, who had my parents in her car, and the normally busy I-5 freeway was unusually quiet. I drove cautiously, not wishing to jolt Giles unnecessarily. I hugged the right hand lane and drove at a snail's pace so that I was ready to pull over if he showed any sign of distress. Giles looked very nervous. I glanced at him out of the corner of my eye and saw him gripping the handle on the door, his knuckles white against his pale skin.

About halfway home, Joanne pulled off on the side of the road, so I pulled onto the shoulder behind her. My father was running back to the car, waving his hands for us to stop. My heart sank when I thought something must have happened. Visions of another catastrophe flashed through my mind.

"I think it's going to rain!" he shouted—as though it never does in this part of the world.

We had the soft top of the Spitfire down. Even though it was cloudy, it was a warm sultry day. We stopped for a few minutes and pulled the canvas top over us and continued on our way—but it didn't rain.

Bill was waiting for us at the door when we arrived at the house, his eyes wild with anticipation; at last his family was together again. It was quite a struggle to get Giles out of the car. We organized our strategy, one on one side and one on the other, to lift him out of the seat and into the wheelchair. It was very awkward, but it was our first time. It certainly made it much easier to be able to remove the top of the car, and because the Spitfire is built so low, leverage was good. I'm sure we will get better at it with all the practice we will have in the future.

We settled Giles down in a corner of the sofa. He looked exhausted and soon flopped his head down and dropped off to sleep, despite all the noise around him. It was wonderful to be home. All the familiar sounds and smells began to heal my soul. The birds lingered on the bird table and chirped their welcoming song. The air was filled with voices and giggles of normalcy as I bustled around the kitchen thinking of something to have for supper. These mundane tasks which I have taken for granted are precious to me now.

We turned on the evening news and the top story was of Giles leaving the hospital. I was moved to tears when I realized Dr. Hikes was weeping during the interview when he said, "We will miss him. We have become quite fond of him."

### July 10th. to 23rd.

*Dear Giles:*

*I just wanted you to know that I and all of America learned of your miraculous survival with grateful hearts. Yet I realize the personal cost of your survival has been enormous, and I know this is a most difficult time for you and for all who love you.*

*Giles, you have suffered tremendous losses, and yet I'm confident that the same courage that inspired you to climb Mount Hood will be your guide as you undertake perhaps the greatest challenge of your life.*

*As you may know, my son Teddy had to have an amputation, and I know from his experience, a positive attitude and a strong faith are more important than all the miracles of modern medical care. I'm sending you stories about Teddy in the hopes they will bring you some encouragement.*

*We hold you in the embrace of our prayers, Giles.*

*Sincerely,*

*Ted Kennedy…Thinking of you.*

G iles has been close to death for such a long time and there have been so many issues to deal with just to ensure his daily survival—the fact that he is a double amputee has been almost a secondary concern. Now, reality looks us squarely in the face and the amputations are the major issue for Giles in his rehabilitation. I have no idea what the outcome will be, and the doctors can't give me any clear answers, mainly because they too have little, if any, experience in dealing with a similar case. I don't have anywhere to turn. Will Giles ever walk again? Can we expect him to look forward to a normal existence?

Roy brought a book to the hospital for me to read. He said a well-known author in Portland asked him to give it to Giles. There hasn't been time until now for me to read it, but this week I delved into the book absorbing every detail, hoping it might give me some idea about what to expect for Giles. The book, *Reach for the Sky,* is a true story about a young Englishman who was severely injured in an air crash when he was eighteen years old, and had both legs amputated to save his life. The coincidence is quite extraordinary really. Giles has exactly the same amputations, a right knee disarticulation and a left below-the-knee amputation.

The story of Douglas Bader begins with his hospital stay when, due to his injuries, he lost enormous quantities of blood. In those days, blood transfusions and dialysis weren't available and there wasn't much the doctors could do except hope for the best. He was close to death for several months and it was doubted that he would recover. However, after five months in the hospital, he did recover and embarked immediately on the use of prosthetic devices. Years ago prostheses were made of metal and wood and were held on with big shoulder straps. From the beginning, Bader refused to use a walking stick or a wheelchair and his first attempts at walking were soul-destroying. He tottered about trying to get his balance until he finally was able to stand. Slowly but surely he took one step at a time until he was walking. Then he tackled stairs on his own, he even tried dancing, playing tennis and golf. Eventually, golf was the sport he enjoyed throughout his life when he regularly walked the entire golf course unassisted. It was noted in the book that he was probably the first person ever to walk on two artificial legs without assistance.

Douglas Bader, a pilot in the Royal Air Force, had been injured in the line of duty. He was forced to retire because of his disability. However, about the same time, the Second World War broke out and he managed to talk his way back into the Air Force because of the shortage of experienced pilots. He flew in the Battle of Britain and was renowned for his skill and fearlessness. He was known as the "Legless Wonder". Inevitably, his plane was shot down over France. When he tried to eject himself he found that he was trapped in the cockpit by his artificial legs; he pulled himself out of the legs and left them behind, which saved his life.

He landed by parachute and was captured by the Germans who took him to a prisoner of war camp in France where a new set of prostheses was sent from England. It wasn't long before he contacted the Resistance and planned an escape. He tied sheets together to make a rope, anchored it to his bed, dropped five floors to the ground and walked six miles to a secret meeting place. However, he was recaptured and sent to a camp in Germany where he made several more attempts to escape. The Germans became so frustrated with his tireless efforts to seek his freedom that they took his legs away. He was put in a maximum security prison where it was impossible for him to escape, but it didn't stop him from trying. He remained a prisoner for three more years until the end of the war when he went back to England as a hero. He lived there for the rest of his life and died at the age of seventy-eight, having lived a fulfilling and happy life relatively unaffected by the fact that he didn't have any legs.

I read his story over and over again, memorizing how long each step to recovery had taken. What attributes did Douglas Bader have to overcome the enormous hurdles which he faced? What came through clearly for me was his absolute, sheer determination to conquer his disability and to master the physical challenges which he faced. It is an inspiration to know that there has been another person who experienced the same loss and was able to overcome it. Surely Giles could do the same.

Perhaps I make too many comparisons to Douglas Bader without realizing it. I have to take into account the damage to Giles' arms and hands, the surgeries, the procedures and the illness associated with his injuries, all of which contribute to his debilitating weakness. Nevertheless, I must inspire him to search his soul for the same determination that Douglas Bader had. There will be moments of despair and despondency, but the important thing is the hope of *walking in the future*.

We have settled into some kind of routine at home. My parents have returned to England and Elizabeth to Vancouver, British Columbia. Joanne has an apartment in Portland and comes to Longview a couple of times a week. Ross is here for the summer and he spends most of his time practicing his guitar. He is a tremendous help to me by staying with Giles while I work at the clinic. Bill is working there too, but we are like ghosts passing in the night. We rarely have time alone these days and I am so exhausted by the end of the day I hardly have the energy to say good night.

Giles' activities are minimal and we keep things as simple as possible. He sleeps well over twelve hours a night and for an hour or two during the day. He sorely needs this rest to rejuvenate his body which has endured such terrible onslaughts. We arranged for a physical therapist and an occupational therapist to come to the house to work with Giles, but he has very little energy—however, with sleep and high-calorie food he gains strength each day. The home-health nurse comes in a few days a week to help with bathing and dressing changes, and on the whole we are managing much better than I expected.

AK and BK made their way home with us, and it is my job to haul them around. They are so heavy and awkward, I can't imagine them being attached to the body all the time. They are quite smart though, their color is a perfect match to Giles' skin tone and they have a simulated roughness to look like hair. The feet are perfect, the toes curl up to resemble natural feet and the ankles look muscular as though they work out regularly. The legs seemed out of place in the house, so I changed their shoes to make them feel more at home. When Elizabeth dropped in to see us on her way to Vancouver, I laid them down in the doorway and crossed the feet over one another as though someone were asleep in the hallway. It looked hilarious from outside, and I was sure she would get a laugh out of it, but she walked right past them acting as though it were normal to have a spare pair of legs lying around.

It is two weeks since Giles left the hospital; he has regained enough strength to go to Frank's clinic in Portland to make an attempt at wearing the prostheses. The office is well over an hour's drive from Longview and by the time we arrived both Giles and I were full of excitement and anticipation. This was the moment we had been waiting for, and Giles was ready.

Frank was waiting for us and helped to unload AK and BK. Within no time at all he had applied profuse amounts of lubricant to Giles' legs and put the prostheses onto his stumps as he sat in his wheelchair. I held my breath. Giles was about to stand. I stood on one side of him and Frank on the other, we put our arms underneath his shoulders and lifted his frail body onto the artificial limbs. His body shook as his weight transferred, but then he flopped back down into the chair.

"I can't," he cried, "it's too painful." He was trembling with pain and weakness.

"Oh, it will be at first," said Frank, quite unperturbed. "I'll make a few adjustments and they will fit better the next time. The stumps have changed since the first cast was done in the hospital, but in time you will get used to them."

I was confused. This wasn't the way we had expected it to be. Giles had been looking forward to standing up and had hoped to be able to do it that day. I didn't know what to say, he was obviously disappointed. I thought about Douglas Bader. Did he have a lot of pain at first? I suppose there is bound to be some discomfort; after all, man isn't built to carry weight in this way.

"It's just the beginning," I reassured Giles. "Next time I'm sure it will be easier."

Giles had tears in his eyes. Voices of despair screamed within me. "Oh God, what can I do? What can I say? I don't know anything about this." When Dr. Hikes explained the use of prostheses, it sounded so easy. I expected him to put them on and off he would go.

"Let's get out of here!" Giles exclaimed.

I told Frank that Giles was exhausted and we were leaving. We said our goodbyes and made an appointment for the next fitting.

I thought of the Beatles song "The Long and Winding Road". Using that scale, Giles had hardly started on his journey. I resolved to read more about how Douglas Bader fared. In his day, there weren't any of these things—no plastic, Seattle feet, hydraulic knees, custom toes, nothing except wood and metal. The prosthetics must have been terribly heavy and awkward to manage, modern legs are bad enough.

I gathered up AK and BK again, thinking if I have to haul them around much longer I will probably dislocate something. Maybe I could hire someone to carry them like a caddie carries golf clubs. I wonder what they call such a person? I'll call myself a squire for now and think about my advertisement.

We went to Frank's office again, but it was the same story, excruciating pain, useless adjustments and absolutely no progress. However, we don't know what to expect, so I suppose this is the way it will be. When he goes to Shriners Hospital it will be better I'm sure. They will sort this out.

Although Giles' weight is still well below normal he is far too heavy for me to manage; his arms are quite useless and he doesn't have the strength to help himself. There have been times when I have been alone in the house and unable to move him. I can't manage the stairs at all so I have been calling on Jason to help me. Jason is an old friend of Giles' and lives just a few doors down from us. He was always in and out when Giles and he were young; they played football and baseball; they went to middle school together. They grew apart when Giles attended OES, but have renewed their friendship since Giles has been home from the hospital. Jason takes Giles with him on his Saturday night jaunts, when he loads the wheelchair into his car and off they go to town. I worry all the time they are gone, but I know it is important for Giles to go out with his friends rather than have them come to visit him all the time. It must be difficult for him to face up to how much he has changed, but he must get back into life again sooner rather than later and Jason fills a void which I certainly cannot. He is particularly kind to Giles and does what he can to help and support him, which is highly commendable in a sixteen-year-old boy, I think.

## July 24th.

An investigation committee, made up of independent climbing experts, held meetings to reconstruct the Climb, and to give parents, the school and the community a report on how this unparalleled accident might have occurred. I felt confident that they had done the necessary groundwork and were ready to give us their report.

A meeting was held in the administrative offices at the school where the parents of the climbers and those closest to the Tragedy were invited to attend. Giles and I went with Paul, our attorney. There were probably about fifteen people crammed into the small designated room.

I struggled to maneuver Giles' wheelchair through the door and found a prominent place for him to settle. The atmosphere was strained when we entered, one or two people acknowledged Giles, but others appeared shocked to see him so brutally injured. It is only two weeks since he was discharged from the hospital, he is emaciated and looks very sick indeed.

A hush descended on the room as the chairman of the committee began to review the Climb. We listened intently to the details of events leading up to it, of the time they left the lodge, of the equipment they took and of the training they underwent beforehand. We were given a minute-by-minute report of the ascent and of the three days the climbers were trapped on Mount Hood. They gave us a detailed description of the school Basecamp Program, how it was structured and how it was conducted. We were given information on how decisions were made, and how the hierarchy of leadership worked on a climb of this nature.

The investigator's voice was calm, unfaltering and without emotion. Most of us stared at the floor unable to look at each other's faces which mirrored our grief. Soon, a soft sobbing was heard as someone in the group relived the experience of losing a loved one.

The investigation left no stone unturned. There was no declaration of guilt, no cover-up, no speculation as to the reasons why; simply a detailed account of the circumstances which led to our children and the two teachers being trapped on Mount Hood for three days. It took about an hour to explain everything and at the end silence reigned for an interminable moment. Then the investigators invited us to ask questions.

"Do we have an explanation as to why they didn't turn back earlier?" The question came from a parent.

"Father Tom had the only watch available although there was another in Ralph's pack. We don't know whether Father Tom didn't realize how late it was, or whether he simply chose to ignore it."

"It's my understanding that one of the rules of a climb is that climbers must turn back before noon, regardless of where they are. Do we know what happened in this case?"

"That's true. We have no explanation as to why this fundamental rule was not adhered to."

"Why didn't the leaders carry an altimeter? Wouldn't that have helped the rescuers to locate the cave?"

"An altimeter isn't standard equipment for a climb of this nature, but certainly in retrospect it would have helped. The purpose of this climb is not to reach the summit under any circumstances, but to make a token effort if time and conditions allow."

"Do we have any explanation as to why they were lost?" I asked this question which had bothered me ever since Giles gave his account of the Climb to Paul. "I mean...do we know how they came to be so far off track. Had they stayed on the same trail of their ascent, on the descent it would have brought them back to the lodge."

The answer was: "By the time the climbers began their descent, many of them were already critically hypothermic. The compass reading to come off the summit is 180 degrees, but as they were afraid of Zig-Zag Canyon they veered to the left. Although we are not absolutely sure, we understand Father Tom instructed that a 160-degree direction be followed. We feel they were much higher up the mountain than they realized and therefore, by veering so far to the east, their path led them to White River Ridge. We think this is the most probable explanation. The group placed wands on their ascent, but the blizzard was so fierce the markers were already buried by the time the climbers reached them on their descent. By then visibility was down to a few feet, and weather conditions were very severe indeed."

"How did you know all this?" one of the parents asked me.

"I was on the mountain during the entire rescue, except for Tuesday," I replied. "I spent a lot of time talking to rescuers, trying to ascertain where the cave could be. There had to be an explanation as to why they were so far from their original path."

"Why did Ralph leave the cave on Tuesday morning?"

Questions continued to come from the parents.

"By Tuesday morning many of the climbers were too weak to hike down the mountain. Ralph felt the best thing to do was to get help. He marked the entrance to the cave with a yellow raincoat, but it was soon covered with snow. He probably did the only rational thing possible under the circumstances, and we have to assume that he too, was affected by the cold."

"Why didn't they have adequate equipment to survive in the cave?"

"The climbers were adequately equipped for what they set out to do, which was to make a token attempt at the summit and turn back at noon. However, when Ralph was digging the snow cave they put their packs, containing extra food, clothing and other survival equipment, on a tarp nearby. The snow drifted so quickly, by the time the cave was made there was over two feet on top of the packs, making it impossible for them to retrieve their things. In our opinion, they should have dug in earlier, probably when they stopped to rewarm the student suffering from hypothermia. At that time, when they had more strength to take charge of their equipment and to do the job properly, they could have made a larger cave. Although rewarming the student would be the correct procedure under normal circumstances, they wasted valuable time. The other members of the group became cold as they stood around and waited. It's like a burning house…you have to get out as quickly as possible."

We sat in silence, unable to think of another question. Some people prepared to leave, to go back to their jobs and families. There was nothing else to say. That was it. Giles looked agitated so I stood up and began to maneuver him out of the door. The air was thick in the small meeting room and I felt lightheaded after being in the tense atmosphere for almost two hours, and relieved to get outside. It was a lovely summer day. The wind rustled in the trees and the shrill sounds of songbirds and civilization were the background music for our sobbing. Life continues to go on; seemingly oblivious of our grief.

The group disbursed rapidly with some people almost running towards their cars. One or two, who stopped to wish Giles good luck, said they were relieved that the meeting was over and they could begin to put their lives back together.

There was nothing left to do except to go home. We said goodbye to Paul and drove back to Longview in silence. I didn't feel relieved at all nor did I feel it was time to get on with our lives. Perhaps I felt that way because Giles was going back to the school, where he will have to relive the experience over again in the same environment with the same people. The investigators did a commendable job of explaining the circumstances to us, but there is so much they couldn't explain, so many "what ifs". It's easy to be wise after the fact, but there are still many unanswered questions.

My eyes rested on Giles beside me in the car. He was so pale and thin, a mere shadow of the boy who drove back with me just three months earlier to buy a tuxedo, shoes for the prom and clothing for the Climb. Why? How could this happen to him and all those innocent people? Will it ever be fully explained?

The *Oregonian* published a full account of the investigation in the Sunrise Edition on July 25, 1986.

Apparently that was the end of that.

## *July 26th. to 31st.*

*Dear Giles,*

*I'm making another pitch to get a letter from you— preferably with pictures of you enclosed. The bait this time is a stamped addressed envelope. I hope it works.*

*In any event, be assured of my very best wishes for a fun-filled year and a future that will be the accomplishment of all your aspirations.*

*Sincerely,*
*Judge James Pearce Kelley*

Judge Kelley writes to Giles almost every week and sometime calls from his home in Iowa. His handwriting is very difficult to read. We are trying to find time to reply to all the letters which we have received from him.

Giles spends his time resting and eating whenever he can and is gaining his strength back rapidly. As his strength returns so does his motivation; he talks more and more about activities and sounds optimistic about going to Shriners. He has a long road ahead of him, I pray there won't be any more disappointments along the way. It is almost three months since this fiasco began, which isn't a long time, but it is as though we have been doing this all of our lives.

Dr. Hikes made arrangements for Giles' rehabilitation to be done at Shriners Hospital for Crippled Children in Portland, a wonderful facility for children with orthopedic problems, fully supported by the fundraising efforts of the Shriners Masonic order. We arrived there on a cool August Sunday evening, prepared for another two-month stay in hospital. We hauled the stuff up to the second floor where Giles was to share a room with another boy. That evening the staff held an orientation meeting for new patients and their parents when nurses and social workers explained what to expect. The next day (Monday) there would be a multi-disciplinary conference, where therapists, doctors and other professionals would review and discuss Giles' case and develop a plan of care for his rehabilitation. More doctors! More examinations and prodding; more explanations. I could see the look of dread on Giles' face.

Later that evening a young girl passed us in the hall wearing a prosthesis, and I noticed she hardly limped at all. I asked her how long she had been wearing her artificial leg. "Oh...about a month," she replied and skipped off. I was encouraged. A month...that doesn't seem long at all to be walking as well as she does. Perhaps Giles would be at her stage in a month also and be ready to go home.

When it was time for me to leave, I said goodbye to Giles and promised to return the next day. I hated to go. Surely he has had enough of hospitals, even though this is for rehabilitation. But he is sixteen and I have to realize he will be alright on his own. Nevertheless, I traveled back to Longview feeling anxious about him. We are used to having him at home and I miss him; the house seems empty without him.

Early the next day, I was back at Shriners to meet with the prosthetist on staff. I proudly presented AK and BK to Carl, a small unassuming man who picked up the finely crafted limbs which were almost as big as he, and hauled them off—one under each arm. Some time later he returned with them. "We can't use these prostheses," he announced.

My mouth dropped open. "What do you mean?"

"In the first place, they're much too heavy." Carl leaned against the sink and peered at us over his glasses. "Giles is very weak and has to start slowly to build up to something like this. It takes time for his skin to be conditioned. We will make a pair of temporary legs to begin with."

"But what are we to do with these? I believe the insurance paid over ten thousand dollars for them. Can't you use any of it?" I couldn't believe my ears.

"Not at this point," he replied matter-of-factly. "You might be able to make use of some of the parts later on, but at this stage we will have to start all over again."

I looked at the legs in all their magnificence. Such a work of art! But what could I use them for? It's difficult to find a use for a pair of feet and a hydraulic knee when the rest of the family already has a working set. I could put plants in them I suppose. I visualized them standing in the garden with ivy trailing over the ankles and perhaps geraniums in them in the summer. Other than that, I couldn't think of a use for them.

I called Dr. Hikes immediately and told him the news. He was confused about Carl's assessment, but assured me Shriners has the latest technology and is the cutting edge in prosthetic devices. He said he would break the news to Frank, and emphasized that the important thing is for Giles to have the best of care.

I have another plan. I vaguely remember reading an article in the *Daily News* about a prosthetist in Longview who made a special artificial arm for a Japanese boy. The boy came over from Japan especially to see him. If Giles goes to this prosthetist he can live at home, but then I wonder about physical therapy and occupational therapy, the problems with Giles' hands and all the other unre-solved issues.

I asked Carl if he had heard of Milo Collier. "No," he said dubiously, "but I can't believe there is anything in Longview. There couldn't possibly be a facility as good as Shriners. We even have computer equipment to monitor walking here. It's unlikely that he has anything like that." I didn't want him to think I wasn't impressed, but after our experience with Frank, we had proof that Portland couldn't necessarily meet our needs.

"Would you mind waiting before you start making another set of prostheses? I would like to explore the possibility of going to Milo."

He could see there wasn't any point in arguing with me and left.

A look of dismay clouded Giles' thin pale face. "Why don't we just get on with it," he said angrily. "Here we are, another week has gone by and I'm still not walking. Who is this guy anyway? I can't imagine he has anything as good as they have here."

"Just let me find out. It would be so much better if you could be at home. You can't use these legs anyway, so you'll have to start all over again. If it can be done in Longview it will be better for you and easier for me." Giles looked thoroughly fed up with the whole thing, and I sensed his enthusiasm waning.

I drove to the hospital every day and watched Giles become more and more despondent. He was having physical and occupational therapy which only took about an hour each day, and occasionally a doctor visited him. He was very bored and lay in bed with nothing to do except watch TV, which must be the worst thing for him. I encouraged him to read and play games with the other patients his age, but he wasn't interested.

"Would you like to go outside?" I asked, trying to drum up some enthusiasm.

"There isn't anywhere to go," he replied grumpily.

There weren't any gardens or places to go outside at Shriners, but it had been the same at Providence. Giles was cooped up in a controlled atmosphere day after day. It was hot and stuffy inside during the day and cold at night with air conditioning. Fresh air is so important for the psyche, I could imagine how Giles felt.

"Maybe we could find a place nearby to get something to eat," I suggested.

He was a little more enthused about this prospect. We loaded the wheelchair into the van and looked for a restaurant nearby. We found a small pizza parlor some distance away and after struggling with the wheelchair, found a convenient table. There were a few people sitting down, but no one offered to help us, they just stared as though we were some sort of freak show. I heard people muttering and passing comments to each other about the boy in a wheelchair without legs. I was overcome with anger and could hardly control myself. This was Giles' first appearance in public and it was devastating. People can be so cruel without realizing it. They made us feel as though we didn't belong, and made no attempt to ease the obvious difficulties we were having. I hated it there and couldn't get out fast enough.

There were a number of other children on the same ward as Giles, but they were much younger. Some were recovering from surgery for congenital hip disorders and wore casts up to their waists which held their legs at right angles to the body. Others had casts after surgery for club feet. From what I could see most of the children had congenital disorders, so Giles was rather out of the ordinary.

By Thursday, I felt something had to be done. This was not the place for Giles; he wasn't happy and neither was I. It wasn't long before I reached for the phone and called directory assistance to find Milo Collier's number in Longview. I was apprehensive as I waited for him to come to the phone.

"My name is Ann Holaday," I started off confidently. "I am calling from Shriners Hospital in Portland. I'm here with Giles Thompson, the boy who was injured in the recent Mount Hood accident. He is my son."

"Oh yes, I have been following the story in the newspapers. What can I do for you?" Milo's voice was soft and deep; I felt comfortable right away.

I told him the story about AK and BK and how Giles came to be at Shriners. "I'm worried about him being in hospital again. He has good care here, but I think he would do better at home."

"Absolutely," Milo's resolute statement gave assurance to my judgment.

Milo explained how he could make the prostheses in Longview and provide local rehabilitation services under Dr. Reynolds, a rehabilitation specialist from Portland. Dr. Reynolds had experience with complicated cases and would supervise Giles' program. "I would like to start right away," he added. "Could you bring him in tomorrow about four o'clock? We can do the preliminary work and then on Saturday we can get him to stand up."

"Do you really think so?" I was doubtful, but at the same time excited.

"We will try. See you tomorrow!" Milo hung up and I stared at the phone.

I suddenly felt anxious about telling the nurses and doctors that Giles was leaving—but it was too late, I had to follow through with my bold plan and hope for the best. I found the nurse, and when I asked her to discharge Giles she sent for the doctor. "Please!" I explained. "It's not because of you. Giles has spent so much time in hospital, I think he needs to be home." They were obviously disappointed, but were supportive and said Giles was welcome to return if things didn't work out in Longview.

The next day, I arrived at noon as planned and Giles was ready to go. He was relieved to be leaving and excited about the appointment with Milo, although we were both afraid to get our hopes up too much after all the recent disappointments.

We drove straight to Milo's from Shriners Hospital and arrived shortly after four o'clock. Milo was standing at the door as we pulled up, his kind face beaming and his huge arms folded in front of him. He was a big man, I guessed about forty years of age. He looked more like I imagine a prosthetist to be, with plaster on his shoes and a well-worn white coat with evidence of his trade wiped all over it. He came over to the van to help us unload all the paraphernalia.

His office was just one room with a few chairs in it, in one corner there were parallel bars and a mirror at one end. A door led off to a little workshop where the prosthetic devices were made. There was plaster of Paris everywhere, with legs and arms lying around and bits and pieces which I didn't recognize, but I had a feeling we were about to become very familiar with them.

Milo asked his physical therapist, Richard, to come in to help. He too was an enormous, muscular man—there was certainly enough muscle to pick me up if I became weak at the knees. Milo spent some time introducing himself and his staff to Giles, and asked him how he felt about the loss of his legs. Giles explained the surgeries and his experiences with prostheses. Meanwhile I hauled AK and BK into the shop and stood them up in all their glory for Milo to admire.

"Can we use these?" I said hopefully. Milo looked at them with disdain.

"They are very nice," he said, turning them over and viewing them from every angle. "They are well made and finished beautifully. However, they are too heavy for Giles. He is extremely weak and his skin is still tender. Although it's healing nicely, it needs time to toughen up. We will start with 'training sockets' which have to fit precisely and he will gradually learn to walk on these temporaries. He will wear those until he gets used to wearing prostheses, during which time the stumps will change constantly. Therefore we anticipate making several sockets over the next year or so.

"The BK is the most challenging because the knee and lateral tissues take the weight. With the AK it's the pelvis which bears most of the weight, but of course it will be more difficult to learn to use that leg because he has lost his knee."

Milo was examining the scars on Giles' legs as he spoke. "The surgeon has done a really good job. We will have to be careful with this grafted area on the outer side of the BK, it's extremely tender and won't tolerate friction. You are fortunate that the surgeon was able to do a knee disarticulation because a whole new set of problems arise if the bone is severed higher up."

"What shall we do with these?" I pointed to AK and BK, determined to find a use for them.

"We may be able to use some of the parts later on," he smiled, "but at this point, we don't know exactly what he will need. You could make a couple of planters out of them."

"Oh, very funny," I retorted. I caught my breath when I realized that the prostheses had stimulated the same idea in me a few days earlier. From then on I knew Milo and I had a lot in common.

"I think I'll send them back," I added. "I'm sick of looking at them and even more tired of hauling them around."

Milo got to work immediately. He gave Giles a pair of shorts to wear; he and Richard lifted him onto an examination table; Milo wetted down some plaster bandage and wrapped it around each of the stumps. It was a long process and Giles had to do contortions to be fully casted all the way to the groin.

"It's important to have legs to wear as soon as possible," Milo muttered as he fiddled around. By then, he had plaster in his hair and a big blob of it on his face. "You will feel better when you can look down and see legs and feet. First of all, we will make the lightest pair of prostheses which we make for elderly people, we will use simple feet and you don't need a hydraulic knee at this stage. We should have these relatively finished when you come in tomorrow. When you will stand up for us."

"Really!" Giles' face lit up with delight. "Standing tomorrow!" I breathed a sigh of relief. At last there was some progress and my prayers were finally answered. To see Giles looking so ecstatic was worth every minute of waiting.

"We have quite a bit of work to do," Milo explained as he leaned back in his chair, waiting for the plaster to dry. "The first step is to make a negative cast of the stumps, which we have done. Then we fill the molds with plaster of Paris and leave them to dry thoroughly overnight. First thing in the morning, the positive mold will be hard enough for us to shape a plastic material on to it to make the check socket. It will take a while to make the necessary adjustments in order to be sure there aren't any pressure points. We don't want you to have any pain, especially in the beginning."

"This man is an angel!" I thought.

"Once we have a well-fitting check socket, we will attach a pair of temporary feet for you to try." Milo continued as he eased the mold off Giles' thigh. "Then we'll see how you get along. Plan to be here most of the day tomorrow, but you will be able to leave the office while we work on the legs. See you about nine o'clock." Milo disappeared into the workshop, carrying the molds.

Richard helped to clean up the profusion of plaster which seemed to be everywhere.

It was quite late when we left and it felt as though a huge weight had been lifted from our shoulders now that we could see some progress. We were both exhausted and did little else except eat and fall into bed. It was wonderful to have Giles home again.

We were back at the office bright and early the following morning, to find Milo and his staff already at work. They had broken out the casts and were cutting pieces of plastic to shape onto the molds. It was a fascinating process, similar to mold-room work in radiotherapy and I wanted to roll up my sleeves to help.

"You don't have to stay here, if you have errands to run," Milo said addressing me. "We will be busy most of the day, but we should be ready to get Giles standing up by about three o'clock. If you come back then, you will be here to see it."

I felt like a spare part and wished they could have given me something to do. Suddenly, I realized Giles doesn't need me so much anymore; this is his journey. I have been totally consumed with his care, I hardly remember a time when I had a life of my own. I told them I had some shopping to do and gave Giles a big kiss. "Can I bring you anything?"

"I'll have a Coke," he replied. It was wonderful to have a mundane request like that, perhaps life is returning to normal after all.

I arrived at 3:00 on the dot, to find Milo and Richard still working. They had already lubricated Giles' legs and were placing the prostheses onto the stumps in preparation for his first "stand". He was ready and the moment had finally come. I held my breath in anticipation and prayed that they would be successful. Milo positioned himself on one side of Giles and Richard on the other. Together, they eased him up, holding him under his armpits. Slowly but surely Giles rose up from his wheelchair and stood on his new legs and feet. He trembled a little, but then pulled himself upright and stood straight and tall.

"It doesn't hurt!" he exclaimed, his voice ringing with excitement.

"It isn't meant to." Milo leaned back in his chair smiling with satisfaction.

It was odd to see Giles standing before us. It has been over three months since I have seen him vertical, and I don't remember him being as tall as he is now.

"I'll be able to pee standing up," he smiled; his pale, drawn face looked elated. Everyone laughed. After a few seconds he dropped back into his wheelchair—exhausted.

"We can't expect much more than this at first," said Milo. "It takes a lot of energy to walk on prostheses and you will build up your strength gradually, but you did well for a first attempt."

Milo was right, but Giles had stood up, at last there was light at the end of the tunnel.

"Thank you so much! You will never know how grateful we are for this."

"Believe me...it's my pleasure." Milo smiled, obviously more than pleased with the progress. "That's all for today. Take the prostheses home with you and try them on for a few minutes each day. Stand up in them if you feel you can, but don't push it. Listen to your body."

Milo and his staff were already cleaning up the mounds of plaster and dust left over from the day's efforts and were preparing to leave. It was Saturday after all.

"We will devise a plan on Monday," Milo continued, running his fingers through his hair, leaving a white dusting over his head. "Dr. Reynolds will be here next week. He will do a complete evaluation and decide on a plan of action. Firstly, you must build up your strength with physical therapy and at the same time have occupational therapy to exercise your hands and fingers. Our therapist's name is Carol Samson, and she happens to specialize in hands. We will consider swimming as an integral part of your rehabilitation program. There happens to be a therapy pool at the YMCA here in Longview, and I believe Carol often takes her patients there."

Everything sounded so promising and optimistic. Giles was finally on The Long and Winding Road.

I gathered up both AKs and both BKs, filled with renewed hope and anticipation. Milo is a gift from heaven and here he is on our own doorstep. Giles can live at home, the therapists can come to the house if necessary and he can have his friends over. Most of all, Giles will feel the healing air on his face instead of being confined to the hospital. It is surprising how many professional services we have in Longview. Apparently Milo moved here a short time ago from California because he wanted to live in a small town.

D r. Reynolds is a big, thick-set person who is himself confined to a wheelchair after being stricken with polio as a young man. He is kind and understanding. Of course, he knows what it is like to be disabled and is familiar with the hurdles to overcome. He has extraordinary upper-body strength and is totally independent, even though he is paralyzed from the waist down. He has a hydraulic lift in his van which enables him to haul himself in and out without assistance. He slips into the driver's seat and lifts the wheelchair into the van behind him. I marvel at his attitude towards his disability. He is such a gregarious person, always laughing and joking with his patients, I feel he is already part of our family. He is completely at ease with himself and apparently does everything he wants to do. It can't be easy for him. I try to imagine the struggles he must have encountered just to live as normally as he does. I feel we are fortunate that Giles can look forward to walking again.

Dr. Reynolds spent several hours evaluating Giles' complex medical history and devising a rehabilitation plan. He instinctively knew what has to be done and what progress to expect. He is an important counsel for Milo and the therapists, and spends many hours with them discussing the various options for rehabilitation.

W hen Giles stood up, it was just the beginning of the long road to rehabilitation. He spends all day and every day at Milo's office. I am trying to get back into a regular routine again and I leave Giles there every morning on my way to work at the hospital. This week I was waiting for Giles at Milo's when I noticed a man watching me. Eventually curiosity got the better of him and he asked me how I had lost my leg. He soon lost interest in me when he realized I had tucked my leg under and I was just sitting on my foot.

Richard works diligently with Giles to build up his endurance a little at a time. Giles could only stand and balance himself on the prostheses at first, then he took a step and then another, gradually gaining strength. It's exhausting work and takes a great deal of effort, but after a week or so of constant training he was using the parallel bars. Next, he practiced walking up and down the stairs, but the most difficult task is to walk on a slope.

There are many adjustments to the prostheses, minor nuances which we take for granted when we have a normal set of feet and legs. The ankle and knee have to be accurately aligned in order to attain correct balance, and these adjustments are done by trial and error. There is a significant amount of extra work to be done on the right leg because Giles doesn't have a knee on that side. Milo fitted a hydraulic knee which automatically swings forward when he takes his weight off it so that he doesn't throw his leg forward as some people do with an artificial leg.

Finally, he had a set of prostheses which were correctly aligned. However, they were too high and Giles was almost seven feet tall. He walked from one end of the house to the other in a couple of strides, or so it seemed. Milo shortened them, but then they were too short and Giles looked odd and out of proportion because he has such a long body.

"You can be any height you want to be," Milo said jokingly. "If you have a tall girlfriend we can heighten you, and if you have a short one we can bring you down a bit."

We laughed together. They are so kind and compassionate. How fortunate we are to have found them. The outlook is so much brighter.

D r. Asaph's group asked Giles to come back to Providence for a follow-up visit. They examined him and went over all the changes which have taken place and were delighted to see the progress he has made. His chest wound has healed and his lungs are clear.

Dan Lagrande organized a reception where the doctors, nurses and hospital staff could come to see Giles. They had refreshments and a cake on which was decorated a skier. It was wonderful to get together with everyone, although I still can't put a name to them all, their faces are familiar. I must say I feel much better now that we are not so dependent on them. I still remember those feelings of helplessness and being out of control, I hope I never have to face that again.

While Giles was at the party, I went to administration and found Sister Karin in her office. She looked tiny behind the huge oak desk, but her spiritual aura made her larger than life. She wrapped her frail arms around me as though I were one of her family, and I felt an instant peace being next to her body.

I sat down and reached into my bag to look for the crucifix and the little statue of Jesus which I had taken off the wall the night I arrived at Providence. I apologized for stealing it and explained I had kept it on my person from that day, it wasn't until then that I could give it up.

She smiled gently and wasn't at all surprised that I had it. She said the crucifixes are there for people to take, and they do so all the time. "They are part of my budget," she added. We laughed. It was strange to think of a crucifix as part of a budget, but it is the twentieth century after all. I apologized for the fact that it was broken and that the statue was off the cross. I told her it happened in dialysis and how I felt empowered at the time, thinking that perhaps we didn't need God's help anymore.

"That's right," she said in a matter-of-fact tone. "Jesus came down off the cross to save mankind."

For a moment I was spellbound and couldn't find words to respond. She had explained in one sentence what I had felt so profoundly over the past months when I looked for signs of salvation. I thought these were fantasies of mine, but here was a holy woman who experiences signs from God every day and understands them. She nodded thoughtfully. "Signs like that are shown to us all the time, but we don't always have the humility to recognize them. Keep the crucifix. It's yours now. Hold it close to your heart, it will help you again." I wrapped Dr. Dreisin's bow tie around it, and put it back in my bag to carry with me for the rest of my life.

She told me how affected the hospital staff had been by Giles' miraculous recovery and how his presence meant a great deal to everyone involved. She thanked me for bringing him back for them to see him. Sister Karin went on to say how much the staff had missed the family around the hospital and wanted a full update on everyone.

I went back to the reception to find Giles deep in conversation with the nurses. He had got to know them even more than I realized, and I had to drag him away. I felt at peace as we left. We had been anxious to leave Providence and we couldn't have stayed there forever, but in a way I was sorry that we couldn't continue with the relationships which were formed there.

As we drove past Providence on our way home, I noticed again the whistle coming off the stretch of road in front of the building. "There it is again!" I thought. The high-pitched sound in my ears was quite distinct. I asked Giles if he could hear it, but he said he couldn't. I wonder what it means.

## *August*

*Parent's Creed*

*Help me to guide this child of God whom You have entrusted to me.*

*Help me to make her life worthwhile and to give her the ability to see*

*That beauty abides in the common place, in the things that around her lie,*

*In the glories of the rising sun and in the myriad of stars in the nighttime sky.*

*For in the sereneness of night, when man's daily work is through,*

*She renews her strength for the morrow, for the tasks she hopes to pursue.*

—Anonymous

Giles' first public appearance in prostheses was Joanne's graduation from Portland State University. He wasn't ready to walk, but he was able to wear his prostheses in his wheelchair. The ceremony was held outside in the grounds of the university on a beautiful Pacific Northwest summer afternoon. It was a hectic day—first arranging the strategies and maneuvers to take Giles and then helping Joanne to organize herself.

Giles spent a long time getting ready, sprucing up his hair and deciding what to wear. He wore dark sunglasses, to look "cool" or maybe to hide behind. Ross was with us when we sneaked in at the back of the crowd minutes before the proceedings began, but we were unable to avoid the stares and whispers. Perhaps it was my imagination, but I felt conspicuous as people turned to look at Giles as though they were wondering if they recognized him from the news.

It was a long ceremony with long speeches and long lines of students. Joanne's was near to the last name on the never-ending list. I was relieved when it was over; we were able to slip out and wind our way through the back streets to the car.

We returned to the hotel where Bill was waiting for us. We went out for dinner and had a simple family celebration which fitted the occasion. Once again, we went out into the world with the wheelchair. Public buildings are obstacle courses when it comes to manipulating a wheelchair, making it impossible to participate in everyday life. At the hotel, we were unable to get the wheelchair through the bathroom door and when I finally got Giles in there, there was no room to maneuver and I was trapped behind the toilet. These are things which we don't consider until faced with a disability.

The next day Joanne announced that she was going back to Texas. She has a boyfriend in San Antonio whom she has known for years. I have objected to the relationship from the beginning, mainly because I don't want her to make the same mistake I made by marrying her first boyfriend. I have attempted to split them up, but haven't succeeded and now she is determined to go her own way. She is twenty-one after all and beyond my influence. She must make her own decisions.

My reasons are selfish; I dread the thought of Joanne going away. She was so much support during the rescue and Giles' hospital stay, and has been a pillar of strength for Giles in his recovery. I feel as though my lifelines are breaking. She won't listen to my pleas and insists on leaving. My mother said, "It's better to go along with it, otherwise you will drive a wedge between you, and you don't want that." Of course I don't want that, but it doesn't make it any easier to let go of her. After all the years of taking the children with me wherever I went and having control over their whereabouts, I now have to accept their independence. I must step back from my daughter which is so much more difficult after what we have been through recently.

Joanne made arrangements to leave after graduation. I helped her pack up her apartment and brought her furniture to Longview—cheerful on the outside—crying on the inside. It is the end of an era, but I am thankful that she has been here over the last two months. What would I have done without her?

We said goodbye at the airport and through my tears I appeared to support her decision, but in my heart, I hoped it wouldn't work out, and she would come back. The children and I have become much closer lately, after drifting apart through their teenage years. It is the only good thing I can think of which has come out of the Tragedy. I have gained a greater understanding of youth and through that I have changed my attitude towards them. Until now, the children had seemed remote and I didn't know how to reach them. They didn't want me around them nor did they seem to need me, but I found out we needed each other more than ever before. They are insecure, like fledglings on the edge of a nest preparing to fly, but like birds they will come back, feel their way and attempt to fly again. Flying from the nest will be different for Giles, but he will do it. He wants to be independent, as I did at his age. It will take him a little longer...that's all.

G iles' right hand and arm are still very worrisome. Carol, the occupational therapist, made another set of splints for both hands so that the tendons won't contract from disuse while the nerves are growing back. The left hand is recovering satisfactorily and although weak, at least there is some dexterity in it, but the right shows no sign of improvement. There is very little movement in his fingers and Dr. Reynolds is uncertain as to whether they will ever return to normal function. Apparently, the right side of Giles' body was up against the ice in the snow cave and the nerves on that side have suffered more severe damage than the left. A great deal of muscle has been removed from both arms, but the right was more extensive.

Dr. Reynolds assured us that the nerves will grow back in time, but it may take several years. He is unable to tell how far up the arm the damage has occurred and has recommended a test to see if the nerves are still intact to give a more accurate assessment. He didn't admit it, but I surmised he was concerned that the nerves may have been severed during surgery.

We made an appointment with a specialist in electrodiagnosis at Emanuel Hospital in Portland, who had a special machine which sends electrical impulses down the nerve. By evaluating the pain (described as discomfort), it can be determined whether the nerve is intact and approximately how long it will take to grow back. I didn't know what this test would be like, but instinctively felt it would be an unpleasant experience.

Dr. Radecki was a neurologist (I don't remember whether Giles saw a neurologist at Providence, but he certainly hadn't seen this one). He was a slightly built, soft-spoken person—in fact he didn't say much of anything, except—"Hello! Get up here.—Can you do this?—Can you do that?"

The first half hour was spent evaluating movement in the arms and prodding with a needle to see if there was any pain. Finally, the doctor was ready to use his machine. When he located a nerve in the shoulder he placed a probe next to it and turned on an electrical current which sent an impulse down the nerve. Giles' arm jumped for an instant and he winced with pain while the doctor asked where he felt it.

It took several hours to test all the nerve groups—a quick zap and then pain. Giles grew more and more tense and perspired profusely. It was torture, just what he didn't need after all he has been through. The test showed that there wasn't any feeling below the elbow. Dr. Radecki explained that nerves grow back at the rate of an inch a month and, in Giles' case, it may take years for them to recover completely. If they don't grow back, there isn't a thing that can be done. The test was simply a way of measuring progress. As far as I could see, it was unnecessary and purely academic.

We were relieved when Dr. Radecki finally finished and said he would send the results to Dr. Reynolds. He printed out a series of graphs which looked like an electrocardiogram to report on the extent of nerve damage. We gathered up our belongings and left as quickly as possible. I felt angry about Giles being put through another procedure and wished I had intervened earlier. He was amazingly tolerant and didn't fully understand the futility of this particular test. I'm sure the doctors believe they are doing the right thing, but Giles must be considered. I know one thing, they will never get him back for follow-up.

We arrived home late that afternoon, relieved that one more procedure was over.

We have been approached by Mark and Bob, the reporters from the *Daily News*. They want to do a detailed article on Giles and his recovery. We have agreed because we feel his is a story of the extraordinary accomplishments of a local boy. I felt they were hoping to get a unique slant on the Climb, but Paul made it clear that the emphasis must be on Giles and not on the circumstances that led to his injuries. I think they were disappointed at first, but then realized that Giles' story was more unique and newsworthy.

I remembered Mark from those dark days at the mountain. He was tall and youthful, probably in his late twenties. Bob was a little older I thought. They were amiable people and eager to start the long arduous process of gathering material for their article. At first they were businesslike and somewhat impersonal, but they soon relaxed and became part of the family. They followed Giles everywhere: to rehabilitation, doctor appointments, Milo's office, with Giles setting the pace; if he didn't want them around he let them know. At first, it was intrusive to have two reporters follow us like shadows, but after a while we hardly noticed them. Mark, the photographer, clicked away and must have taken hundreds of photographs. They interviewed the doctors at Providence and documented the hospital stay and even came with us to Dr. Radecki's office.

We are concentrating on getting Giles to consume as many calories as he can, as often as possible. He is gaining weight, but not nearly as much as I am. On our way to Milo's, we often pick up breakfast at McDonald's drive-through where Giles has a square egg and square hash browns in a box. What a peculiar way to serve food! It doesn't taste like food to me, but it's calories for him which is important.

Giles has enjoyed cooking ever since he was a little boy when he made ready-mix cakes. We used to have more cakes around than we could possibly eat, and they were really quite good. We are encouraging Giles to cook our meals at home. I am not a particularly enthusiastic cook and am happy to let him do it. The minimal exercise of chopping, stirring and especially gripping small objects such as kitchen utensils is quite beneficial for his wrist and arm. He can't use his right hand, so he is becoming left-handed, but it is still important to use both hands as much as possible. We work at exercising his hands all day long.

## *September to December*

September is fast approaching and we have to decide whether Giles will return to OES as a boarder. The doctors feel he can go back to school even though he is still weak and underweight; however, he is gaining strength and walking more each day. I feel it would be better for him psychologically to start the year with the other students and not to fall behind in his education which might cause additional stress. But perhaps that is not as important as facing up to the old routines as soon as possible.

We go to the school frequently and meet with the teachers to make plans for his return. The physical layout of the school is not conducive to a person in a wheelchair and handicap access isn't a requirement. The school hasn't had to accommodate anyone with a disability before, but they have made every effort for Giles. They are making a ramp inside the main building and another that leads into the dorms, but there are still areas which he won't be able to access at all. Bars and rails are being fitted in the dorm bathroom and his room is close to an exit door to avoid steps.

We plan for him to dictate his written work and for a secretary to transcribe his papers. Giles likes that idea because he doesn't have to think about spelling, which isn't one of his strong points. The Longview medical community have donated a computer which we will set up in his room. The minimal pressure required to press the keys is much easier than holding a pencil or using a typewriter.

The day finally arrived for Giles to return to school. We loaded up the car with all the necessary stuff: AK and BK, wheelchair, crutches, computer and other paraphernalia for school.

Robindra was at the dorms to greet us and help us unload. She couldn't restrain a giggle as I handed her a leg to carry to Giles' room. The other students seemed uncomfortable, after all this was a new experience for them also. By the look on Giles' face I could see he was dreading it and wishing he could hide away. Last year he was so popular and active, but he has to face up to it, putting it off would only delay the agony.

I unpacked his things, put them away and busied myself with meaningless tasks. Giles had tie-dyed a sheet which he asked me to hang from the ceiling in his room. Meanwhile, he sat in his wheelchair staring at the wall with thoughts in his mind which I could only imagine. "Oh God!" my voice screamed inside me. "Help us!" I wanted to gather up his things, load them back into the car, forget the whole idea and protect him from it all. I fussed around for a while, hoping to hold back my tears long enough to get out. Finally, I couldn't find any more excuses to stay, said goodbye and left. I got into the car, drove around the corner and wept. "How can I endure this?" I cried. "How can I make it go away?" If only I could have done it for him. It was the same feeling I had the first time I left him as a baby when he cried for me not to go. But then I reminded myself that I would go, he lived through it and was fine when I came back. I prayed it would be like that again.

The school had a picnic at the beginning of the academic year, for parents, staff and students. This year it wasn't a particularly nice day, but by evening it had at least stopped raining. The picnic had already started when I arrived and there were about a hundred people gathered under the shelter at the back of the school. There were lots of new faces, as always at the beginning of the year. I looked for Giles and caught sight of him amongst some people in a corner of the courtyard. I joined them, but felt awkward. Giles seemed alright, but sad and despondent. I asked him how things were going at school. "Okay," he shrugged. The others left us alone and I tried to make conversation.

"Shall I look for something to eat?" I asked. "Please yourself," he answered sullenly, "I don't want anything." I left him and wandered around in a daze. I felt awful. Everyone was acting as though nothing had happened. We were ignored except for one or two close friends of Giles' who came over, said a few words and left. I felt most uncomfortable and wanted to run away. Didn't these people realize Giles had moved heaven and earth to be there? No one seemed to notice him. Perhaps he was too much of a reminder of the terrible sadness and guilt bestowed on the school.

I was heartbroken. Giles sat in his wheelchair watching the other students running around. This was worse than anything we had experienced so far. Maybe Giles wasn't ready to go back to school after all. Maybe it wasn't a good idea for him to go where there are so many memories, so much pain and regret.

We stood on the very place where less than five months ago, at the summer barbecue, Marion and I had helped to serve food on one of the stalls. Marion had been excited when she told me she was going on the Climb with Giles. I don't remember seeing Giles at all that day, he was probably with his friends.

"I mustn't hang on to Giles," I thought. I wandered to the back of the school to the memorial stone laid in memory of the seven students and two teachers who died on the mountain. Vases of flowers were placed lovingly on the ground nearby. Nine names— what a waste. I reflected over the last months—all the machines, all the treatments and surgeries—and realized how close we had come to having ten names on the stone. I wondered how it would be if all of the climbers had survived like Giles, all lost their legs, and were at the picnic to remind the rest of the dreadful episode.

Emotion overwhelmed me and anger boiled inside. I wished to be thousands of miles away. Does life go on? Will it ever return to normal? I had forgotten the meaning. Ross was making plans to go to music school and Joanne was working in Texas. My parents had returned to England, my sister to Canada. Bill was getting on with his life, but we were still in the thick of it. In fact, it was as though we were just beginning.

I pulled myself together, swallowed my tears and dabbed my eyes. I didn't want Giles to see I had been crying, although he was used to it by then. I had to remain strong, but I could feel my strength waning. "Please, God, help me," I cried.

I returned to the picnic to find Giles sitting alone again. I considered leaving. I didn't feel right there and perhaps my presence was preventing his friends from coming over. "I think I'll be on my way," I said, my voice faltering. "Do you need anything? Shall I take you back to your room?"

"It's okay, someone will help me." Giles' voice was flat and unemotional, but his face said it all. I hoped he was right. I hoped that someone would help him.

"Wear your legs a little bit each day?" I added. Giles didn't answer. I circled around looking for an excuse to stay, but at the same time I was anxious to leave.

"I'll be back on Thursday to take you to Milo's." I tried to sound cheerful as though the prospect was an exciting one.

"Whatever…" Giles' voice was empty. I kissed him goodbye, but I could see he would rather do without it. My heart was heavy as I left. How would he get on? Surely people would help. He needed so much help. I drove home slowly, thinking and crying. It was four months since the accident and I felt we were only just beginning the climb back.

The phone rang early the next day. It was my father calling from England to say that my mother had been taken to a London hospital for cancer treatment. There was evidence that her breast cancer had spread to her spine and she needed further therapy. She fell in the hospital and fractured her hip.

"Oh, no!" I cried. "What else could possibly happen?" I would have to deal with it later. Maybe it could wait a while, at least until Giles was settled back at school.

R oss was accepted at the Conservatory of Music and the following week we drove to San Francisco. Ironically his first interview had been scheduled on May 15th, the day that the cave was found. The Conservatory accepted his excuse for not attending and he interviewed later.

I left Ross to get his things together and he appeared to be ready, with piles of books, music and instruments. I didn't have time to help him and hoped he had everything he needed. San Francisco was a twenty-four-hour drive from Longview and we spent the night in Ashland on the way.

San Francisco is a daunting city after Portland, which looks like a village by comparison. We searched the map and found San Francisco University where Ross was to board, but when we arrived there we found we had the wrong University. I think our minds were preoccupied. We found San Francisco State University, which was the right place. Poor Ross—he looked so bewildered, striding out on his own after the summer we had with so little support for his needs. We hauled his belongings to his assigned room and I helped him unpack his things. I was appalled to find he had simply stuffed his bags with dirty clothes—very dirty clothes which hadn't seen soap and water for months.

He hustled me out before I saw any more, and told me it didn't matter. I was ashamed when I realized how much I had neglected him. I assumed he was managing, but he had taken a back seat and I was oblivious of his needs. I had no choice except to leave him and hoped he would manage on his own. I flew back to Longview and prepared myself for my next trip: to England.

*Hi Giles:*

*Just a quick note to let you know I'm thinking of you. By now you've got your computer. Sorry it took so long. Southern California is hot, but the beaches cool. I want to take this opportunity to tell you how much you've taught me about courage and kindness these last few months. You are a brave young man. And a kind one too. With this you will go far and influence many people. It is so good to see you taking such an active role in your destiny. I'm proud to be your friend.*

*Take good care,*
*Jack*

I drove to OES every few days to find Giles in his wheelchair and discovered that he had not been wearing his prostheses at all. This week Jack was with him when I arrived to take Giles back to rehab, and the prostheses were in the closet.

"Have you been wearing your legs?" I asked.

"No," Giles answered defiantly.

I felt my temper rising and blood rushing to my face. "How are you ever going to learn to use them when they stand in the closet!" I cried. "Do you want to spend the rest of your life in a wheelchair?"

Jack was obviously embarrassed by my outburst, but I pressed on trying to contain my rage.

"You *must* wear them every day, even if it's only for a few minutes." I marched over to the cupboard and grabbed the legs, exasperated.

"I will do it in my own time," Giles said calmly.

He was right, he had to do this, but he didn't seem to have the necessary determination. Later, he asked me if I thought he could do it. "You know how I am," he said. "You know how I can be, how I lack the will to try difficult things."

"You *will* do it," I told him firmly, "because you don't have a choice."

My remarks were cruel, but I think they helped. He started to wear his legs an hour or so each day. After a couple of weeks, he told me triumphantly that he wore them all day; not walking on them of course, but wearing them.

The visits to Milo's office are tiresome for Giles. The other day he was particularly despondent and obviously fed up with the whole business. He loathes his legs as they are a constant reminder of what he has become.

"Mom! I don't want to walk on these," he said angrily as we were leaving Milo's office.

"What are you going to do then?"

"I'll just stay in a wheelchair," he replied.

"Giles, it's now or never!" I was calm, at least on the surface. "You have come this far and I'm not going to let you give up now. I understand how you feel; I understand how difficult it is, but it must be done—and you can do it."

It breaks my heart to be so unkind. I don't want to nag, but if I don't push him, who will? I hope and pray he will understand in the end that I only do it out of my love for him.

Our plans to help Giles do his schoolwork turned out to be futile, his level of concentration was minimal and he hardly studied at all. He was unable to read a book or concentrate for any period of time necessary to complete an assignment. Bill told me it was a common side effect of being on a respirator; apparently the effect on the brain can last for years. I was concerned about Giles, but maybe I was expecting too much. He was struggling with many issues, both emotional and physical, it was bound to take time and perhaps it didn't matter if he had to spend an extra year in high school. The computer turned out to be a tremendous asset. He adapted to it quickly and was able to produce remarkable things on it. He designed a thank-you letter to the Longview physicians and put a Grateful Dead skull-and-crossbones graphic on it. Giles thought it was "cool", but the doctors didn't quite understand. I explained to them that it was just a logo and that I had been upset about it at first.

I took some photographs of Giles and sent a copy to each of the doctors to thank them for their outstanding kindness and attention. A week or so later Dr. Bietz wrote a handwritten reply:

> *Thank you for the card and the picture of Giles.*
>
> *As time goes on the intensity of that emotional event dims slightly, but the tremendous support that all of the family gave Giles and his own personal drive and dogged will to succeed will always be a high point in my medical career.*
>
> *Dr. Bietz*

Giles was fair game for the press once he came home, and the phone rang constantly. We put Paul in charge of requests for interviews which came almost daily. Giles agreed to appear on *Good Morning America*, and arrangements were made for interviews to be held at the house. As the day approached we grew apprehensive about being TV stars; a television interview was a unique experience and our expectations were cloudy to say the least. I asked Paul to be present to monitor sensitive questions. Giles' immediate concerns were about his hair, he wanted a certain style—it had to be just the right length at the sides and short on the top. I asked Alan, my hairdresser, to come to the house to style it for him.

It wasn't long before the locals knew that we were going to be on national television and a landscaper dressed up the house with wonderful plants. Never before had we been so adorned.

A huge van, which almost filled the street, parked outside our house. We didn't have any complaints from the neighbors, but I'm sure they must have had an eyeful. The four-man crew arrived exactly on time, carrying enormous cameras, microphones and other equipment. They bustled around deciding on lighting and the best place for the interview. It wasn't long before the front room looked like a recording studio.

Giles was in good spirits that day and was ready to talk to the world. The interviewer's name was Steve Fox. He was a kind man and talked at length with Giles prior to the official interview. Paul laid down the guidelines for questioning making it clear that the Climb was off limits. Steve held a notepad on which he had prepared questions and I guessed they were all about the Climb, but he wouldn't allow us to review them first. I began to feel nervous about agreeing to talk because it soon became obvious that their questions were beyond our control. Steve was a warm person and seemed impressed with Giles, but I sensed he might cajole him into saying something sensational. He soon realized it wasn't going to be easy and put aside the "hot story" and was more interested in what Giles had to say.

Some of the questions bothered me, but Giles handled them well. Paul remained silent and they pressed on with the interview.

"Did you ever think you would die up there?" Steve began.

"No never," Giles answered without hesitation.

"Really!" said Steve in artificial surprise. He paused for a moment, expecting Giles to say more, but he didn't, so he went on to the next question.

"I have been told that you were surprised when you woke up."

"Yes...That's true...I couldn't figure out where I was...I was lost. There were all these big people in white. I didn't know who they were...I thought I was in my dorm room at school."

"Is that so!"

"Yes, really!"

"Were you afraid to go out on your own after this?"

"Yes...I was scared. I was afraid in case I might get into another accident, in case something might happen to me again."

"Indeed! When did that feeling go away?"

"When I drove home from the hospital with my mom!"

The crew and Giles laughed. Paul gave me a knowing smile. Mmm, Giles hadn't admitted he was nervous about driving with me.

"Do you ever feel guilty that you survived and the others didn't?"

Giles looked down, obviously uncomfortable with the question. "Forgive me, for that untoward question," said Steve.

"I think I was just lucky," Giles began thoughtfully. "I don't put guilt on it. I sometimes think that I want to do things…for those who don't have a chance anymore."

"Do you look at the world differently now?"

"Yes…now I have a second chance…and I'm not going to screw it up this time."

"But you didn't before."

"No…but I put a lot of things off before. It has made me appreciate life more. I appreciate a cloudy day. I look at the flowers and think, 'That's a lovely yellow'…I watched the moon go from a little sliver to a full moon. I made sure everyone else saw it too, because some day they may not have a chance to see it again."

"How do you get through things when you are down?"

"I just accept it and go on. I have a future at least; I've got my mind, I can imagine things, I can't run, but I can walk…I will be walking in the future. There is a lot to get used to, so much that we take for granted when we have all our faculties. The other day I almost jumped out of bed to take a shower when I was late…I forgot that my legs were gone."

Paul whispered, "They will put that in I'm sure." But they didn't air that comment, strangely enough.

Later in the day, the crew filmed Giles being fitted for his prostheses at Milo's office and swimming in the YMCA therapy pool. Walking into the "Y", Steve said:

"Are you ever surprised at how quickly you have progressed?"

"Sometimes. When I walk into school without my crutches, I realize I am doing well."

The program was called "A Survivor's Tale". Giles was inspirational in the interview, making his recovery sound easy. Those were early days and I felt the impact of what happened hadn't really sunk in.

After his first month back at school I realized how difficult it was for Giles to get around. There were a lot of uneven areas on campus, many sets of steps to tackle and slopes between buildings. He had to rely on other students to push him in his wheelchair, and could only walk on his legs for limited periods.

I believed a car would help. At first, I thought a golf cart would be the answer, but if he had a car of his own, he could drive himself to Longview and relieve me. He went to take his driving test in Portland as a handicapped driver. We thought he might have to have a special car with hand controls, but it wasn't necessary. The only restriction was that he must not drive a manual shift car. We bought a Jeep Wrangler. It's sporty, a big psychological boost and gives him much-needed independence.

The school doesn't allow students to have cars, which is a policy I favor under normal circumstances; but these are hardly normal circumstances. At first, the headmaster refused to give permission and although I understood he didn't want to set a precedent, I was incensed that the rules couldn't be bent to accommodate Giles. I decided to send Giles to school in the car anyway and see what happened. Later, administration called to say they would allow him to have his car at school as long as he didn't transport other students. Giles agreed. I don't think he was interested in taking anyone in his car and he certainly wanted to cooperate.

The winter ski season was fast approaching and Giles wanted to ski with the school team. I had mixed feelings about it. Apart from the obvious reasons, I was afraid he might damage his knee and it is the only one he has. Kathy Woods, who is herself a handicapped skier, offered to take him skiing at Mount Hood.

It seemed an impossible task, but Giles wanted to try.

Milo made a special prosthesis for the BK held on by shoulder straps as well as the suction method of his "walking" leg. It had to be particularly strong in order to withstand the stress of manipulating one leg on the slopes.

I wasn't involved in Giles' learning to ski. He and Kathy went to Mount Hood after school on Friday nights and Kathy worked with him while the ski team practiced. How they managed all the gear, I can only imagine. In addition to his walking legs, he had the ski prosthesis with a ski boot attached and outriggers which are ski poles with small skis attached to them. Kathy told me Giles' first attempts were painfully difficult; she even had to help him put on his hat and gloves. He still has limited function in his arms and his grip is weak. Apparently there were many tears, but he was there trying to learn to ski again, even though it couldn't be easy.

When we moved to the Pacific Northwest, skiing was the main family activity. Giles was a good skier and was on the OES ski team. He loved to ski before the accident, but this wasn't the way it was meant to be for him and now he is faced with an enormous challenge. It is frustrating to find learning again so difficult, something which was so easy before. However, week after week, he and Kathy persevered, progressing a little at a time until Giles skied the slopes with ease.

Although I often go to the cabin, I can't bring myself to go back to the mountain with Giles and Kathy. We made several attempts to drive up there, but only managed to get as far as a certain bend in the road, where suddenly Mount Hood looms up. I know this vision is there, but I am never prepared for its effect on me. I became hysterical and sobbed uncontrollably. Bill was confused by my reaction, unable to understand how I felt as I begged him to turn back. I trembled with fear as emotions flooded back. It isn't just the sight of the mountain which affects me, the atmosphere brings back memories. The air on the mountain is different somehow—clean, cold and damp. There is an eerie silence which engulfs my soul, broken only by the rustle of the wind in the cedar trees, the whistle of songbirds and the rush of distant traffic. Normally it is exhilarating and why I have enjoyed that area in the past; but now it reminds me of those terrible days, and I can't face it again.

*Dear Giles:*

*I wanted to write and let you know how much all of us are pulling for you and wishing you a speedy recovery.*

*From what I now understand, you have had double amputations in your lower legs. Giles, no matter how grim things might seem now, a full, adventurous and challenging life awaits you.*

*I lost my leg above the knee at age twelve, but it has not stopped me from pursuing activities I loved so much—from skiing to sailing, swimming and dancing—everything is still possible. It may take a little more effort—I'm not saying it's going to be easy—but the thrill of meeting your challenge and overcoming your disability will transcend into all aspects of your life and make you more of a stronger-willed and free-spirited individual.*

*You will be stronger willed because you will have to fight for something, and you will be free spirited because you will learn at an early age not to be troubled by things in life which have no consequence and things that you cannot change.*

*Giles, like everything else in life, you can look at your situation in two ways: either as a burden that you'll have to live with, or as a challenge to overcome and you will become a better person for it. You have many friends pulling for you...and many more people you don't even know.*

*I look forward to your full recovery and to meeting you real soon.*

*Your friend,*
*Ted Kennedy, Jr.*

A magazine article about Ted Kennedy, Jr., was included in the letter. It explained his rehabilitation and what he learned through his experiences, and how he realized that recovery has a lot to do with attitude. It's up to the individual to chose how he or she faces up to his or her disability. Ted Kennedy, Jr., started an organization called Facing the Challenge which helps young people with disabilities to become involved in sports and activities which they *can* do rather than worry about things which they can't. Skiing is considered to be an important part of rehabilitation for amputees whenever possible. Ted Kennedy, Jr., was trained by Hal O'Leary, a ski instructor at Winter Park in Colorado. It so happened that Milo had an office at the University of Colorado and went there regularly. He made arrangements with Mr. O'Leary for Giles to spend a week with him in training. The reporters from the *Daily News* went with Giles; it was a relief to know he had help with all his gear at the airports.

Giles gained a lot more confidence on the slopes after the week with Hal O'Leary and later skied with the other students on the OES ski team.

NBC's Tom Brokaw contacted Paul to do a feature on Giles, to make the necessary arrangements with him to interview at home and film at Milo's office and on Mount Hood.

This time there were even more cameras and microphones. Giles was interviewed extensively, and the crew followed him to rehab, the pool and school. During filming at the YMCA, I asked a cameraman how long the program on Giles would be. He told me it would be about three minutes on the Tom Brokaw show. I couldn't believe that they would go to all that trouble for just three minutes. I was expecting at least an hour documentary. On the news clip which aired about a week later, Giles talked in the background over old news footage of the rescue.

"I appreciate things much more now. I look at the mountain and I think what an awesome thing. I think of what it did to me and my family. I am alive...I'm breathing, I have a lot more going for me than those who didn't make it, and that always brings me back."

The interviewer, Dave Barrington, asked him what he thought when he realized he had lost his legs.

"I woke up in the hospital and they were gone."

"Giles says the hardest thing is going out in public," continued Dave Barrington. "He still has a lot of therapy, but now feels he has to take charge of his own recovery."

The crew went up to Mount Hood to film Giles skiing. I was somewhat perturbed that they would interview Giles on the mountain when Paul and I weren't with him, especially when I realized many of the comments were about the Climb.

Dave Barrington's voice: "Giles has memories of being cold and of being trapped under the snow, memories of panic. He says that he is scarred mentally as well as physically, but he has come back to the mountain. Not to mull over what happened here, but to challenge it again."

"It has set me on the road to recovery," Giles' voice came over again. "It gives me confidence. I want to make it...I want to do it!

"It slows me down...it slows me down a lot. But it doesn't stop me...and that's all that matters."


When Giles was relatively settled in school and able to drive himself to Longview for rehabilitation, I decided I had to do something about my mother. She was still in a London hospital and I knew how difficult it was for my father to visit her. They lived in the suburbs and he traveled by train to see her every day. They were isolated in England with no family to help them. To be of any real assistance I would have to stay indefinitely, but my commitments are here in the States with Bill, the cancer clinic and my family. The only solution was to persuade my parents to come to America until my mother recovered.

Bill and I found a little house for them in Longview and the next thing I knew I was on the plane to England. I didn't tell my parents I was coming, I simply turned up at the hospital. My mother couldn't believe her eyes when she saw me, but she was obviously relieved. After much persuasion, they agreed to fly back to Seattle with me and we went straight to Heathrow airport from the hospital. My mother never saw her home in England again.

Bill met us at Seattle airport with a hospice nurse to care for my mother on the journey back to Longview. It was very thoughtful of him, but she really didn't need it; she was in good spirits and didn't require any extra assistance. Giles came home to see them and when he walked into my mother's bedroom and bent over to kiss her, it was the greatest tonic she could have received. The last time she had seen him, he had been very ill, and she was surprised to see him so strong and walking as well as he does.

We busied ourselves furnishing my parent's new house; hanging plants and pictures. Soon it was their home away from home. They felt secure being close to the family in spite of their crisis. Elizabeth, in Vancouver, B.C., was just a short distance away and Giles could visit them whenever he came home. A few weeks later, we celebrated Christmas with my mother. It was a wonderful gift for her. At last, she had her family around her, a treat which she hadn't enjoyed for a long time.

## *January 1987*

The *Daily News* section on Giles is finished and I asked Bob and Mark if we could review it before publication. I don't want to edit the article, but be assured that their slant isn't put on the story. Mark and Bob are apologetic and explain that it is against the rules to do that. This doesn't make any sense. Where are the rights of the individuals who are at the mercy of the press and what they decide to write? Many of the reports about the accident aren't exactly untrue, but because a story can be told in different ways, they are often inaccurate. The press picks up on off-the-cuff comments and reporters take these comments out of context. When they appear in the paper, the final commentary comes from a totally different aspect than intended because the reporters put their own slant on the interview. These observations are troubling, but it is too late for the *Daily News* article.

Giles was comfortable with Mark and Bob, spent many hours alone with them and probably confided in them. We have to believe that they will keep to the facts and adhere to our agreement, but the final say is up to them. I have to put my trust in them and hope they won't sensationalize the story.

The newspaper article came out on January 16, 1987. It was much longer than I expected—a twenty-page insert in the daily paper. Bob and Mark obviously put a lot of effort into it. However, they did ask Giles about the Climb because he commented about the other climbers. I suppose he must have volunteered the information. On the whole, the article was well done. We were relieved.

Shortly after the publication, Bob and Mark came to the house to say goodbye. They were almost in tears showing their obvious affection for Giles as they hugged him. In the end, they realized they had unfolded one of the most remarkable human stories ever told. We were sad to see them go, they had become part of the family and we knew we would miss them.

## *February*

A fter the Christmas holidays, Bill talked to me privately about my mother, saying she had more advanced disease than I realized. He thought she would probably only live a couple of months. I was startled to hear this, because even though I understood the seriousness of her illness, I thought as long as she stayed on medication, she might live a long time. She was hoping to go back to England to enjoy many more productive years, but it was not to be. Bill's predictions of the life expectancy of his patients were almost always right, so I took his estimates seriously. He was accurate almost to the day. Exactly six weeks into the New Year, my mother slipped into a coma and died. She had asked Bill not to allow any heroic measures to be taken to prolong her dying. Her wish of being with her family had been fulfilled and she was ready to go.

She died in the hospice on a sunny spring day, to the music of the blue jays singing their song of renewal. Her funeral, held three days later in Longview, was a strange occasion. Her closest family were there, but she had never known the other people who attended. Ross played a favorite piece of music for her on his guitar as her casket was wheeled out of the church. She had asked us not to cry when she died, but to wear a bright dress and a flowery hat to her funeral. Joanne didn't let her down.

After the ceremony, a limousine took her body to be cremated. Her ashes were put in a wall of remembrance at the church and a little plaque, inscribed with her name and the dates of her life, closed them from the world. That is all we have to remember her by. No notation of her wit and of her simple faith. No remembrance of her creativeness except in the hearts of those who loved her. The end of a life devoted to bringing up children and running a home, never counting the cost or expecting anything in return.

Her funeral was an inadequate tribute to her memory, but it was the best we could do under the circumstances. After the service, we went to our house and there was a message from the children's aunt in England saying that their father's brother had died the same day. A wave of doom swept over me. When will this ever end? Surely the grim reaper has taken all he can from this family.

I didn't really grieve over my mother. It is as though her spirit lives on with me. I miss her of course. I miss our endless conversations and her long recitations about the past. I miss her infectious laughter setting me off into uncontrollable giggles about something quite silly. Perhaps I don't have the capacity for any more grief, but I am comforted in the knowledge that she was ready to die. Perhaps she preferred to live on with me in spirit and not to add more to our overburdened lives.

Soon after, my father dismantled their house in Longview, packed up his things and flew back to England. Within a few weeks, he had sold their home and disposed of most of their things. I wished I could have gone with him to help with this unenviable task, but he seemed to cope; at least on the outside. In April, he was back in the United States where he stayed for a while to sort out his life. Later he moved to Vancouver to be closer to Elizabeth.

A short time after my mother's funeral, Ted Kennedy, Jr., came to Portland to talk about his organization, Facing the Challenge. Giles was invited to introduce him. Once again he was on the television and I burst with pride as I listened to his speech. He was very articulate, his voice strong and confident. He wrote the speech himself and his choice of words was that of a more mature person, his sentences beautifully constructed, with a poetic lilt to them. He was such an inspiration.

Giles continued with his interest in the arts for the remaining two years at OES. He became quite good at pottery and spent many hours in the art department on the potter's wheel, turning beautiful bowls and vases. I think it became a refuge for him, a place to go where he could indulge himself in his creativity while his peers played soccer and other outdoor games. It was truly a gratifying pastime and therapeutic for his hands and his mind. I remember when I tried my hand at the potter's wheel at school, but I was never able to produce anything recognizable. Giles' creations were wonderful.

## *June 1988*

J ust before graduation, Jack displayed the work of his students at an OES art exhibition. The paintings were mounted on partitions which stood in the center of the Great Hall. I was casually browsing, admiring the amazing talent of young people when I turned a corner and saw Giles' artwork before me. For a moment, I was shocked and unable to move, my body frozen. There were two pictures. One showed the back view of a nude, male person facing the mountains and a mass of dark gray clouds. The figure had blond hair and its arms reached out to the side with the palms turned upward. I moved closer and saw that the right leg was missing at the knee and the left missing below the knee. The outstretched pose of the figure seemed to plead to God, "Why me?" At the same time it faced the horizon, ready to begin *walking in the future*. The other painting was of a swirling blizzard with vague features peering out of the snow depicting his survival. Giles and I never really discussed how he felt about losing his legs. But after seeing his paintings, I hardly required an explanation. They said it all. The Climb and the effects on his self-image still preoccupied his mind, and will probably continue to do so for many more years. Perhaps he will heal through his art, just as Ross heals through his music.

G raduation time for the class of '88—and Giles' graduation from OES—this rite of passage was far-reaching in its dimension, not only for him, but for all those involved in the Tragedy. This graduation was beyond the limits of anyone's expectations, far beyond the realm of academic achievement represented by the diplomas which Giles and his class will have for the rest of their lives. It was a milestone for them, a place in time to look forward to a new beginning and bring closure to the previous two years.

We decided to have a graduation celebration for Giles, an informal party to show our gratitude toward the many people who contributed to his remarkable recovery. Time would pass and the accident would fade into a distant memory, except in the hearts of those closest to it. We wanted to grasp the moment of victory, one of the few there were to capture, among the disappointments and perceived failures which have dominated the recent past.

We invited our friends, both known and unknown, who were involved in the accident. We asked Portland Mountain Rescue and other rescue team members, the medical teams from Providence and Emanuel, the Life Flight, the Air Force Reserve, county officials, staff and students from the school and friends from Longview.

It seemed inappropriate to celebrate such an important milestone for the survivors at the school where there was still a profound aura of loss. We decided to have the party on more neutral ground, at a restaurant in Portland. I worried that only a few people would come, but the attendance was outstanding, everyone who could be, was there. It was a wonderful occasion with only one problem, it was too short and there wasn't enough time to tell everyone how much they were appreciated. I feared that it was probably the last chance we would have to see such a unique group together.

"Let me introduce you to this young man," said Al Radys, the head of Portland Mountain Rescue. "He was one of the rescuers." I looked up at a tall, broad-shouldered, handsome young man, probably about twenty years of age. His blond hair clung to his head in tight curls just like Giles'. He told me he fell down a crevasse during the rescue and the operation was held up for a couple of hours while a helicopter pulled him out. Miraculously the only injury he suffered was a broken rib.

I walked away feeling quite lightheaded. For a moment, my mind drifted back to the hours of waiting on Mount Hood when we were so engrossed in the intensity of the search and didn't think about the people who were risking their lives by participating in the rescue. This young man wasn't much older than Giles. He had a mother and father who must have been worrying about his safety. There could have been many more fatalities and even more lives lost. After all Giles barely made it out alive.

I was suddenly brought to my senses by a commotion at the door. It was Milo looking for help to bring Dr. Reynolds up the stairs in his wheelchair. I was pleased to see them because they were an important part of Giles' triumph. Later, I found them talking to Dr. Hikes when Milo was explaining the strategy he used for making Giles' prosthetic devices. Dr. Hikes expressed his disappointment at not being involved throughout Giles' entire rehabilitation.

"The main thing is that the best thing was done for the boy," he said.

"Absolutely," Milo responded. "It was a privilege to take care of Giles."

"We learnt an important lesson through Giles," Dr. Hikes added, standing proud and tall. "Patients must remain in charge and be given the responsibility of making their own decisions." I smiled. I knew it must have been difficult for him when he realized

Giles had gone his own way, and I remembered his tears of sadness the day Giles left the hospital.

Dr. Long, the trauma specialist from Emanuel Hospital, was making his way towards the door when I intercepted him. He smiled and shook my hand vigorously. "I must go," he said. "I'm on call. I want to thank you for having this party. You have no idea how much it means to those of us who were involved to see Giles and Brittany doing so well. The accident was devastating to the Portland community, particularly to the medical community. To lose so many young people in such a senseless way. Everyone was affected."

"I know," I had to shout above the noise of chatter. Dr. Long is so tall he had to bend down to hear me. "We wanted to do something for graduation which marks such a big milestone. Were it not for the tireless efforts of the rescuers and medical teams, Giles and Brittany would not be here tonight. We wanted to celebrate their victory with everyone."

Dr. Long replied, "I want you to know how much we appreciated your support in taking care of Giles. Your medical background and cooperation made a big difference in our being able to make very difficult decisions. Your support of us and of Giles contributed to his successful recovery."

I almost cried when I heard him say this. I often felt like an interfering idiot in the hospital, and it was a comfort to know the doctors supported me. Suddenly, I had been thrown into a situation in which I didn't know my place, I felt infinitely powerless and dependent on others. It helped to be a part of Giles' care.

"Your support helped us work as a team," Dr. Long continued. "There are fierce politics between the hospitals in Portland and they seemed to come to a head over this accident. We had to work together and pull in the same direction—we learnt a great deal from it."

"Thank you again for everything you did," I bellowed over the noise of the crowd. "I want you to know how much we appreciate you and the rest of the medical community. We were fortunate to have so much expertise available to us."

Dr. Long was practically running as we said goodbye. That was the last time I saw him. A man who played such an important role in making this party possible left our lives as abruptly as he had entered.

I fought my way through the people to where Dr. Asaph and Dr. Dreisin were talking to a group of doctors from Longview. We greeted each other like family; these men were like my brothers, we had become so close.

"The doctors at Providence didn't want Giles to go back to Longview," I shouted. "I think they felt we couldn't handle him in the country. I told them we had electricity and hot running water."

We laughed over what seemed silly when we could reflect on it.

"We were pretty possessive about Giles, you know. He was our baby and we were unwilling to let him go," Bow Tie remarked.

"Believe me, I know how it feels," I added.

Just then, there was a disturbance in a corner of the room as Giles tried to get attention. Gradually a hush descended as the crowd stopped talking and turned to face him.

"I want to thank everyone for being here," he shouted. "I see faces which I remember clearly from the hospital, but many of you I haven't seen before. Heroes both known and unknown. Thank you for the extraordinary effort everyone here put into making this party possible. My only regret is that those who didn't survive are not here to celebrate graduation with us. I want to thank my family, friends and teachers from school for your continuing support; without you I wouldn't have made it. I wish to thank the doctors and nurses from the hospital and to everyone else involved, names too numerous to mention. Thank you! Thank you...and enjoy."

Everyone applauded and cheered.

There were many familiar faces at the party and countless others I didn't recognize. To have an opportunity to show our deep appreciation was the beginning of a long healing process and I think our guests also found it a healing experience. It was especially difficult for the school personnel to be there. It was yet another reminder of the absence of close friends and students.

However, it was a positive although painful rite of passage, one where we could celebrate with the people who had made it possible. Giles received many gifts and cards for graduation, but the plaque from Life Flight is imprinted on my memory.

> *Many have touched the edges*
> *of our lives…*
> *coming and going,*
> *scarcely leaving an impression.*
>
> *But you are an uncommon person,*
> *someone who has made a difference*
> *in our lives.*
> *So it is not surprising*
> *that we find ourselves remembering*
> *how special you are.*
> *And knowing your strength*
> *and spirit*
> *will continue to bring*
> *new joys to light your way.*
>
> *Your Life Flight Crew,*
> *Michele Kelly, Barbara Dubbert,*
> *Mark Kohnstadt, Sue Galeski, Mike Fletcher*

A formal graduation ceremony was held at the Episcopal cathedral in Portland. The church was again packed with people and the usual group of reporters and photographers were waiting outside. We only invited a few of our closest friends and family to be there to see Giles graduate. It was a happy occasion, but at the same time sad when we remembered the students who would have been there to graduate with Giles and Brittany. The remaining class had had many difficult issues to deal with over the past two years — their youth snatched away by the Tragedy. Nevertheless they were there with their heads held high with pride, they had made it through the most critical period, now it was up to them to go *walking in the future*. At the end of the service, I felt an air of relief from the crowd. Perhaps the formal closing of a chapter at school gave everyone permission to leave it behind.

There wasn't any particular attention paid to Giles and Brittany, who lined up with the others to take their diplomas. However, when they marched out of the church, it was as though the people couldn't contain themselves a minute longer and a big cheer went up. A crowd gathered around them, some with tears in their eyes. They clapped for several minutes while Giles and Brittany smiled at one another.

I was glad that everyone realizes what a struggle it has been.

### *August 1989 to May 1990*

Giles has decided to attend Colorado College in Colorado Springs, not only because of the opportunities to ski there, but because Milo has an office in Denver. Colorado College has a "block system" which means instead of taking all subjects throughout the year, the students can take one subject for a three-and-a-half-week period. This system solves many problems for Giles. He won't have to change buildings for different lectures and he can take a block of time off during the school year without missing class. He has always been interested in set-design from his days at OES and will take a liberal arts degree, majoring in drama.

We packed up Giles' car and traveled across the country to Colorado. We stayed at a hotel close to the Air Force Academy and watched boys with their short cropped hair, dressed in uniform, saying goodbye to their parents. Ross came to help his brother to settle in and make sure that this really was the best place to leave him so far away from home. Giles will share a room with another boy who is a football player, I think. He is athletic and muscular, and I wonder how Giles will get on with such a person. I did my usual dorm room decor and helped Giles to unpack. He seemed ready to embark on this new phase of his life. Although I felt he was a little melancholy when I left, I think he is ready to stride out on his own. Nevertheless, I struggle with worry about how he will manage and how he will deal with the world without us.

"I will always be with you," he said as he started up his car when he left me at the airport.

That is Giles. Even with all that he has to face, he still finds a place in his heart for others.

The college years were somewhat of an enigma to me. I couldn't afford the time to go to Colorado and Giles usually came home for the holidays. I learnt some time later that he was almost in an accident when driving back after a Christmas holiday. His car skidded on black ice on a bridge, and by the grace of God, he managed to gain control before it hurtled over an embankment. He didn't tell me at the time; it's a good thing I didn't know; the drive in winter is too treacherous and I would definitely have found an alternative. Another time, he was driving back with a friend when the friend fell asleep during his turn at the wheel. Fortunately, Giles was awake and managed to take control of the car before it went crashing into the center divide. I sometimes think that he must have nine lives, but at the rate he is going he is using them up rapidly.

Joanne and I went to see a play put on by the drama department at Colorado College in which Giles was instrumental in the design and construction of the set. He was very proud of his work and talked about it for weeks beforehand. While in college, he was commissioned to build a theater for a children's museum in Colorado Springs. Bill and I went out to see it and couldn't believe the amazing accomplishments he had achieved in such a short time. I was most impressed and proud that he could do such commendable work which is held in high regard at the college.

Dr. Radeki's assessment of Giles' arms materialized. The left arm recovered in about a year, but the right is still weak and doesn't have full range of motion. There is obviously permanent damage, but we see subtle improvements all the time. While working on construction he has to stand for many hours at a time, climb ladders and scaffolding, but it doesn't seem to bother him a bit. Using heavy tools must be a struggle, but is wonderful exercise for his hands and arms.

G iles never discussed his difficulties with dating with me; after all I am his mother. Nevertheless, I instinctively knew there were issues which were painful for him. I knew he was unable to participate in many college activities because he feels different—he is different. He can vividly remember being an active participant in student life when he played sports and had a circle of friends. In college, he felt alone. I could only imagine his inner struggles and prayed that he would find some peace. Apparently, he sought counseling when he sank into a deep depression while dealing with the changes in his personal image. I silently hoped that he would find a girl he could love, someone who would be good to him and give him the affection he deserves. On top of everything he has to deal with, I pray he won't get hurt and experience the heartache of breaking up, of lost love and lost egos.

Giles often seemed complacent about his plight, but there were times, especially when he was learning to ski, that he was overcome with anger and frustration. Who wouldn't be? Life has few limitations at sixteen and to have that suddenly change, he had every reason to be angry. However, I felt it was important for him to express his anger as part of a normal grieving process. He suffered a huge loss and it would take time to heal. It was painful for me to watch him because there was nothing I could do except to be there for him.

Whenever I walk, I think of Giles constantly and how he is unable to do the same. I can't enjoy activities knowing that he can no longer do them. I have always been active—I love to dance, walk and I have skied, but now I don't want to do any of these things.

It is three years since the accident. Giles asked me to go skiing at Mount Hood. I don't want to go, I dread having to watch Giles struggle with the paraphernalia which he needs, but rather than let him know—I will go. Sooner or later I have to face up to the mountain again and make some sort of peace with it. After all it's absurd to feel that a mountain was somehow to blame.

I managed to drive past the bend in the road without breaking down, but found myself reliving those hours gazing at the mountain, wondering where the climbers could be. I stared blankly at Plymouth Rock and White River Canyon where the cave was found. I heard helicopters hovering overhead and saw rescuers like black specks dotted over the mountain looking for clues on the ground.

I was sick inside as the feelings returned, but struggled to get a grip on myself for Giles' sake. "It's in the past," I thought. "I have to move on…it's just a place."

I made it to Timberline Lodge, only crying on the inside. No one knew how much I hated every moment. Giles was already there, preparing for a day of skiing. He was changing in his car parked in the handicapped parking close to the slope. He was dressed, had put on his ski prosthesis, attached the ski, grabbed the outriggers and was on the slopes in no time at all.

I watched him in awe. I knew how difficult it must be for him, but he did it with apparent ease. We skied to the chair and went to the top. As I maneuvered myself and struggled with the awkward equipment, Giles flew by me. No one on the hill could keep up with him. I was flabbergasted, he hardly fell down and when he did, I ran over to help him. "Leave me alone," he said, "I can do it myself."

I feel ashamed. I have been virtually immobilized all this time over an injury that isn't mine. I haven't even taken my dogs for a walk and meanwhile Giles has moved on. It is time for me to do the same. He doesn't need me any more and I have mixed feelings about it. I have worked so diligently for him to gain independence, but in a way it has been a fulfilling experience. Through the months of caring for Giles we became interdependent, but now it's time for me to let go. This is what I have worked for. I don't want him to remain dependent on me and yet it's hard to accept that he is standing on his own two feet. I must look after myself now, take care of my own needs and the other relationships in my life.

G iles decided to take some time out of college to train for the National Handicapped Ski Team in Winter Park, Colorado. A competition was held at Mount Hood in which he participated. Bill and I went to cheer him on. It was a unique experience for us to be with young people without arms and legs, watching them having the time of their lives.

One fellow without arms or legs was flying down the mountain on a "sit ski" which is rather like a sleigh with a ski in the center. We watched in amazement as he got on and off the chair without any help at all. Another man was on the edge of the stairs in his wheelchair, and I thought he would go hurtling down. When I rushed over to help him, he shrugged me off and disappeared down the stairs. He had a bar on the chair which allowed him to use the stairs in his wheelchair. The disabled skiers referred to people with limbs as "normies" and we did feel out of place without something missing. Some of the skiers were spina bifida children, and were affectionately referred to as the "wobblies". They were quite awkward while walking, but when they were skiing it was difficult to tell there was anything wrong with them.

The atmosphere of excitement at Timberline Lodge was exhilarating. The young people bustled around the lodge on crutches and in wheelchairs, tucking into hot dogs and Coca Cola, just as obnoxious as any other teenagers. "Everyone should have the chance to see this," I thought. "It is so inspiring." In sporting competition such as the Olympics, challenging the human physique is often discussed when records are beaten. This is what challenge really means. It's easy for athletes with all their faculties to challenge their bodies, but these people have enormous obstacles to overcome just to get started.

Giles went on to compete in the Handicap Olympics. When he raced in Alberta, Canada, Elizabeth and I went to support him. He won a bronze medal of which he is very proud. He did well in competition, but after a while he felt the need to move on. He found the political climate in handicap sports quite tedious, where the emphasis is more on excelling in competitive events rather than enjoying the sport. Anyway, I think it's more important for Giles to feel normal, and it is the everyday challenge of participating in life itself which matters more.

P*M Magazine* went to Colorado to film Giles skiing at Winter Park. Neither Paul nor I could be there to monitor the questioning, so Giles was in charge. The media seemed to focus on his skiing prowess, but nevertheless they were persistent about details of the Climb.

Giles talked in the background over the filming.

"I knew in many ways that I was going to do it. I didn't know how, or how long, but I was going to make it. To be looking up at this magnificent mountain, and have no idea where your son, your daughter or your brother is, really frightens me."

When asked if it bothers him to be in the cold or the snow again, he answered,

"It's not the place I remember…it's the event. To be sixteen and to find yourself in something unimaginable…something that you see on TV. To know that I almost died. To realize that someone had opened my chest and handled my heart…knocks my socks off. I don't have any socks—but it's overwhelming.

"It's really weird, when I was in the hospital, I was with my family and all the people that I love…it doesn't make any sense I know…we were watching this movie. It was really stupid, and we started laughing, there was so much noise coming from the room that the nurses came in. They saw this family laughing their heads off…and said 'What the…?'

"I knew, from that moment on, that no matter what, my family would always be there for me, and as long as they were there, there would always be a turning point."

My heart leapt for joy when Giles mentioned the time in the hospital when he was so terribly sick and we were in the midst of tragedy, yet we were able to share laughter. It had meant such a lot to me at the time, and I was grateful that he remembered.

"There are visions in my mind, I'll never forget.

"I don't want to say that perhaps I was the chosen one, but

that's the only word that comes to mind...I sometimes think, if I hadn't been on top of Brittany, the girl, keeping her warm, maybe she wouldn't have made it. To think they were only fifteen minutes from calling the whole thing off, blows me away. There was nothing anyone could do—everyone tried their hardest.

"When things are going well, which they are a great majority of the time, it's as though...it almost never happened.

"It isn't a matter of how fast I'm going—it's the fact that I'm going. That's what matters."

Asked if there is anything he would like to tell the others, he said they already knew.

"If I could tell them anything I would want them to know that I'm trying really hard. I'll make it for them—and do it for me."

This TV program was the last one that Giles agreed to do. He was frequently invited to speak at clubs and conferences, but the novelty of being in the limelight wore off. He told Paul and me that he didn't want any more; public appearances took up too much time and energy. This decision was part of getting back to normal again.

During college vacation, Giles tried other sporting activities. Boating is a wonderful sport for people with amputations and he had a Hobbi-Cat which he and Jay, his stepbrother, took out on the Columbia River. The river is quite dangerous with the presence of large container ships and strong currents, but the boys thoroughly enjoyed the wonderful wind, while I sat on the beach and worried.

The children are getting older and I feel there probably won't be many more opportunities to have a vacation together. We planned a horseback riding holiday at a dude ranch in Canada. I haven't done anything like that before and have a dreadful head for heights, but I was willing to try it for Giles' sake. Horseback riding wasn't easy for Giles, he felt insecure perched on top of the horse and it was uncomfortable for him to sit on the socket of the AK. I don't think he enjoyed it as much as we did, but maybe he will take up riding again in the future. We have many funny stories to tell and wonderful memories of the short time we spent together riding horses.

## June 1990

After Joanne completed her degree, she worked in a nursing home in San Antonio as a counselor. She loved the work and was very good at it. Her relationship with Mike continued and I knew she was happy with him, but there wasn't any sound of wedding bells until a spring day when she was visiting Longview. She lay on the sofa nervously twirling a piece of paper, and I knew something was coming. "I'm going to get married," she announced, "to Mike." She waited for my reaction, watching me out of the corner of her eye. "I'm going to marry him, Mummy, whether you like it or not," she added. I saw her determined expression and realized her intentions.

I had to accept it, but I felt defeated after all my attempts at keeping them apart. Their love for each other had certainly stood the test of time and I could only pray it was the right thing for her. I couldn't do anything other than support her.

Joanne and Mike made all the arrangements for their marriage which was held in a park in San Antonio beneath live oak trees. Joanne worked for months beforehand making garlands and flower arrangements. Their wedding day must have been the hottest day of the year. It was 102 degrees as we drove in a limousine to the wedding, however, the trees provided welcome shade from the sweltering heat. The ceremony, which was conducted by a Lutheran minister whom Joanne knew from her work, was held outside in the afternoon in the hottest part of the day.

Giles and Ross gave her away. It was the first time Giles had had to cope with such extreme heat, and wearing a black tuxedo added to the problem. His body-temperature balancing mechanism has been affected by the loss of his legs and his temperature doesn't regulate in the normal way. I worried as I watched him in his dark suit with a tight tie round his neck. Beads of perspiration formed on his brow and were rolling down his face as he stood beside Joanne.

I couldn't control my weeping as I watched my three children walk towards the pastor. I was overcome with emotion as I reflected on the struggles to get them this far. I asked God to protect them from further trials and prayed that Joanne would be content in her marriage, and that nothing will come between her and her husband.

As Giles walked away from the procession he took off his tie and jacket, reached for a long drink of cool, refreshing water and rushed inside to the air conditioning. The photographs were taken before the ceremony which seemed odd to me at the time, but it turned out to be a blessing for Giles, because he didn't have to go through more posing after standing in the heat through the service.

The reception was quite informal, but truly lovely. Joanne was radiant and obviously happy. Mike was ready to make a commitment and love was written all over his face. "I'm a very lucky man," he told me after the service. They are both lucky, to love one another and have a chance of a future together. I am learning to accept him, he loves Joanne dearly—that's all that matters.

In September Ross packed up and left for England to study at the Royal College of Music for a year. A few days after he arrived the phone rang at the clinic. It was Ross in tears calling from the center of London. He was lonely and couldn't find a place to live. It was all I could do to persuade him to stay. His voice quivered as he said goodbye and I put the phone down in despair. It was so far away and there was nothing I could do to help him.

The year in England was difficult for Ross. His girlfriend, Ann, joined him a few weeks later when at least his living situation was solved. I don't exactly remember when I first met Ann, she seemed to slip into our lives unobtrusively without our noticing. I was hardly aware that I stopped worrying about Ross as long as she was with him. Ann is very quiet, silently going about her own business, but she is effective and determined in her objectives. She has big brown eyes, silky auburn hair and a laugh that you can never forget. We were a little wary of one another at first, but ours is a long-term relationship and I know we will be close friends.

Bill and I went to England with Giles the following April, to find Ross a completely changed young man. He told me that he had turned to alcohol for comfort in the early months and hit bottom very quickly. He decided to stop drinking, lost weight and became a new person. His guitar playing rose to unprecedented levels during his studies in Britain. We went to several of his concerts with Jack, who happened to be in England at the same time. I was proud of Ross and in my heart I hoped he would find a future in Europe, which would give me an excuse to return.

On our way back to the States, walking through the airport, Bill complained of breathlessness. Soon after, it became obvious that he was having severe problems and within a couple of weeks, he went into a Portland hospital for open-heart surgery. He was diagnosed with heart valve stenosis which meant that the surgeons had to replace the diseased valve with an artificial one. I asked Dick to stay with me while Bill was in the CCU, because I didn't know how I would react after all the hours I had spent there with Giles. I followed the nurse down the hallway to Bill's room with the pounding of the respirators hammering in my ears. The familiar odors engulfed me and left me dizzy. I watched the green undulating lines on the monitors and listened to their monotonous beeping. Bill was hooked up to a huge machine which measured fluids flowing through translucent tubes. He was already conscious, although he still had a tube down his throat and was fighting the forces of the respirator. He recognized me and tried to communicate; all he wanted was a bowl of Häagen-Dazs ice cream. As it happened, I didn't need Dick at my side, once I got over the initial shock of being back in the CCU. I was alright, and I remembered what Giles said when he went back to Mount Hood: "It's not the place—it's the event."

Bill only stayed off work for a month and in September he returned to the clinic. Six weeks later the phone rang again. It was

Joanne calling to tell me she had been diagnosed with Hodgkin's disease, and she didn't have health insurance. What was I to do? I turned once more to Bill. After long hours of conversation between doctors debating on the best course of treatment, we decided to bring her to Longview to be treated where I knew she would get the best of care. In January of 1992, she had exploratory surgery and two weeks later, she began a long course of radiotherapy. She was treated on the same table and for the same disease, as the young girl whom I had come back to treat when Giles was in the hospital. Ross came home to be with Joanne and pampered her by cleaning her shoes and making sure she had plenty to eat. Her treatment ended in April, when she returned home. We were confident that she was cured. Everything had gone well, and we had no reason to believe otherwise.

## *January 1993 to June 1994*

The year 1993 started off with our losing all three of our pets—Smoky, Rufus, and Kitty, the cat. I took Smoky and Kitty to be put to sleep, but when it was time for Rufus, I was emotionally drained, and Bill had to take him. I wasn't prepared for the sadness I felt over the loss of such old friends, and I missed them terribly. The house seemed empty with no little soul waiting patiently every time we opened the door. I missed Rufus and Smoky barking at night over something or nothing, and the sense of security they gave us when we knew they were protecting us.

Giles took time off to ski during his years at Colorado College and had to complete course work before he could graduate. He was interested in theater architecture and decided to include in his studies an internship at an architectural firm in Seattle. It was wonderful to have him nearby again and although we didn't see him very often, just to know he was a short journey away was comforting. He came to Longview to work with Milo once in a while.

Marie was Giles' new girlfriend. We met her in February when she flew to Seattle to see him. She is a very attractive girl with the darkest, biggest eyes I have ever seen. Perhaps she was a little nervous around us at first; she had an infectious giggle which ended almost every sentence. I liked her immediately and was particularly impressed by her attitude towards Giles' disability; she recognizes it, but doesn't treat him differently because of it.

In May, the phone rang and it was Marie looking for Giles. A couple of days later he came to the clinic and said he was leaving for Colorado.

"I can't tell you why I have to leave so abruptly," he said. But I could guess.

I determined there could only be a couple of things to cause Giles to leave in such a hurry. Either they were breaking up, and he had assured me it wasn't that, or Marie was pregnant. How could I talk to him without interfering in his life? How could I say I didn't want them to have an abortion?

"Just do the right thing," I told him as he left. "You will know what that is when the time comes."

A week or so later, as we prepared to go to Colorado Springs for graduation, the call came from Giles.

"There is something I have to tell you," he said. "Marie is pregnant."

"I guessed that," I replied.

"Well, what do you think? Are you mad or upset? Are you disappointed?"

"Compared to what we have had to deal with, Giles, it's nothing. Nothing at all, a child will give you more happiness than you can possibly imagine. You must look after each other. Are you going to get married?"

"We have decided to wait," Giles replied.

"You must," I implored, "for the sake of the baby. You could stop off in Nevada, and have a formal wedding later."

"We don't want to get married just because Marie is pregnant. We want to wait until we are ready, if you see what I mean. Does that make sense?"

"Not really," I said. It didn't make any sense at all. It appeared to me that a baby would be the one reason they would want to get married. Surely they wouldn't want the child to find out later his parents weren't married when he was born. Times have changed, perhaps it doesn't make any difference as long as they are together.

"We haven't told Marie's mother yet," Giles continued, "so don't let on that you know anything at the graduation."

"What do you mean? I won't say anything."

"You know, fussing over Marie and that sort of thing—how mothers do."

Giles was in a miserable state when we arrived in Colorado. His legs had been giving him trouble and he was in a great deal of pain. There had been celebrations with Marie's family who had come from Switzerland for the graduation including parties and dances. I sensed that Giles was depressed.

I felt powerless, with little to do except be supportive. However, I do know how important it is to commit the time to ensure the prostheses fit properly, and because his legs are constantly changing, it is an ongoing process. I also know Giles hates to deal with it. I can't blame him, but he can't escape reality— it is a choice only he can make.

The graduation ceremony was a rousing experience held outside on the campus of Colorado College. Giles' name, starting with a T, was near the end and Marie, an R, was just before him. There wasn't any attention paid to Giles, he was one of the crowd—one of the graduating class going out into the world to find his way.

After graduation, Giles announced that he and Marie were moving to Seattle. They felt there were opportunities in the theater business and they wanted to be closer to us. "Not too close," he added. I was thrilled that they were coming to live nearby. Again I suggested that they get married on their drive through Nevada, but they said they weren't ready.

B ill's open-heart surgery made him realize he wanted something else in his life other than dealing with the daily stress of medical practice. He decided to retire in June. I couldn't understand why he gave up the practice which we had both spent so long building up, and was at its peak. I went through the motions of celebrating his retirement, but I was sad inside. I was just getting into my stride in my career and felt all the years of experience finally paying off. I didn't want to leave my job. However, I was a mere pawn on the chessboard of hospital politics and a month later I was disposed of. I felt a loss which I have never felt before. I have been in radiotherapy for thirty years and I don't know any other profession. What was I to do? The hospital and patients had been my entire professional life—it was like giving up my family. When the children were young, I never had any trouble finding a job, there was always a demand for my expertise and experience. It is ironical that now that they have grown up and gone away, I am at home.

Bill signed up with an agency to do *locum tennens* and accepted a position in Texas. Another irony is that Bill was the one who wanted to retire, but now he is back at work and I am retired. I had to get away from Longview for a while and I decided to go to Texas with Bill.

We settled in Texas and life was going smoothly, until one day in October Joanne told us that her cancer had come back and she had to take chemotherapy. It's odd how things work out. I could be there with her while she went through her treatment. Her doctor said she had a good chance of being cured, but she had to have aggressive therapy for at least six months. We decided to stay in Texas until she finished her treatment.

B aby Lewis John Rubin Thompson was born on November 24, 1993 in a Seattle hospital. He weighed nine pounds one ounce and was bursting with health and energy. I flew back from Texas a few weeks before and was at the hospital in no time at all. The first thing I did was look at his feet and count his ten little toes with ten tiny little toenails.

## *July 1994*

L ewis was eight months old when Giles and Marie were married. I still couldn't understand why they waited so long, but it was better late than not at all. The date was set for July when Marie's family could come from Switzerland, and Giles' relatives from England.

The ceremony and the reception took place at their little house in Seattle which has a beautiful naturally wooded garden. Father Roy conducted the wedding and christened Lewis on the same day.

Soon after Christmas, Giles began the project of building a stone wall by hand which surrounded a grassy area in their garden where the ceremony was to be performed. One day I found him sitting on the grass in the rain piling stones on top of one another to shape the wall. He worked for weeks and weeks through the winter months, hand picking each stone from the quarry and carrying it home. It was his first attempt at building a dry wall which was a work of art when finished, stretching almost across the entire width of the garden. It was truly a labor of love built to tell their guests that at last he had found stability and was firmly rooted there with his new wife and family. He and Marie planted the garden with a wonderful array of color which blended into the gray stone making it look as though the wall had been there forever.

Excitement mounted as the day approached. Two months before the date, Giles and Marie decided to rip out their living room carpet and lay a hardwood floor. I still don't know how they finished it in time, but it was ready and looked fabulous.

I was given the tasks of picking up salmon for the reception, entertaining our family from England and bringing them to the wedding. Giles and Marie organized caterers and friends of ours from Longview offered to cook the barbecue. I provided the flower baskets which we hung from the eaves of the front of the house.

I was dubious about having the wedding outside, knowing the way Seattle weather can be, but when the long-awaited day finally arrived I didn't have to worry. It was a beautiful clear day as only warm summer days can be in the Pacific Northwest. We drove to Seattle from Longview on the morning of the wedding with the "aunties", Bentley, the cat, Bonnie, the dog, and the salmon which I had picked up on sale. We dropped off the animals and the salmon at the house and then went on to a hotel to get ready for the wedding — cool — calm — and collected.

When we arrived at the wedding, confusion reigned, but it was organized. Ross had made signs to direct the guests to the house and was already on duty in the street. Joanne was frantically sticking flowers on my hat with her glue gun. It was gorgeous. She had dyed her hat the night before with tea and it wasn't quite dry. It was difficult to imagine that we could be ready in time, but there was no turning back. The atmosphere of excitement, the sounds of laughter and chatter, the smell of perfume and flowers filled the air. Everyone had news to catch up on, but there wasn't any time — we had to get on with the wedding.

Roy stood in the center of the living room robed up and ready to go. We hugged each other for a long time, and in his eyes I recognized the realization of what a milestone this event was going to be. Who would have thought eight years ago that we would be in Giles' house for such a joyous occasion?

"I've been trying to catch Giles and Marie," he said smiling. "I stopped by several times yesterday to talk to them about their vows, but they were always at Costco. I began to think we might have to have the wedding at Costco." Roy never changes, always finding humor.

"Anyway," he added, "I think we're ready."

"Will you do the wedding first or the christening?" I asked.

"Oh I think the wedding...definitely the wedding."

"Yes, but Lewis was here first. It's difficult to know the right order, isn't it? I bet this isn't in the *King James Prayer Book.*"

"It's different these days. Sex was such a big thing in our day, when the bride was expected to be a virgin. Nowadays, couples usually have lived together before they get married and they have long since got over the novelty of that side of their relationship. Young people pay more attention to the relationship itself, to being friends and being supportive of one another, and that's what's important—love—love of the heart."

I contemplated what he had said for a moment and I remembered my own struggles when I got married. Attitudes have changed and society is so much more accepting of what were considered unconventional unions in my day. I am sure that the vicar who married Giles' father and me would not have agreed to marry us away from the church and certainly would have had difficulty in accepting a christening on the same day. I couldn't imagine a wedding like this one ever taking place in the sixties in England. I tried to pinpoint what differences there were between our respective weddings. I decided they were in the sincerity, in the genuine love and commitment that Giles and Marie demonstrated with a determination to marry under their own terms when and how they wanted. They asked God to bless their union and He was there to do it through Roy.

I squeezed Roy's arm. We had so much to be thankful for on that day: the opportunity to witness Giles' wedding, the baptism of Lewis, family and friends and Roy to initiate the proceedings after all the history we have had with him.

At last we were ready to begin. Giles and Marie organized themselves around the corner as Ross played the wedding piece which he composed for the occasion. Giles stumbled in his haste and Roy ran over to help him. Giles shrugged him off. "I'm alright. I can do it by myself. I don't need any help," he said.

Roy waited for the couple to appear on the grassy stage which Giles had prepared. They walked together slowly between the rows of chairs arranged on the lawn; Giles' family on the right and Marie's on the left. Giles strode confidently, trying not to tread on Marie's dress. When they reached the steps in front of Roy he told them to change places—Giles should be on her right. They both looked jubilantly happy and determined to make a commitment to one another.

Their vows were quite traditional. Roy's voice rose above the garden sounds of birds and the gentle rustle of leaves and echoed across the still summer air. The guests stood motionless, listening to every word. I glanced at Jack and saw tears rolling down his cheek. Many of us wept as we witnessed another miracle in the cycle of life. Bentley played with the tassels on Roy's robe while Marie giggled nervously through the ceremony. How fortunate we are to have her. I couldn't have chosen a more perfect daughter-in-law—even if I had been asked.

After their vows, the wedding party proceeded towards a table set aside for the signing of the registry. Marie's sisters were the bridesmaids and Ross the best man. They looked so grown up and handsome and I wanted to hold the moment forever.

Many of Giles' close friends from OES were at the wedding and although I knew them as though they were my own children, I hardly recognized them. They looked a lot older and were acting more like adults. Robindra never misses an opportunity to come to our family occasions and is firmly rooted with us. She is close to Joanne and Ross and they regard her as a sister and she is like a daughter to me.

I met Jason from Longview in the kitchen later, he looked much older than I remembered from the days when he helped me carry Giles up and down the stairs. His hair was shorter and he looked businesslike in his dark suit.

"I would like to find a good woman like Marie," he said. "I would like to marry and have a family like Giles. He is a lucky man. He has what most men dream of—love, a beautiful baby and a nice home. He has what is important in life."

"Most never realize these things at the time," I replied. "I didn't recognize them until they were gone."

I was surprised to hear Jason share his personal thoughts with me. He will be close to my heart forever. I have watched him grow from a gangly boy to a fine, handsome young man who has come to realize such priorities.

Roy set up a table in a different part of the garden where he performed Lewis' baptism. As the moment approached, I took Lewis inside to change him into a christening gown which I had made for the occasion. Marie's mother bought the material and I sewed it, making it a family effort. I wrapped him in the shawl which his great grandmother had crocheted for Joanne's christening more than twenty-five years earlier. Both Ross and Giles were christened in it also. I am glad that I have kept it and hope it will be a family heirloom for future christenings. Many things from the past have disappeared over the years, but they are important to me now, especially for occasions like this.

The christening was even more moving than the wedding. Roy wrapped his arms around Lewis and held him high, offering him to God. Lewis looked around from his lofty perch and surveyed the crowd as though he knew what it was all about. It was as though he realized that he truly is the triumphant ending to the worst tragedy that Mount Hood has ever seen.

His life marked a new beginning and proof that life really does go on.

# PART III

*No man is an island, entire of itself; every man is a piece*
*of the continent, a part of the main;...*

—John Donne, 1622

I n May of 1986, I suddenly found myself plunged into the despair and profound inner suffering of a parent facing the loss of a child. It was impossible to find solace. Grief took over my whole being and I drifted into a world where I became totally focused on Giles, wishing I could put the clock back. I longed to go home and look in the bedroom to see my children safe and sound. Nothing else existed for me.

Perhaps if I had been able to look into the future, see my world as it is now and see Giles so strong and vibrant with his little family struggling with day-to-day mundane problems, I would not have allowed myself to spiral downwards. I could have reminded myself that life has a way of returning to normal even if it is a normal that is quite different than what we imagine at the time. Although our lives are forever changed, we are richer because we will never take life and what it has to offer for granted again.

I was fortunate that I had Douglas Bader to look to as an example—a man who was similarly snatched from the jaws of death, and went on to lead a memorable and fulfilling life. His story showed me that the will to survive comes from the individual. Giles had to find determination within himself, my role was to nurture that will and push him forward until he no longer needed me. It wasn't easy. I wanted to take on his pain, live his struggles, but he had to do it himself.

There was much speculation as to why only two survived. The rescuers felt that the likelihood of anyone at all being alive after three days of being trapped under the snow was extremely remote. Yet there were two, and although they were colder than anyone who has ever been revived, they recovered.

The question was never completely answered, but I think because Giles was close to the entrance of the cave and Brittany directly underneath him, they had a minimal air supply. Perhaps because their bodies had slowed down to such an extent due to hypothermia, they didn't need much oxygen. Giles was active for a longer period because he was working on keeping the entrance of the cave open, therefore, he didn't become hypothermic until later. He sustained more serious injuries than Brittany, because he had more muscle mass and his limbs were in the ice. Brittany's body was more protected by Giles being directly above her, although their temperatures when they were found were almost the same. In the end, their survival was determined by very marginal factors. However, a couple of hours more in the cave and it would have been too late.

Some rescuers, maybe even all of them, suffered emotionally after the Climb, blaming themselves for almost giving up, reliving the search over and over, and all the "what ifs". Apparently, Sergeant Harder didn't fly in the 304th. Air Force Reserves again, but continued to serve as a fireman. He died suddenly of natural causes ten years after the Tragedy, still a relatively young man and in the prime of his life. Coincidentally, some of his crew who were in the Mount Hood rescue were killed in the line of duty just a few days later. I regret never having had a chance to talk to Rick Harder again to tell him myself how much his efforts were appreciated. However, Giles went to his memorial service to pay our respects to one of the most dedicated professionals in the field.

There is no doubt that Giles and Brittany would not have survived without today's technologies, and it is ironic to think that a little technology could have prevented the accident. The school and mountain rescue representatives worked diligently to get a law passed which will allow climbers to use tracking devices in Oregon so that, should they become lost or trapped, rescuers can find them. Giles and Brittany went to Salem to advocate the law during legislation. Yet people still climb the mountain without signaling devices, and continue to get lost and die in climbing accidents; but *the mountain never cries*.

As I reflect over that terrible time, it is the people I remember, thrown together to struggle with a situation for which no one was prepared. There were a number of people whom I never met, but I think about them and include them in my prayers. All of us were deeply affected by the Tragedy, and have a unique story to tell.

It was a long time before I could bring myself to go back to OES after Giles left the school. Most of the faces have changed, but there are still some I recognize. The school has altered, buildings have been taken down and new ones put in their place, but the trees and the gardens behind the school where the memorial stone lies are still there. The teenagers look much the same as they did in '86, although fashion identifies a new generation. Jack still teaches at the school. He looks a little older and his hair is thinning on top, but to us he doesn't change. He still inspires his pupils and runs a thriving art department, putting on three plays a year. He has remained a part of our family over the years, Giles and Ross see him whenever possible.

Gerri was appointed by OES to be the school's liaison with the parents after the Tragedy. I first met her when she brought in meals for us at the hospital and later we went out for lunch together quite frequently. She would tell me about the dreadful effect the

Climb had on the school and about how the staff, teachers and pupils were coping. She knew the climbers and teachers involved personally, especially Father Tom, and would often talk about him. She obviously thought highly of him.

"He was a very religious man," she told me. "He and his wife had a house in Portland where they took in people who were down on their luck for one reason or another. They gave them shelter until the people could get back on their feet again. It was his ministry. They didn't make a big thing of it, it was known in the community that there was a safe place to go. They didn't have much, but what they had they shared."

I listened intently to her description of this wonderful man whom I had talked about so much since his death, a man whom I had never met. When Ross first went to OES, Father Tom taught "Origins of Western Civilization". I remember how thrilled I was to hear Ross' account of his class when he was so stimulated and enthusiastic, especially about his teacher he called "Father Tom".

"He loved the mountain," Gerri continued, "he took parties of kids up there on numerous occasions over the years and was a very experienced climber."

"What went wrong?" I asked.

She shook her head. "It was totally out of character for him to behave the way he apparently did. He was known for being extremely cautious and never took unnecessary risks. I don't understand what happened to him that day."

"Perhaps he was sick," I said. "Perhaps he had hypothermia. I know it doesn't seem to take much of a drop in body temperature to distort judgment."

"Maybe. Perhaps that was it."

"Who knows? There are many unanswered questions."

I often think about the people and wonder where they are now. I heard that Marion's daughter, Amy, went to live in England after her mother's death, I wonder how she is getting along. I'm sure she is an English girl by now, probably married and maybe with children of her own. She will be almost the same age as I was when I left England; perhaps she is facing the decisions which I had to face about leaving her homeland and settling abroad.

I remember years ago when we arrived in Longview, how strange it felt and how I worried whether I would ever be accepted being a foreigner in a small Northwest town. For years after the Tragedy, the support we received was extraordinary. People who didn't know us, but had read about Giles in the paper would interrupt their busy lives and do what they could to help. Individuals would come up to me in the street with tears in their eyes and say they were praying for Giles. I don't feel alone here. I know there will always be someone around if I need anything again.

One of my friends set up a dispatch center in Longview when the climbers were missing. She relayed information back and forth and dealt with inquiries from doctors and friends in the Longview community. She helped my children by giving them an ear to listen and a shoulder to cry on. She told me that Joanne had said: "Giles will be fine...it's Mummy we're worried about."

She brought friends to the hospital, brought little gifts and offered to take me away from the endless routines. I will never forget these caring people.

Jo, the Red Cross nurse, has remained my friend. She calls me occasionally to tell me about the latest disaster mission which she has been on—sometimes an earthquake, sometimes a flood. I wouldn't have known these silent crusaders existed had they not been there for us in our time of need. Jo has had her share of personal tragedies, but still manages to be there for others.

We have lost touch with most of the doctors and nurses at Providence, although we see Dr. Asaph and Dr. Dreisin from time to time. Dr. Asaph looks the same, and when I see him, it's like coming home. His strong personality and professionalism will remain my most vivid recollection of him. I still have Dr. Dreisin's bow tie wrapped around the crucifix and although I don't take them with me wherever I go, they are never far away from my heart. For many years we saw Dick at Christmas time, but I haven't seen him since the day that Bill had his surgery. His infectious laugh and keen interest in people made a lasting impression on our family and we have fond memories of the many hours we spent together.

Giles sees Milo less frequently these days. Although I make a point of keeping in touch with him, I rarely see him. Subsequent to the publicity he gained from Giles' case, his business grew explosively. He still practices in Longview, but now has offices throughout the country. He serves humanity in his own untiring way and recently went to Bosnia on a mission to make prosthetic devices for children injured in the war.

Paul was with us from the beginning, helping us to make decisions and to say the right things. He dealt with the medical bills, all the media inquiries and ended up with an enormous job. He had the patience of Job and often came to the hospital to gain absolutely nothing and I know it was a full day's work for him. He always came whenever I asked him to be there—nothing was too much trouble. He has remained and will always be a close friend.

Roy is still the Dean of the Parish of St. John the Baptist at OES and we make every effort to see him whenever possible. I believe God sent Roy to be with us during our time of trouble. He was always there, keeping our spirits up and reminding us to pray. I didn't see much of Roy immediately following the accident and many years passed before I had an opportunity to tell him how much his presence meant.

"It was important for me to be with a survivor," he said. "With Giles, there was hope amongst so much despair—that gave me the strength to carry on."

Roy is such a holy man, yet humble, to admit that in his humanness he needed us.

"When we were told Giles had to have his legs amputated," he continued, "I was mortified. It was the last straw. What else? I asked myself. It was you who pulled *me* through when you said it was the only thing that would save his life. You gave me strength."

I often wonder how we survived those hours of worry and uncertainty. Hours which ran into days which ran into weeks, months and then years. Certainly, the love which surrounded us gave meaning to the horror which we were experiencing. The sense of humor which never left us, even in the most unlikely times, helped us to keep our sanity and held us together. Then there was prayer. From the very darkest hours to our most joyful moments, God was with us and to reach into my inner soul and to pray has been my salvation. In suffering, it is our inner traits as mere human beings which determine our ultimate survival.

In retrospect the most important support was that of the family as Senator Kennedy so eloquently stated. We had such a tumultuous family life, with very little time to talk to one another. I haven't been much of a mother, always concerned about being successful and assuming that if I made it then the children would also. Even though I thought I was doing the right thing, I failed my children in many ways. When faced with losing one of them, I realized there wouldn't be any time left to say and do the things I should have done years ago. It's really a shame that it takes a tragedy to bring a family together, to open doors which have been closed for years, to build bridges in relationships which have long since broken down. The family is the most important to nurture, because it has been there for the longest time and will continue to be there in the future after everyone else has forgotten.

I will always be grateful that my family were around me. My parents were always in the background, although sometimes I thought they felt neglected and in the way. My father still lives in Canada with a woman he loves and for his age has good health. I don't see him as often as I would like and feel we have drifted apart, but I hope he understands that I will always be here for him.

My sister gave up valuable time out of her busy life to be there for me, but more importantly, she was available for Joanne, Ross and our parents. She is married now and has two little girls. She moved to California a few years ago where her life continues to have its trials, but she is happy, I know.

It was by a strange twist of fate that Joanne happened to be in Portland during that time. I still don't know what I would have done without her. We shared the same feelings — she as a sister and I as a mother. She understood what I was saying from my heart, and likewise, I felt her trepidation. Joanne and Mike still live in Texas and have a thriving business. I think she would like to start a family, but knows it may not be possible after all the chemotherapy and radiation she has had. She tells me she won't feel completely confident to try until five years after her treatment have passed, which is almost to the day. I believe she is cured, but there is always a ghost which nags at the back of my mind and tells me we can never be sure. Nevertheless, each day brings us a little closer; another day without a phone call.

Ross and Ann were married in a Catholic cathedral in San Francisco, on September 6, 1997. Giles was best man at the wedding. He stood tall and confident at the altar as Ross and Ann took their vows. Lewis was the ring bearer and although he was confused about what he should do at the rehearsal, he did a commendable job at the service. Ann is a lovely girl, she and Ross have a bright future together. I feel fortunate to have two such wonderful daughters-in-law.

There were several young people at the wedding who were at the school at the time of the accident. Robindra lives in San Francisco and works with the handicapped. She said she feels she must give something back to life after her experience. What a fine young woman she is.

Ross was particularly affected by the Tragedy—not only did he have to stand by and watch his brother fighting for his life, but he had to go back to OES and deal with the deaths of his friends and teachers as well. It was the last straw when Joanne became ill. Ross was always available, and he was the one we all turned to, to listen and console us. He was the crutch of our family, just as he had been when his father died. We took him for granted, because he appeared to be so strong.

Ultimately he was the most human of us all when everything built up inside of him and he finally had to deal with his own grief. He battled a problem with alcohol until he finally hit the depths of despair and took a grip on himself. Even then the pain didn't go away and demons haunted him for a long time. Ten years after the accident, Ross spent many months composing and producing a series of classical guitar pieces as a memorial to his brother, his friends and teachers who died on the Climb. He called it *Winter's Book*. When the CD was completed he was at peace and able to look forward to a future with the woman he loves without fear of his world collapsing around him. Ross is now a successful professional guitarist and continues to perform and produce CDs in the San Francisco area. I gave Ross his father's car which he took to San Francisco. He and Ann enjoy driving the Triumph Spitfire in the big city.

Bill has worked more than ever since his retirement, but I haven't returned to radiotherapy, although I have considered it many times. However, new doors have opened and given me happiness, although moving on from a lifetime career has not been easy. I have at last found the time to do things which have been put off in the past and I feel fortunate to have the opportunity to redirect my life.

There are many things for which I am thankful, especially in Bill. His quiet support made such a difference to our survival. It must have been difficult for him. Giles wasn't his child and in many ways he was on the outside, but was expected to play the role of a parent when I know he didn't necessarily feel it in his heart. There was a lot to do, things to keep going, members of his own family who needed attention, but he was always there for us. Every night, he would be at the hospital doing what he could. I think some feared that perhaps our relationship wasn't strong enough to endure so much chaos, separation and emotional turmoil, but it did, and perhaps is stronger because of it. Knowing that we could survive when it seemed that all the odds were against us, makes me realize that we can make it through anything—it was the ultimate test.

Giles and Marie still live in Seattle and have another baby boy, Colin Andrew Rubin Thompson, born almost exactly three years after Lewis. He is a delightful child and quite different in personality and appearance to Lewis. Colin was baptized by Roy at the church of St. John the Baptist at OES, and was the first baby to be christened in their new font. I have never been to an Anglican baptism similar to it. It was another of Roy's moving ceremonies. He completely immersed the baby, except for his head, in the warm water, over and over again. Colin gasped at first, but then seemed to enjoy it. He smiled at the congregation as Roy lifted him high above his head and walked with him triumphantly down the aisle.

I think Giles has come to terms with his memories of the Climb. As he said, "There are visions in my mind I'll never forget." But those visions do not haunt him as they used to. The prostheses are a bother of course, but they are hardly an issue anymore.

We have seen very little of Brittany over the years, but we make certain that we keep current with her activities. The last report we had was that she was going to medical school and I believe she is doing well.

Giles is still passionate about the theater and works for a large theatrical company in the Seattle area as well as trying out a business for himself. He is an avid gardener and an attentive father to his boys. Marie continues to support him and they nurture the love they feel. They are both good to me and make me feel an active part of their family. I visit them as often as I can, but not nearly as frequently as I would like. The role of grandmother has been new and exciting for me, quite different from being a mother. I feel fortunate to have them close by and privileged to have Giles, who has brought Marie and the two babies into my life.

The whistle of the road in front of Providence haunted me for many years each time I drove by the hospital. However, I noticed recently that I can't hear it any more. I wonder what it meant. It was definitely there, but why was I the only person who could hear it? Whatever it was it has gone away.

Everyone connected to the Tragedy was a hero to me, the medical and rescue teams, the communities both near and far, but there is one whose courage and strength will forever be a lesson — and that is Giles. His quiet determination and refusal to give up even at the lowest ebb, is testimony to what the human spirit is capable of. If this book leaves the reader with any one thought, I would like it to be the celebration of this human spirit which brings us closer together in times of trouble. I don't think we will ever

completely recover from the accident, but it is possible to move on and get on with life.

The memories are still vivid and in many ways it is as though it happened only yesterday. Yet at the same time, it seems in another life, another world away. There doesn't seem to be a place to bring closure to such an experience, but I hope that in closing this chapter, we can close that chapter too.

Not that we will ever forget, but we will not be haunted anymore by the memories.

# EPILOGUE
by
Michael Henderson
May 29, 1986

I can never look at Mount Hood in quite the same way again. In its beauty and starkness is shrouded the mystery of the forces of nature and the ways of God.

It might so easily have been our precious daughter, Juliet, who lost her life in the mountain's worst disaster. As it is, family of friends whom we had just made, children we had watched on the sports fields in our daughter's teams, children we had applauded just the week before as they performed joyfully in the school play, staff members we were beginning to appreciate, are no longer with us. And our hearts go out to every one of the bereaved.

The words of an experienced mountaineer, Bob Pierce, capture what it must have been like in those hours on the mountain: "The world around you turns into a swirling, dingy whiteness in which there is no real bottom. It is hard to know if you are going uphill or down, stepping into a hole or running up against a wall. You cannot hear your friends, cannot see what is around you. The world shrinks to the immediate. You move along unsteadily in freezing isolation, every minute seeming like an hour."

The words of the Book of Wisdom printed in the service sheet seem to epitomize the restful spirit at the Memorial a week later: "The souls of the just are in the hand of God, and torment shall not touch them. In the eyes of the unwise they seemed to die, but they are at peace."

From the fear on the mountain to the faith at the service it has been for all a painful journey. Sadness and solace, anger and love, despair and hope, have moved through many a heart, and many a tear has been shed. But as the Oregon Episcopal School headmaster, the Reverend Malcolm Manson, told the nearly two thousand who attended the service and the many more who watched the live telecast, "No storm in God's creation can rival the power of the love we have felt in these last few days."

A comparative newcomer to Oregon, I can only say: what a marvelously loving community we have. I think of the heroism of those who risked their lives in search and rescue, of the commitment and skill of doctors and nurses, of the sensitivity of the media to a grieving school and its families. "The support we have received," says Oregon Episcopal School counselor Bonnie Stanke, "will make our transition back to purposeful and joyful living a little easier."

…Thanking the community for its support, as all of us connected with the school do, Father Manson said, "Please don't stop. We will need you and need you deeply in the months ahead. We have found a great treasure. In great tragedy we have come upon the soul of our school and its name is love."

—From a broadcast, radio KBOO

A portion of the proceeds of this book will be equally divided between two funds in the Lower Columbia Community Trust:

**The Mountain Signal Fund** was established in memory of the climbers who lost their lives in the 1986 Mount Hood Tragedy. The fund provides:
- Signaling devices to be used by climbers on Mount Hood to prevent a similar accident ever happening again.
- Licensing and maintenance of the devices.
- The opportunity to develop a universal system as technology advances.

**Disability International Foundation** is a non-profit, educational foundation providing global awareness, consultation, networking, publishing, and training in fostering progress for the inclusion of people with disabilities—children, youth and adults.

The Lower Columbia Community Trust is held by
Community Foundation of Southwest Washington
703 Broadway, Suite 610
Vancouver, Washington 98660

*Winter's Book,* music CD by Ross Thompson
*The Mountain Never Cries,* book on tape
available through
***BookPartners***
P.O. Box 922
Wilsonville, Oregon 97070

Contact the author at www.amholadaysbook.com

# ABOUT THE AUTHOR

**A**nn Holaday was born in Wales and raised in England. She was educated in therapeutic radiology at the Christie Hospital and Holt Radium Institute in Manchester. She emigrated with her family in 1970 to Puerto Rico where they lived for seven years. She moved to the mainland and worked as a manager in radiation therapy in San Antonio, Texas, and Longview, Washington. Ann Holaday now resides in Washington where she pursues her profession and continues to write. She and her husband enjoy traveling and sailing the Northwest waters.

To order additional copies of

# THE MOUNTAIN NEVER CRIES

Book: $14.95    Shipping/Handling: $3.50


Contact: ***BookPartners, Inc.***
P.O. Box 922
Wilsonville, OR 97070
Phone: 503-682-9821
Order: 1-800-895-7323
Fax: 503-682-8684
E-mail: bpbooks@teleport.com